DEMOCRACY ON
THE GROUND

GABRIEL HETLAND

DEMOCRACY ON THE GROUND

Local Politics in Latin America's Left Turn

Columbia University Press / *New York*

Columbia University Press
Publishers Since 1893
New York   Chichester, West Sussex
cup.columbia.edu

Library of Congress Cataloging-in-Publication Data
Names: Hetland, Gabriel, author.
Title: Democracy on the ground : local politics in Latin America's left turn /
Gabriel Hetland.
Description: New York : Columbia University Press, 2023. | Includes
bibliographical references and index.
Identifiers: LCCN 2022048899 | ISBN 9780231207706 (hardback) |
ISBN 9780231207713 (trade paperback) | ISBN 9780231557092 (ebook)
Subjects: LCSH: Municipal government—Venezuela. | Municipal
government—Bolivia. | Torres (Venezuela)—Politics and government. |
Sucre (Miranda, Venezuela)—Politics and government. | Santa Cruz de la Sierra
(Bolivia)—Politics and government. | El Alto (Bolivia)—Politics and
government. | Right and left (Political science)—Venezuela. | Right and left
(Political science)—Bolivia. | Venezuela—Politics and government—1999- |
Bolivia—Politics and government—2006-
Classification: LCC JS2759 .H47 2023 | DDC 352.14098—dc23/eng/20221206
LC record available at https://lccn.loc.gov/2022048899

Printed in the United States of America

Cover design: Elliott S. Cairns
Cover image: PSboom / Shutterstock.com

CONTENTS

PART II

BOLIVIA: REFRACTING PASSIVE REVOLUTION, PERPETUATING CLIENTELISM

PREFACE

Democracy is a maddening concept to write about and think with. This is partly due to the linguistic and theoretical stretching it is subject to when scholars, journalists, and politicians use it to refer to forms of rule, such as that found in the contemporary United States, which are demonstrably oligarchical in key respects.[1] It is also maddening because it is a profoundly contested concept. To some, e.g. followers of Joseph Schumpeter, democracy refers to a form of competitive elite rule. To others it means a system in which ordinary people can and do exercise real control over decisions affecting their lives. To further complicate matters, democracy is used to refer to a broad array of political—as well as social, economic, and cultural—processes, procedures, rules, institutions, structures, beliefs, practices, and more.

Given all this, why bother with the term at all? One reason, of course, is that it can hardly be avoided. Another is that democracy does not only madden; it also inspires. This is true not just of those who write about it but also the millions of ordinary people who have lived and often died for it. As exasperating as it may be, democracy has long been a horizon of popular struggle. It has been the goal of peasants struggling against despotic landlords, workers contending with arrogant bosses and owners, the unemployed butting heads with unsympathetic and abusive state officials, women seeking to free themselves from the shackles of patriarchy, and racialized populations fighting for respect and dignity—in short, those challenging what they feel are illegitimate forms of power and authority.

Like all books written about democracy, this one will find its adherents and its detractors. My hope is that those who take the trouble to read the pages that follow will grapple with some of the challenges democracy raises, and perhaps they will do so in unanticipated and interesting ways. One of the greatest conundrums democracy poses is the question of its limits. Many scholars have come to the conclusion that democracy is possible only when it is "safe" for elites. The reason for this is that the classic, and still literal, meaning of democracy—rule by the people—is profoundly threatening to those with power and privilege. Because they have money and guns, and much else, the rich and powerful have often been able to prevent democracy from being established and end it when it becomes too threatening. One of the main historical solutions to this thorny issue has been to make democracy "safe." This has been done in many ways, from weighing the votes of the rich more than the votes of the poor, to corporate lobbying, gerrymandering electoral districts, union busting, inducing leftist parties to moderate, and building conservative parties that give the rich political voice. More subtle means of taking the risk out of democracy include shaping public opinion through advertising and scrubbing school textbooks of "controversial" and "offensive" material like slavery.

Each of these ways of resolving the "problem of democracy"—the threat it poses to elites—is alike in seeking to make democracy more safe by making it less real. That is, each is an attempt to keep the "will of the people" contained within clear limits, to make sure that democracy does not pose such a threat to the rich and powerful that they reach for their guns, and use their money, to make it go away.

In this book I argue that a different way of resolving the problem of democracy is possible. This resolution rests on what I term *leftist hegemony*. By this I mean a situation in which a left political force succeeds in establishing moral and intellectual leadership such that other political forces, including forces on the Right, are compelled to "play the game of politics" on the Left's terrain. I contend that one effect of this is the widening of the space within which democracy can operate, conceptually and politically. This is because the Left has historically been closely associated with efforts to make democracy more real by extending it from the political to the socioeconomic realm and deepening it through the creation of new participatory institutions.[2] If a left party committed to extending and deepening democracy establishes hegemony, non-left parties will be forced to embrace, or appear to embrace, these practices. (The concepts of Left and Right are discussed at length in the introduction to this book.)

In the pages that follow I seek to illustrate this argument by comparing Venezuela and Bolivia during Latin America's "left turn," the period from the early 2000s to mid-2010s when leftist parties governed across the region. I chose these countries since they are often seen as the two most radical left turn cases, in part because of their leaders' greater embrace of deepening and extending democracy. Through my research I found that the countries differ in an important and theoretically productive way. Drawing on nearly two years of fieldwork, I argue that Venezuela's Hugo Chávez established a form of leftist hegemony, which compelled the Venezuelan Right to embrace his ideas, including those regarding deepening democracy. I argue that Bolivia's Evo Morales failed to establish a similar form of leftist hegemony, with one result of this being that the Bolivian Right acted in a more "typically right-wing" way vis-à-vis democracy. The key import of my research is that the limits of democracy may be more extensive than much existing thought holds. I contend, specifically, that when leftist hegemony is present the Right can be compelled to tolerate, and even champion, democracy even if it takes a "dangerous" form.

A NOTE ON TIMING

Latin America has gone through three historical cycles in the years I have spent researching, writing, and revising this book. I conceived of and conducted most of the research for the book at the height of the left turn, circa 2009–2011. This was a period of profound hope for many and unalloyed fear for others. During the years I spent writing the book (2015–2020), Latin America experienced a contrasting "right turn," with the rise of leaders like Brazil's Jair Bolsonaro, Argentina's Mauricio Macri, and Bolivia's Jeanine Áñez. Other countries that did not see the Right return to office, such as Venezuela, became mired in profound crises. All this considerably dimmed the hopes felt at the peak of the left turn. In the time I spent revising the book for publication (February 2022 to February 2023) Latin America appeared to be entering yet another cycle, dubbed by some the left turn (or pink tide) 2.0. This has generated new hopes, and fears, within and beyond the region.

These changes raise many questions, including what lessons the "first" left turn might have for the second? Some of these lessons are extensively dealt with in these pages; for instance, I spend considerable time thinking about the conditions in which participatory democracy is more and less likely to thrive, and about how the presence or absence of leftist hegemony shapes political action by forces of the Right, and the Left. Other aspects of the left turn "1.0" are treated in a more cursory way; this is true of the question of the material and political conditions of possibility for different types of left projects to emerge and thrive. And some issues are touched upon only in passing. This includes the crucial question of climate change. One of the most heartening features of the left turn 2.0 is the determination of Latin America's new crop of leftist presidents—particularly Chile's Gabriel Boric and Colombia's Gustavo Petro—to tackle the challenges and opportunities of climate change head-on. Amongst the greatest conundrums climate change poses is how resource-dependent countries, like Venezuela and Bolivia, will be able to navigate the necessary-but-still-uncertain-and-murky transition to a fossil-free future. It remains to be seen how Boric, Petro, and others, such as Bolivia's Luis Arce, Mexico's Andrés Manuel López Obrador, Argentina's Alberto Fernández, and Brazil's Luiz Inácio Lula da Silva, will navigate these and other challenges, particularly how to deliver on their promises of social justice, inclusion, and real sustainability amidst the continuing fallout from the COVID-19 pandemic and global economic turbulence. This book, like all books, is limited in scope. If it is able to shed some light on how those committed to building more just, equitable, and democratic societies might best confront, and to some degree overcome, the difficulties of doing so, it will have served its purpose.

ACKNOWLEDGMENTS

Like its subject matter, the production of this book has been an eminently collective and participatory process. My debts—personal, intellectual, and professional—are many and deep. These debts begin in UC Berkeley's Sociology department, which provided an extraordinary intellectual community during my years of graduate study. For me and many others Michael Burawoy stands at the center of this community, not only because of his brilliance and charisma, but above all for his ability to forge collectivities that make the task of producing knowledge not only bearable but joyful and transformative. Michael, my dissertation chair, offered critical guidance and unflagging support for this project at all stages: from the unwieldy prospectus I presented him with long ago, through fieldwork and years of writing and rewriting. I remain awed by and grateful for Michael's unmatched ability to devote so much time and attention to his students while maintaining an incredibly active schedule of research, teaching, administrative, and organizing work. I'm also grateful to the other members of my dissertation committee: Peter Evans, Laura Enriquez, Dylan Riley, and Michael Watts. The book bears the marks of each of them, and

I feel so fortunate that all five of my committee members are models of engaged scholarship who show that far from being mutually exclusive, the relationship between ethical-political commitments and rigorous research can be synergistic and productive. Peter and Laura deserve particular mention for going above and beyond the call of duty in offering comments on many articles and book chapters upon which this book builds.

I owe an immense debt of gratitude to residents of Torres, Sucre, Santa Cruz, and El Alto who graciously put up with my many questions about their lives, work, and dreams. These dreams—of a more just and equal world—continue to inspire me. In Torres, I'm especially grateful to Myriam Giménez and Victor García, who welcomed me into their home, and are models of lives well lived. I thank Johnny Murphy for his warmth, boundless good humor, and willingness to open so many doors, and Julio Chávez for his time and openness. In Sucre I thank everyone from Fundasucre, who showed me such generosity and warmth, and the many organizers and activists I spoke with in Petare and elsewhere. In El Alto I thank officials from all levels, and the leaders and members of Fejuve, MAS, and other organizations for their willingness to speak with me time and again. In Santa Cruz I thank leaders and members from district associations, neighborhood councils and the MAS throughout the city, and the many city officials who agreed to speak with me. For help making my fieldwork in Venezuela possible and enjoyable I thank Lisa Sullivan, Kendra Fehrer, Alejandro Velasco, David Smilde, Sujatha Fernandes, the *compañeros y compañeras* of the Antimano hostel, Mariya Ivancheva, and Carlos Martinez. In Bolivia I am grateful for the support and camaraderie of Sinclair Thomson, Luis Gómez, Noah and Jean Friedman-Rudovsky, Susan Ellison, Jorge Derpic, Sara Shahriari, Lesli Hoey, Sarah Hines, Ana Arendar, and Adriana Soto.

In Berkeley, New York City, and elsewhere I've had the good fortune to be surrounded by bright and committed scholars and friends who have supported this project in many ways. I thank Adam Reich, Ben Gebre-Mehdin, Becky Tarlau, Marcel Paret, Edwin Ackerman, Michel Estefan, Mike McCarthy, Jeff Goodwin, Susan Spronk, Jeffery Webber, Zach Levenson, Fidan Elcioglu, Kate Maich, Laleh Behbehanian, Emily Brisette,

Siri Colom, Elise Herrera, Roi Livne, Ben Shestakofsky, Cihan Tuğal, Mara Loveman, Raka Ray, Kim Voss, Gill Hart, Nathan McClintock, Elif Kale Lustavali, Mike Levien, Abigail Martin, Abigail Andrews, Trevor Gardner, Sarah Anne Minkin, Dan Buch, Gowri Vijayakumar, Graham Hill, Quinlan Bowman, Brian Palmer-Rubin, Mareike Winchell, Ilaria Giglioli, Matteo Stiglich, Ramon Quintero, Katy Fox-Hoddess, Louise Ly, Manuel Rosaldo, Alex Barnard, Ruth Collier, and Samuel Handlin.

My interest in participatory budgeting led to long-term involvement with the Participatory Budgeting Project (PBP). I've benefitted immensely from my interactions with people involved with PBP over the years, including Josh Lerner, Pam Jennings, Ginny Browne, Aseem Mulji, Daniel Schugurensky, and the original PB Vallejo crew.

For their generous feedback on articles and papers that are incorporated herein I thank the late Erik Olin Wright, Fred Block, Benjamin Goldfrank, Tim Gill, Rebecca Hanson, David Ost, Archon Fung, David Smilde, Patrick Heller, and Stephanie McNulty. I'm appreciative of editors of popular-press publications who gave me the opportunity to sharpen my ideas in their pages: Roane Carey and Christopher Shay of *The Nation*; Bhaskar Sunkara, Shawn Gude, and Micah Uetricht at *Jacobin*; Alejandro Velasco, Laura Weiss, Leo Schwartz, and Heather Gies at *NACLA*; and Elí López at *The Washington Post*. I'm immensely thankful for feedback I received on the full manuscript or parts of it from Gianpaolo Baiocchi, Alejandro Velasco, Sinclair Thomson, Michael Burawoy, Javier Auyero, Adam Reich, David Smilde, Naomi Schiller, and anonymous reviewers at Columbia University Press. I'm similarly thankful for comments I received when presenting the book (in whole and part) and material related to it in talks and workshops at the University at Albany, NYU, Tulane University, University of Wisconsin-Madison, New College of Florida, Skidmore College, Seton Hall University, Rutgers University-Newark, CUNY Graduate Center, and York University. My colleagues at University at Albany have offered critical support to this book, and I'm pleased to thank Pedro Cabán, Bret Benjamin, Alejandra Bronfman, Johana Londoño, Barbara Sutton, Ron Friedman, Tom Narins, Matt Ingram, and the late Richard Lachmann. I'm grateful to Dan Wilcox for offering a wonderful home away from home during my years of commuting. I also thank students in my Fall 2022 Latin America seminar for engaging so thoughtfully with the book. I owe a major debt to the wonderful Columbia University Press team, with particular thanks to Eric Schwartz, Lowell Frye, Marisa Lastres, and Ben Kolstad.

Finally, I thank my family for all their support during the long process of writing this book. I'm forever in debt to my parents, Mary and Paul, who, amongst so much else, taught me to think with passion about issues that matter. I owe a huge thanks to my sister, Mitra, and brother, Adam, for making sure I don't take myself too seriously. I'm grateful to my brother-in-law, Sean, sister-in-law, Michelle, and delightful nieces and nephew, Maia, Cecily, and Bodhi, for their similar efforts. I thank my wonderful in-laws, Vijay and Girija Shankar, for offering me a writing haven and support during many stages of this process. I heartily thank Shreya, Rohit, and my buoyant nephews Kabir and Ishaan, for their warmth, always-open door, and stimulating conversation. More than anyone, I'm grateful to my partner, Karin Shankar, without whom I couldn't have written this book. Karin has endured the book like no one else, and as much as I she will truly celebrate the fact that it's done. Karin: I'm beyond lucky to have your love, laughter, support, and highly astute editorial eye. Words cannot express my appreciation for everything. And finally, there is Sami, who in his three and a half years on earth has repeatedly reminded me that there is much more to life than writing books. I cannot wait to see all the things you'll do, and I hope you'll do them in a more fair, equal, and truly democratic world.

DEMOCRACY ON
THE GROUND

INTRODUCTION

O
n Saturday, April 30, 2011, around eighty neighbors of Caucagüita, the second-poorest parish of Sucre municipality in eastern Caracas, gathered for a public assembly. For several hours the predominantly Black and Brown residents discussed how to spend a portion of Sucre's municipal budget. This happened in three working groups, covering sports and culture, public security, and social infrastructure respectively. I observed two of the working groups. Each had several dozen participants. The first had some hiccups, while the second ran smoothly. When I entered the classroom where the second was taking place, the facilitator, Maribel, was giving each participant a chance to present their proposal. Maribel and the participants then asked questions like 'What's this proposal for?' and 'How many people will it benefit?'[1] After everyone had presented, Maribel guided the group through the process of choosing five of the eleven proposals. She told the group to consider six criteria in selecting proposals: 'Does the proposal involve more than one community? Does it address the problem specified? Does the project have visibility? Will it be done by a legally certified community organization? Does it take place on private land or public land the municipality lacks jurisdiction over? And does it involve ongoing

expenses, like a chauffeur's salary?' The group quickly approved several proposals, including one for a bus. The man advocating it got others on board by saying, 'It can be used to go to other communities, too.' Another proposal, for a jobs training program, sparked disagreement. A man identifiable as a Chavista due to his red hat and communal council vest objected: 'There's already a program [in the neighborhood] providing this type of training.' This led the group to choose a modified proposal to provide the neighborhood with six youth centers. Once the proposals had been discussed and voted on, Maribel read out the list of the five approved proposals. The group warmly applauded after each was announced.

A similar assembly occurred on Thursday, November 26, 2009, in Las Mercedes, a poor parish in Torres municipality in the central-western Venezuelan state of Lara. Over the course of a few hours, around sixty mostly Black and Brown residents discussed how to spend the 850,340 *bolívares* (about 400,000 USD) allocated to their parish as part of Torres's Participatory Budget.[2] These residents came from the popular classes and worked as small farmers, agricultural workers, teachers, and domestic caregivers. Each was elected by their community to be a *vocero* (spokesperson) tasked with communicating their community's priorities and, along with other communities' voceros, collectively determining the parish participatory budget project list. The assembly discussed and approved projects for a cultural center, road paving, electric lighting, water purification, water tanks, an aqueduct, and a tractor that would also serve as a school bus, ambulance, and road leveler. Before any project was approved there was dialogue, at times heated, about its merits and the wisdom of spending limited funds on this versus that. There was lengthy debate on two projects: streetlights and drinking water. Both had been approved the previous year but had not been implemented due to budget cuts. A vocero argued that the frequency of blackouts caused by a severe drought meant they should not fund the streetlights: 'Given the current electricity situation, I think streetlights are not urgent and shouldn't be funded.' A vocera responded, 'Not having this streetlight is a security issue for these communities. If you arrive late, after 10 P.M., it's totally dark and unsafe.' Another vocero spoke for the streetlights, which would 'raise community self-esteem.' The meeting facilitator also favored the lights: 'It was a commitment from last year so we should make a decision on it in this assembly.' In the end both delayed projects were (re)approved.

These two assemblies are alike in a number of ways. Both are examples of participatory budgeting in which ordinary citizens—in these cases predominantly poor people of color—come together to make decisions about how to spend their city's budget money. Both assemblies involved deliberative decision-making, in which participants aired competing views and justified these views through reason-based argument. These discussions were at once mundane (e.g., participants debating whether to fund drinking water or streetlights) and far-reaching, with conversation touching on issues of public safety, women's rights, climate change, national energy grids, and more. The discussions also revolved around and put into practice notions of social justice, solidarity, and fairness.

Nearly a year of fieldwork (six months in Torres and four in Sucre) reveals other similarities between the broader participatory processes these assemblies were a part of. Both cities' processes were inclusive in terms of class, race and ethnicity, gender, and political views, with Chavistas, oppositionists, and "ni-nis" (neither one nor the other) present. And both processes were institutionally and politically effective. Participant decisions were binding, or near binding, and implemented effectively and in a generally timely way. Both processes proved politically beneficial to the local incumbent party. In both cities many citizens, including some political opponents, viewed the mayor favorably, and in both cases the local incumbent party won reelection one or more times. In short, Torres and Sucre both appear to be successful cases of participatory urban governance.

This similarity would not be particularly noteworthy were it not for a significant difference between the two cities: a *radical left* party, and specifically a *movement-left* party with close ties to social movements and a commitment to deepening democracy, governed Torres, while a *right-of-center* party governed Sucre. Torres's participatory success is thus expected, while Sucre's is not. My finding of success in both cities is additionally surprising when placed alongside the outcome of participatory reform in two other cities where I conducted long-term fieldwork: El Alto and Santa Cruz, Bolivia.

At the time of my research, El Alto, like Torres, was governed by a movement-left party, Bolivia's ruling Movement Toward Socialism (MAS), known for its organic ties to social movements and rhetoric of "ruling by obeying." El Alto is world-renowned for its powerful social movements, which toppled consecutive Bolivian presidents in the 2003 and 2005 "gas wars." During El Alto's period of MAS rule, 2010–2015, the mayor, Edgar Patana, and the head of the city council were both social movement leaders who had been active in the gas wars. All this led me to expect robust participatory reform under Patana's MAS administration. However, this expectation was not met. Patana failed to deliver participatory decision-making as mandated by the 1994 Law of Popular Participation. In fact, five months of fieldwork shows that Patana adopted an *antiparticipatory* governance strategy, with Patana officials repeatedly telling me that they wanted *less* popular participation in decisions rather than more.

Santa Cruz resembles Sucre in being run by a right-of-center party linked to dominant classes, who are largely white and notably racist. Santa Cruz's predominantly Indigenous and mestizo popular classes possess limited capacity for autonomous mobilization. All this led me to expect little in the way of (nationally mandated) popular participation. This expectation was more than met. In four months of fieldwork, I found that city residents had virtually no control over local political decisions, which were made by avowedly apolitical experts who openly disregarded citizens' self-professed needs. One official proudly told me that in the last participatory planning process he had attended years ago, he had selected projects in *precisely the reverse order* of how citizens had prioritized them. This official felt entirely justified in doing so, confidently asserting, 'There's a difference between what residents say they want and what they actually need.'

Torres, Sucre, El Alto, and Santa Cruz are among thousands of cities worldwide that in recent decades have implemented participatory reforms purporting to give citizens greater control over decisions affecting their lives. Such reforms have been particularly widespread in Latin America, which has been at the forefront of what some scholars call a "participatory revolution."[3] When Latin America's participatory wave took off in the 1980s and 1990s it was led by innovative leftist parties, like Brazil's Workers'

Party, which instituted Porto Alegre's famed Participatory Budget. In the last two decades, non-left parties have implemented participatory experiments more frequently. Scholars have noted this, but there is little research on participatory reform in non-left-governed cities.

Democracy on the Ground takes up this task by comparing participatory reform in cities governed by left and right parties in Venezuela and Bolivia at the height of Latin America's "left turn." When I began my research, I had little doubt that I would find greater success in the two left-governed cities of Torres and El Alto, with success defined as participatory reform giving citizens real control over local political decisions. This expectation was based on the burgeoning urban participation literature, which shows that participatory reform is most likely to succeed in cities governed by a movement-left party, as Torres and El Alto were.[4] I did not expect to find anything approaching success in the right-governed cities of Sucre and Santa Cruz. At best I thought I might find simulacra of participation in these cases, but I was confident that, should I find even this, it would amount to little more than participatory varnish atop elite-led decision-making.

I was thus genuinely surprised by the results of my research, approximately two years of ethnographic fieldwork carried out on numerous trips to the four cities between 2007 and 2016. As table 0.1 shows, instead of finding success in the two left-governed cities, as I expected, I found success in both the left- *and right*-run cities in Venezuela, and failure in both the right- *and* left-run cities in Bolivia. My finding of greater success in the Venezuelan cities was also a surprise to me, since a left-populist party governed Venezuela while a movement-left party governed Bolivia. As noted above, movement-left parties have been seen as ideal for delivering participatory success. Left-populist parties, by contrast, have been seen as particularly unlikely to do so.[5]

What can explain these doubly unexpected findings?

The answer I give is: the interaction between national and local politics. My argument centers on an unanticipated contrast in the types of national political regimes found in Venezuela and Bolivia at the left turn's height. This contrast is rooted in the distinct way each country's left-ruling party responded to the right-wing backlash that its rise to office elicited.

TABLE 0.1 Expected vs. observed outcomes of research

	EXPECTED			OBSERVED	
	LEFT	**RIGHT**		**LEFT**	**RIGHT**
Venezuela	Torres	Sucre	Venezuela	Torres	Sucre
Bolivia	El Alto	Santa Cruz	Bolivia	El Alto	Santa Cruz

Note: Shaded cells indicate greater success.

Venezuela's ruling party responded with full-out populist mobilization. In conjunction with the post-2003 oil boom, this facilitated the emergence of a *left-populist hegemonic* regime. Bolivia's ruling party responded with a mix of limited mobilization and significant demobilization of popular movements. From 2010 on, the party's demobilizing turn deepened, helping lead to a *passive revolutionary* regime.

This difference in national regime type was consequential for subnational politics, specifically for how left and right parties related to participation at the local level. Venezuela's left-populist hegemonic regime transformed the rules of the game of politics such that *all* parties, *even right-wing opposition parties*, were forced to play the game of politics on the ruling party's left-populist terrain. Participatory democracy was a central part of this terrain. Parties from across the ideological spectrum faced significant pressure to make a show of supporting popular participation. As chapters 2 and 3 show, this helped facilitate participatory success in electorally competitive cities where an opposition party of the Left *or Right* came to office.

Bolivia's passive revolutionary regime differed from Venezuela's left-populist hegemonic regime in three notable ways. First, while Venezuela's ruling party moved left over time,[6] and compelled the right-wing opposition to move leftward as well, Bolivia's ruling party moved to the right from 2010 on. Second, while Venezuela's ruling party governed through populist mobilization, Bolivia's ruling party demobilized the popular movements from whence it came. Third, while in Venezuela participatory democracy was discursively and institutionally central, in Bolivia participation was a secondary and largely rhetorical part of the ruling party's political toolkit:

the party espoused a rhetoric of "ruling by obeying" but did little to link this rhetoric to new institutions and practices. As chapters 5 and 6 show, this meant local Bolivian politicians—both from the opposition and, more surprisingly, from the ruling party itself—faced little pressure to govern in a participatory way. These cases also suggest that, to the extent that Bolivia's ruling party served as a model for local parties, it was one of demobilization. I argue that these combined factors helped contribute to the failure of participatory reform in both right- and left-run Bolivian cities.

The findings and analysis presented in *Democracy on the Ground* are significant for thinking about urban participation, democracy and left-right relations, and the left turn. This book contributes to the urban participation literature by showing how national politics, and specifically a country's national political regime type, shapes the prospects for local participatory success. This challenges the explanatory localism found in some studies of urban participation. The book also contributes to literature on democracy and left-right relations by showing how the presence or absence of leftist hegemony shapes right-wing action toward democracy. It shows, specifically, that when leftist hegemony is present, right-wing parties may not react to a radical left party in office by seeking to end democracy, as has occurred so often in the past, but instead by seeking to extend and deepen democracy. This suggests that democracy may have less restrictive limits than what much existing thought holds. More specifically, it suggests that under certain conditions the Right can be compelled to tolerate democracy even when it is "unsafe" for elites.

Finally, the book contributes to thinking about the left turn, and leftist regimes in general, in three ways. First, it shows the benefits of dynamically analyzing leftist regimes, with attention to how such regimes transform, in sometimes surprising ways, in response to right-wing backlash. Second, it seeks to complicate prevailing ways of thinking about Venezuela and Bolivia as left turn cases by showing that Venezuela provided an unexpectedly propitious context, and Bolivia an unexpectedly unpropitious context, for participatory reform. Third, it points to the need to rethink movement-left and left-populist parties, with attention to the sometimes-unexpected ways such parties enable and constrain participatory democratic reform.

DEMOCRACY, URBAN PARTICIPATION, AND THE LEFT-RIGHT DIVIDE IN LATIN AMERICA AND BEYOND

If the world is experiencing a participatory revolution, a case can be made that it started in left-governed Latin American cities in the 1980s and 1990s.[7] During this time, innovative leftist parties—such as Brazil's Workers' Party, Venezuela's La Causa R, Uruguay's Broad Front, Mexico's Party of the Democratic Revolution, and Peru's United Left—took office and implemented participatory reform in dozens of cities across the region. This took many forms: participatory health councils, city master plans, and, most famously, participatory budgeting (or PB), which gives city residents direct and often binding control over local budget decisions. Porto Alegre's PB emerged as the paradigmatic case of participatory success. Innumerable studies show it democratized city governance, revitalized civil society, helped foster progressive redistribution of city resources, and more (Sousa Santos 1998; Abers 2000; Baiocchi 2005; Wampler 2007; Avritzer 2009; Goldfrank 2011a). Porto Alegre's success inspired mayors throughout Brazil, Latin America, and later the world to implement PB reforms. By 2015 PB existed in over two thousand cities across the globe (Baiocchi and Ganuza 2017, 75; Sintomer et al. 2010), and by 2022 it was found in over seven thousand cities worldwide, according to the Participatory Budgeting Project.[8]

The Right's initial reaction to Latin America's participatory reform wave was firm rejection. Right-wing parties fervently opposed PB when it was first implemented in Porto Alegre, Montevideo, Caracas, and other left-led cities. Notably, this opposition was done in the name of democracy. As Goldfrank (2007, 97) notes, "From the conservative perspective, rather than deepening democracy and promoting government efficiency, participatory budgeting is antidemocratic and unstable." Further, "many within the conservative perspective explicitly link participatory budgeting to totalitarianism."[9] The Right's rejection of participation as antidemocratic highlights the changing ways left and right forces in Latin America and elsewhere have viewed and related to democracy. I turn briefly to this history, as it played out in Europe and Latin America, to set the stage for the analysis of urban participation and left-right relations that are the focus of this book.

DEMOCRACY AND THE LEFT-RIGHT DIVIDE: A VERY BRIEF HISTORY OF EUROPE AND LATIN AMERICA

Democracy is constitutive of the left-right distinction. As Geoff Eley (2002, 17) notes,

> The vocabulary of 'Left' and 'Right' came from the radical democratic ambience of the French Revolution. When the French Constituent Assembly divided on the question of the royal veto and the powers reserved for the king during 1789–91, radicals took a position physically on the left-hand side of the chamber as viewed from the president's seat, facing conservatives on the right. As this alignment clarified, the 'Left' became identified with a strong democratic stance, embracing abolition of the royal veto, single-chamber legislature, an elected rather than an appointed judiciary, legislative supremacy rather than separation of powers and a strong executive, and—most vital of all—the democratic franchise of one man, one vote.

The "Right" became identified with a strong antidemocratic stance on these, and other, issues.

Scholars view the Left, specifically the socialist parliamentarian Left, as the central driver of European democratization. In *Forging Democracy: The History of the Left in Europe, 1850–2000*, Eley (19) dubs socialist parties "the torchbearers of democracy." Rueschemeyer, Stephens, and Stephens (1992) concur. As Eley (2002, 18) notes, the European Left understood democracy in a social way: "In the Left's tradition, some notion of social justice was practically inseparable from the pursuit of democracy." From the 1860s to 1960s this "notion" was socialism—"the social democracy"—which "came to signify not only the most radical form of parliamentary government but also the desire to extend democratic precepts to society at large, including

9

the organization of the economy" (21–22).[10] Socialists in office—e.g., 1918 Germany and postwar Italy, England, France, and West Germany—fought to implement demands like "the eight-hour day; full employment and unemployment legislation; expanded social insurance; housing reform; universal, equal, secret, and direct suffrage, with proportional representation and no distinction of sex; the calling of a constituent assembly; and an end to all wartime restrictions on civil freedoms and the free movement of labor" (166, 295, 312).

The European Right initially vociferously opposed democracy. As Daniel Ziblatt (2017, xi) notes, "[O]ld-regime groups represented by conservative political parties were the most recalcitrant opponents of mass democracy." This was because conservatives shared the Left's class-based view of democracy. Consider England's Lord Cecil's 1861 opinion that suffrage expansion "means . . . the whole community shall be governed by an ignorant multitude . . . that the rich shall pay all the taxes and the poor shall make all the laws' " (28). Prussia's Ernst von Hydebrand similarly "decried suffrage reform in 1912 [as] 'rule by the undifferentiated masses . . . an attack on the basic laws of nature' " (242).

By the end of the nineteenth century the Right had developed two main ways to contain the threat elections posed to dominant classes: fraud, found in Spain, Germany, Italy, and Portugal; and building mass parties to win "clean" elections, which occurred in Britain, the Netherlands, Denmark, Belgium, and Sweden (Ziblatt 2017, 34–37). Scholars view conservative parties as crucial to democratization, since they help make democracy safe for elites (34–37; see also Rueschemeyer et al. 1992; Gibson 1996; Middlebrook 2000). When democracy became (or remained) unsafe for elites, as when the Left won office, the Right became (or remained) firmly opposed. Numerous examples show this, including France in 1851, England after the 1906 "Liberal landslide," and 1930s Spain (Przeworski 1985, 9; Ziblatt 2017, 141, 347).

Left and right ways of understanding and relating to democracy shifted over the twentieth century. The Russian Revolution precipitated a monumental split between the communist and social democratic lefts. Communists rejected "bourgeois democracy," even as communist parties regularly participated in elections. Social democrats embraced elections and by the 1940s supported "making democracy safe for capitalism" (Eley 2002, 301). This facilitated broader right-wing acquiescence to and even championing of democracy, as long as it was safe. Alongside effective conservative parties, scholars view cohesive moderate left parties as key to making this so (Rueschemeyer et al. 1992, 143).[11] Such parties mobilize lower classes enough to overcome dominant classes' hostility to democracy but not too much to make democracy unsafe.

The neoliberal "counterrevolution" of the 1980s and 1990s brought another major shift in how left and right forces thought of and related to democracy. In theory and practice, neoliberals sought to empty democracy of social content. This was done in various ways, including promoting the Schumpeterian view of democracy as elite competition, establishing and maintaining a clear separation between politics and economics, with democracy restricted to the former, and identifying democracy with the market (Friedman 1962, 15; Kohl and Farthing 2006; Slobodian 2018; Olsen 2019). By the 1990s neoliberalism was globally hegemonic in Gramsci's (1971, 181–82) sense of providing "moral and political leadership, posing all the questions around which the struggle rages not on a corporate but on a 'universal' plane."[12] Leftist parties' embrace of right-wing neoliberal ideas is a potent indicator of this (Anderson 2000; Mudge 2018).

The relationship between democracy, the Left, and Right in Latin America has followed a broadly similar pattern to that found in Europe, with some notable contrasts. The Latin American Left came into being over the first half of the twentieth century as an often-contradictory amalgamation of Marxist and populist parties, unions, and social and political movements struggling to advance working-class and peasant demands for political rights and social justice. As in Europe, scholars view this amalgamation, i.e., the Left, as the key agent of Latin American democratization. Greg Grandin (2011, xxii) argues, "In Latin America, in country after country, the mass peasant and working-class movements that gained ground in the middle of the twentieth century were absolutely indispensable to the advancement of democracy. To the degree that Latin America today may be considered democratic, it was the left, including the Marxist left, that made it so."

To an even greater extent than its European counterpart, the midcentury Latin American Left understood democracy in a social, and participatory, way. Per Bethell and Roxborough (1992, 327–28) both the communist and noncommunist Left saw democracy as "a commitment to popular, more particularly working-class participation in politics, and social and economic improvements for the poorer sections of the population. Democracy increasingly became identified with development and welfare." The U.S.-backed Right—comprising conservative parties and institutions, such as the Church and military, committed to defending existing hierarchies around class, race and ethnicity, and gender and sexuality—vociferously rejected what Grandin (2011, 6) terms "this union of a socialized democracy and a democratic socialism [which] produced a powerful threat to the power and privileges of the incumbent order."

During the Cold War period of the late 1940s through 1980s, the Right repeatedly enacted U.S.-supported coups to depose elected leftist regimes that threatened this order. Such coups occurred in Venezuela in 1948, Guatemala in 1954, Bolivia and Brazil in 1964, the Dominican Republic in 1965, and Chile in 1973. Throughout this period U.S.-backed right-wing forces across Latin America engaged in protracted terror against leftists and reformists of all stripes including union leaders, students, guerrillas, and human rights and Church activists. As Grandin (2011) contends, counterrevolutionary Cold War terror had two major effects. The first was to push many leftists to take up arms and reject electoral democracy as impossible. (To be sure, the Cuban Revolution was also an important factor behind the leftist guerilla insurgencies of the 1960s and 1970s, but Grandin compellingly argues that Cold War terror was more central to this.) Second, this terror effectuated a radical "downward" redefinition of democracy "from entailing both liberty and some degree of social equality to meaning just individual freedom," with Grandin (2011, xiv) viewing this "history . . . [as] *the* story of the twentieth century" (emphasis in original).

The provisional endpoint of this story was neoliberalism, which became hegemonic in Latin America, and most of the world, in the 1990s. As in Europe and the United States, this hegemony was manifest in the right-wing shift of historically leftist parties like Bolivia's *Movimiento Nacionalista Revolucionario* and *Movimiento de la Izquierda Revolucionaria*, Venezuela's *Acción Democrática*, Argentina's Peronist Party (*Partido Justicialista*), and Chile's Socialist Party. All of this paved the way for the Right, and the U.S. government, to acquiesce to and then champion democracy when it returned to most of Latin America in the 1980s, shorn of its social(ist) and participatory elements, and ever more firmly linked to free markets and capitalism (Weyland 2004; Loxton 2021).

The end of the Cold War left the Right in Latin America, and elsewhere, feeling triumphant. The Left, by contrast, was thrown into crisis. This crisis had multiple causes: the failure of the guerilla strategy much of the Left embraced in the 1960s and 1970s; the related decimation of leftist parties and movements due to Cold War terror; and, most important of all, the demise of "actually existing socialism." This latter development, symbolized by the Soviet Union's fall, plunged much of the Left into existential despair. It raised the question: if the Left no longer stood for socialism, what was it for?

Democracy was increasingly the answer given. But there was a major divide within the Latin American Left on what this meant. Moderate leftists accepted the downward redefinition and understood democracy roughly as the Right did: as elite competition in elections and as necessarily linked to free-market capitalism. Radical leftists, by contrast, embraced deepening democracy, which replaced socialism as the post–Cold War Latin American Left's new "master frame" (Roberts 1998:3).

URBAN PARTICIPATION AND THE EVOLVING LEFT-RIGHT DIVIDE IN CONTEMPORARY LATIN AMERICA

With the Left out of national office, cities were the main arena in which new left parties in Latin America sought to deepen democracy in the 1980s and 1990s. As noted, right-wing parties strongly opposed this, and they did so in the name of democracy. This is indicative of a major change in the left-right conflict over democracy, which increasingly centered on democracy's form rather than its existence, as Eaton (2014, 80–81) notes: "The examination of recent struggles between left and right in Latin America reveals a deepening conflict between two different models of democracy. Whereas the left has articulated the case for more direct, participatory, and radical forms of democracy . . . the right has often sought to defend liberal representative democratic institutions by trying to protect the constitutional roles played by elected legislatures."

As with electoral democracy, the Right's position on participatory democracy shifted over time, from full-scale opposition to partial acquiescence. Wampler and Avritzer (2005, 41) document this change in their study of participatory budgeting in Brazilian cities. In Brazil's first PB wave, from 1989 to 1992, left parties implemented 92 percent of PB cases, with centrist parties implementing the other 8 percent. By 2000–2004, left parties' share of PB was 57 percent, with centrist parties implementing 35 percent, and right parties 8 percent. Baiocchi and Ganuza (2014, 31) note, "In the 2000s Participatory Budgeting had become completely politically polyvalent." This contrasts with PB's origins "as part of a transformative left project." Goldfrank (2011a, 265) similarly notes that "the Latin American Left's most famous local government innovation, participatory budgeting, has been taken up by parties from across the political spectrum as well as by international development organizations intent on encouraging PB throughout the region and the globe." This raised a question: Would reforms like participatory budgeting succeed when implemented by non-left, and particularly right-wing, parties?

This question has received limited scholarly attention. The handful of studies touching upon it suggests that non-left, and especially right-wing, parties are unlikely to implement reforms like PB in a way that deepens democracy. Montambeault (2015) examines two instances of participatory reform administered by the conservative PAN party in Leon, Mexico, and finds that neither gave citizens a chance to meaningfully influence political decision-making.[13] Montambeault also found this to be the case in Recife, Brazil, where a succession of two center-right parties implemented PB in a way that gave citizens no real input into decisions. In a separate study of PB in Recife under the same succession of center-right parties, Wampler (2007) found the same thing.[14]

In contrast to the dearth of studies on participatory reform in right-run cities, and the near-total absence of research showing participatory success in such cities, there are many studies of successful participation in left-run cities (Sousa Santos 1998; Abers 2000; Baiocchi 2003, 2005; Wampler 2007; Avritzer 2009; Baiocchi, Heller, and Silva, 2011; Goldfrank 2011a; Montambeault 2015; Gibson 2019). Taken as a whole, the urban participation literature is thus broadly consistent with the view that participatory reform is (much) more likely to succeed in left- than right-governed cities. This view seems implicit in many works on participation (Heller 2001, 133; Baiocchi 2003; Fung and Wright 2003, 6; Chavez and Goldfrank 2004). Goldfrank (2011a, 265–66) is openly skeptical that participatory reforms like PB could succeed in non-left-governed cities.[15] Baiocchi and Ganuza (2014, 32) profess "agnosticism" but appear to hold a similar view.

The question—*What type of left party* is needed for participatory reform to succeed?—has received significant scholarly attention. There is a growing consensus that movement-left parties (Levitsky and Roberts 2011a, 15), also called "movement parties" (della Porta et al. 2017), "movement-based parties" (Anria 2018), and "social movement parties" (Baiocchi 2018), are ideal. Such parties are "directly formed by social movement activists and leaders" and have "a core constituency of grassroots social movements" (Anria 2018, 8). Movement-left parties are not vanguardist, with power flowing from the bottom up rather than the top down (Baiocchi 2018, 36). This setup makes this party type ideal for deepening democracy, which requires genuine bottom-up control over decisions. It is not coincidental that movement-left parties led Latin America's first participatory wave.

There is also a near-consensus that left-populist parties are particularly ill suited for democratic deepening (Baiocchi 2005, 27; Sandbrook et al. 2007, 243–46; Levitsky and Roberts 2011, 25). Left populism is a subtype of populism. As used herein, populism refers to a political strategy combining personalistic leadership, state or party-led mobilization of popular and middle classes, and Manichean rhetoric pitting the virtuous people against the amoral elite.[16] Left populism is characterized by the centrality of class as a means of dividing the people from the elite, while right populism tends to use race and ethnicity in dividing the "true" (often white) people from dangerous outsiders (e.g., foreigners and people of color) and an often-amorphous elite. Left populism involves state- and party-led mobilization and rhetoric pitting popular against dominant classes. Anti-imperialist nationalism, opposing the U.S. empire, is also a key feature of left populism in Latin America.

Left-populist parties are seen as poorly suited to deepening democracy because such parties are top down in two senses: they arise from above, as electoral vehicles for charismatic political outsiders, and they seek to direct and control popular mobilization, inhibiting civic autonomy. Scholars view a strong and autonomous civil society as key to democratic deepening. Baiocchi et al. (2011) cogently explain the basis of this view:

> A robust civil society is important because it creates the spaces in which subordinate groups can associate and self organize, increasing the likelihood that these groups will become coherent political actors capable of independently articulating their interests. (25)

> In its ideal-typical democratic incarnation . . . civil society is characterized by voluntary forms of association that are constituted by and protective of communicative power and that seek to exert their influence by specifically engaging with and seeking support in the public sphere. Taken together, these attributes will trend towards the production of the very types of universalizing norms that must necessarily undergird the democratic ideal of collective self-rule. (29)

As Baiocchi et al. argue, for participatory reforms to succeed in generating something approximating "the democratic ideal of collective self-rule" there must be a "robust civil society" in which popular classes have significant capacity for autonomous mobilization. Left-populist parties mobilize popular classes but in a way that tends to undermine civic autonomy—for example, by linking popular mobilization to a clientelistic distribution of benefits. In so doing, left-populist parties inhibit the potential for genuine collective self-rule. Movement-left parties, by contrast, strengthen popular classes' capacity for autonomous mobilization, which enhances the prospects of participatory success. It is important, however, not to romanticize or reify civil society, understood as a sphere of voluntary collective action. Civic associationalism can, and often does, have democratizing effects, but it is by no means guaranteed, as Riley (2010) shows in his book, *The Civic Foundations of Fascism in Europe*, and I show in my case study of El Alto (chapter 6).

THIS STUDY: EXAMINING URBAN PARTICIPATION AND THE LEFT-RIGHT DIVIDE IN LATIN AMERICA'S LEFT TURN

Democracy on the Ground compares participatory reform in a left- and right-governed city in Venezuela and Bolivia at the high point of Latin America's left turn. My research design facilitates examination of two hypotheses, derived from literature on urban participation, democracy and left-right relations, and the left turn, about the conditions in which participatory urban governance reform is most likely to succeed:

> H1: *Participatory reform is more likely to succeed in left- than right-governed cities.*
>
> H2: *Participatory reform is more likely to succeed under a movement-left rather than a left-populist party, such as in a context like Morales's Bolivia rather than Chávez's Venezuela.*

This section details the book's research design, methods, and data. I begin with a brief discussion of Latin America's left turn and its methodological significance.

THE LEFT TURN AS METHODOLOGICAL OPPORTUNITY

Latin America's left turn, or "pink tide," started in Venezuela in 1998 with Hugo Chávez's election. Over the next decade and a half the region experienced an unprecedented political shift, with leftists elected and regularly reelected in Venezuela, Chile, Brazil, Argentina, Uruguay, Bolivia, Honduras, Nicaragua, Ecuador, Paraguay, El Salvador, and Peru.[17] At the left turn's high point, circa 2010, "nearly two-thirds of Latin Americans lived under some form of left-leaning national government" (Levitsky and Roberts 2011a, 1). In addition to its obvious political importance, the left turn is also methodologically significant for scholars of democracy. This can be grasped by comparing the left turn period to Latin America's previous era of neoliberal hegemony.

Under neoliberal hegemony, the question of democracy appeared settled. Within neoliberal common sense democracy meant elections, elite competition, and representative government; all required free-market capitalism. The left turn unsettled all this and generated new questions like: Would newly elected leftists accept the limits of liberal democracy and market economics? Would they seek to extend or deepen democracy? Would they uphold, reform, or seek to overcome capitalism? These questions have received significant attention (cf. Levitsky and Roberts 2011b; Weyland, Madrid, and Hunter 2010). This is less true of the related question of how the Right might react to the real and perceived threats that the left turn posed to dominant classes: e.g., would right-wing forces seek to unseat elected leftists in military coups, as happened so often in the twentieth century?[18]

COMPARING VENEZUELA AND BOLIVIA, THE LEFT TURN'S TWO MOST "RADICAL" CASES

To get at these issues, I compare Venezuela and Bolivia, widely considered the two most radical cases of the left turn.[19] This characterization is reasonably apt, with efforts to extend and deepen democracy going much further in these two countries than other left turn cases. In countries like Chile and Brazil the "moderate left" took office and took few steps to extend or deepen democracy while taking pains to reassure investors and elites that it would not rock the boat.[20] Venezuela's Chávez and Bolivia's Evo Morales, by contrast, did quite a bit to rock the boat: convoking constituent assemblies, nationalizing industry, initiating major land reforms, promoting participatory democracy, and identifying as socialists seeking to transcend capitalism.[21] However modest by historical standards, these actions appeared radical in the early twenty-first century and provoked a strong conservative reaction that put democratic continuity in doubt in each country.

While similar in being comparatively radical, Venezuela and Bolivia's left turns differed in a notable way. Expressing a view common to Latin Americanists, Hylton and Thomson (2007:8) frame this as a contrast between top-down and bottom-up change:

> In Venezuela, political transformation has occurred at the level of the state and has worked from the top down to channel the existing energies of grassroots organizations. . . . In Bolivia, by contrast, impressive popular power has flowed from the bottom up, setting the parameters for national political and economic debate and putting in place authorities at the national as well as regional and local levels. In no other Latin American country have popular forces achieved so much through their own initiative.

Venezuela's top-down process led to a left-populist regime, while Bolivia's bottom-up process led to a movement-left regime (Levitsky and Roberts 2011a, 15; Anria 2018).

Venezuela and Bolivia's similarities and differences make the two countries particularly interesting cases for studying urban participation and the left-right divide in Latin America's left turn. I turn now to the research used to do so.

CASE SELECTION, METHODS, AND DATA

To select the four cities researched, I conducted two and a half months of preliminary fieldwork in 2007 and 2008 in eight Venezuelan cities and six Bolivian cities governed by left and right parties.[22] Through interviews with municipal officials, party leaders, activists, citizens, and academics, I chose a left- and right-governed city in each country where credible participatory governance reform seemed to exist, with care taken to choose two left-run cities that seemed to have similar prospects for success and two right-run cities that appeared to have similar prospects for failure.[23] As noted, I specifically examined participatory reform in a city in each country governed by a movement-left party (Torres, Venezuela, and El Alto, Bolivia) and a center-right party (Sucre, Venezuela, and Santa Cruz, Bolivia). For reasons discussed, I expected greater success in the cities governed by movement-left rather than center-right parties and relatively greater success in the Bolivian compared to Venezuelan cases.

I use multiple methods and data sources to systematically compare participatory reform in the study cities. My primary method is ethnography, which is ideal for assessing democratic deepening in practice (Baiocchi 2005). The book is a multisited ethnography that employs the extended case method (Burawoy 2009) to reconstruct existing thought about urban participation, democracy and the left-right divide, left party types, and Latin America during the left turn. This reconstruction centers on evidence I gathered while seeking to answer the following questions in each city: Who rules? That is, who controls local political decision-making: ordinary citizens, party leaders, political officials, economic elites, civic association members or leaders, or others?[24] What form or forms of decision-making predominate in purportedly participatory arenas such as participatory budgeting: deliberation, aggregate voting, command-and-control, or other forms? How inclusive are decision-making and resource distribution vis-à-vis class, race and ethnicity, gender, and partisanship and political ideology? How do citizens evaluate the municipal executive politically and administratively? Ethnography builds trust, which makes it ideal for answering these and other questions that appear straightforward but are sensitive in politically polarized and charged contexts, such as asking someone what party they support.[25]

My primary data source is twenty-two months of ethnographic fieldwork and over two hundred interviews conducted on multiple visits to Venezuela and Bolivia between 2007 and 2016. I spent a total of six months in Torres, four in Sucre, five in El Alto, three and a half in Santa Cruz, and three and a half in other cities in each country. I collected data on four indicators in each city: the extent and quality of popular control over political decision-making and degree of institutional and political effectiveness. In each city I attended budget-related government and community meetings, party and civic meetings, and events such as protests and secular and religious celebrations. In the four cities I observed over 150 meetings, assemblies, marches, and other events. I conducted interviews with residents, party and civic association members and leaders, local and national officials, and scholars. Roughly half the interviews were formal, and usually recorded, with the other half informal conversations occurring "on the fly." My ethnographic research generated innumerable interview questions. Interviews, in turn, often generated additional sites or foci for follow-up participant observation.

I collected and analyze other forms of data—electoral data, local and national government reports, newspaper accounts, and information culled from secondary sources—to answer questions amenable to more "objective" quantitative assessment in each city, such as the percent of the budget subject to participatory budgeting; budget-execution and project-implementation rates; electoral turnout; and incumbent-party margins of victory and defeat. Qualitative data facilitated assessing the plausibility of sensitive or politically charged quantitative data, such as budget-execution and project-implementation rates provided by incumbent parties facing reelection. To account for potential biases I use multiple data sources and give more weight to data provided by non-administrative sources, particularly people unlikely to sympathize with the incumbent party. For example, if an opposition supporter rates an incumbent party favorably it is taken as more reliable than a party loyalist doing so.

COMPARING THE CASES: A MULTIDIMENSIONAL APPROACH

I examined four dimensions related to participatory governance in each city.[26]

- *Extent of popular control* over local political decision-making. I measured this by examining the following indicators: the percent of the municipal investment budget subject to participatory budgeting (PB); whether there are institutional mechanisms permitting popular control over non-budgetary local political decisions; and turnout within PB or other local participatory processes.

- *Quality of popular control* over decision-making. I measured this by the type of decision-making procedure(s) used within PB and other participatory governance institutions, with attention to whether decision-making approximates deliberation, where competing perspectives are voiced and justified by use of reason-based arguments (of the form "Let's do a because of b. No, let's do x because of y. Okay, perhaps we should do c because of d, which partially furthers b and y, etc."), command-and-control, aggregative voting (not preceded by deliberation), or another method. Other indicators related to quality of popular control examined are whether officials or participants have final say over decisions within PB or other participatory processes; and the inclusivity of decision-making and local-state resource distribution vis-à-vis class, race and ethnicity, gender, and political views.

- *Institutional effectiveness*, meaning the degree to which decision-making inputs are effectively translated into policy outputs. I measured this by using both "objective" indicators, such as the rate of budgetary execution (the percent of the municipal budget spent annually), and the rate of project implementation (the percent of approved projects that are implemented within a given time period), and "subjective" indicators, such as citizens' perceptions of the municipal executive's effectiveness and performance, particularly administratively.[27]

- *Political effectiveness*, the degree to which a city's political decision-making system generates popular consent. This is measured by whether the local incumbent party wins reelection; whether this occurs if the party fields a new mayoral candidate; the party's win/loss margin; voter turnout; and the party's overall relationship to civil society (particularly whether it's cooperative or conflictual).

To determine whether and to what degree participatory reform succeeded I score each study city on the four dimensions. I classify Torres as highly successful, with extensive, high-quality popular control, and institutional and political effectiveness. Sucre is scored as moderately successful, with moderately extensive, moderate-quality popular control, and institutional and political effectiveness. El Alto is classified as unsuccessful, with a low extent and quality of popular control, and institutional and political ineffectiveness. I classify Santa Cruz as highly unsuccessful, with an extremely limited extent and quality of popular control, and institutional and political semi-effectiveness. The next section details a more conceptual way to think about the outcomes found in the four cases.

CATEGORIZING THE OUTCOMES: THE URBAN REGIMES FRAMEWORK

To better understand the participatory outcomes found in the study cities, I categorize each city as a type of *urban political regime*. This concept builds on Baiocchi's (2005) notion of a "state-society regime," which seeks to capture the patterned ways local states and civil societies relate. Baiocchi et al. (2011, 34) further develop this notion by constructing a typology of civil society-state relations organized around two axes: self-organization, meaning "the degree to which collective actors in civil society are capable of independently organizing," and demand-making, which "refers to *how* civil society actors routinely engage the state" (emphasis in original).

The concept of the urban political regime similarly points to the interface between the local state and civil society on two axes. The first is the *form of rule*, which refers to how citizens are involved (or not) in deciding the allocation of public resources and the manner in which these resources are allocated. (This resembles Baiocchi et al.'s demand-making axis in examining how actors in civil society engage the local state.) I distinguish between two forms of rule. In "democratic rule" citizens are involved in decision-making in a direct, participatory, and effective way, and access to decision-making and resources is universalistic, meaning that it follows "rule bound, regularized, and transparent procedures" (34). In "clientelistic rule" political or civic elites, rather than citizens, control decision-making, and access to decision-making and resources is politically discretionary; to gain access citizens and civic associations must provide support to political or civic leaders, resulting in a patron-client relationship.

The second axis is the *state-society balance*, which refers to the respective ability of actors in the local state (e.g., elected officials and bureaucrats) versus civil society (citizens and civic association members and leaders) to determine the form of rule, to shape how decisions are made and resources are allocated, and whether top local state officials have "professional" or "movement" career trajectories. In "state-controlled" regimes, institutional mechanisms give local state actors the ability to determine the form decision-making and resource allocation take, and local officials have professional trajectories, i.e., degrees from prestigious universities or prior government experience. In "socially-controlled" regimes, social actors (citizens and civic association leaders and members) determine the form that decision-making and resource allocation take, and officials have movement trajectories, i.e., prior experience in social movements.

Bringing the two axes together yields the urban political regimes typology shown in table 0.2. Each of the study cities approximates one of the four urban regime types. The types are presented deductively but were induced from analysis of the four study cities.

- *Participatory democracy* is a socially controlled democratic regime. This regime type's key feature is that citizens and civic associations are central to making political decisions and determining the form this decision-making takes.
- *Administered democracy* is a state-controlled democratic regime. Its key feature is the tension between its two axes, with citizens and civic associations central to political decision-making but local state officials determining the form it takes.
- *Technocratic clientelism* is a state-controlled clientelistic regime, with political or civic elites key to making and determining the form of political decisions.
- *Inverted clientelism* is a socially controlled clientelistic regime. This unusual formulation seeks to capture the tension between this regime type's two

TABLE 0.2 Urban political regimes

		STATE-SOCIETY BALANCE	
		"SOCIALLY CONTROLLED	STATE-CONTROLLED
FORM OF RULE	DEMOCRATIC	Participatory Democracy (Torres)	Administered Democracy (Sucre)
	CLIENTELISTIC	Inverted Clientelism (El Alto)	Technocratic Clientelism (Santa Cruz)

axes, with civic actors determining the form that political decision-making takes but civic and political elites controlling actual decision-making. This can be understood as an inverted form of clientelism in the sense that civil society exerts significant control over the local state but instead of generating broad-based participation (as in participatory democracy) it takes a clientelistic form.

EXPLAINING THE OUTCOMES: NATIONAL AND LOCAL POLITICS

As noted, the outcomes shown in table 0.2 are doubly surprising: I expected more success in the two left-governed cities and in the Bolivian cases but instead found success in the left- and right-governed Venezuelan cities and failure in the left- and right-governed Bolivian cities. What can explain these findings?

The argument I advance departs from works on urban participation that rely on what I term "explanatory localism" to account for participatory outcomes. By this I mean explanations largely or entirely based on local variables, like political will, mayoral leadership, institutional design, availability of local fiscal resources, and the character of local civil and political society (e.g., whether local civic associations possess significant autonomous mobilization capacity and the characteristics of the local incumbent and opposition parties).[28] To be sure, these and other "local" factors have been causally efficacious and often central to participatory outcomes in many cities. The issue is that some studies of urban participation give minimal attention to extralocal variables or treat such variables as endogenous. In the following chapters I seek to show that extralocal variables, like national political regime type, can be causally efficacious for urban participation, in part by shaping seemingly endogenous local variables.

My comparative research design facilitates making such an argument. There are notable local-level similarities in the left and right city pairs. Movement-left parties rhetorically committed to participatory democracy and linked to mobilized popular classes governed both Torres and El Alto, and social movement leaders held the mayoralty and top municipal posts in both cities. Sucre and Santa Cruz both had center-right mayors with a professional background and a reformist history that includes past support for participatory reform; the two cities are also alike in having large informal poor sectors aligned with the ruling left party during the left turn. These similarities make the contrasting outcomes found in Torres and El Alto, on the one hand, and Sucre and Santa Cruz, on the other, stand out, and point to the limits of explanatory localism.

If local-level variables seen as crucial to local participatory outcomes—such as the character of local political and civil society—cannot explain the outcomes found in these cases, what can? My answer is the interaction of national and local politics. The starting point of my argument is the contrasting national political regimes found in Venezuela and Bolivia at the left turn's height. I view this as key to explaining the unexpected similarity of the cross-ideological within-country city pairs, namely the success of the left and right Venezuelan cases (with both having a democratic form of rule) and the failure of the left and right Bolivian cases (with both having a clientelistic form of rule). To explain the differences within the in-country pairs—the greater success in Torres than Sucre and the lesser failure in El Alto than Santa Cruz—I point to the cities' balance of class forces.

NATIONAL REGIMES: VENEZUELA'S LEFT-POPULIST HEGEMONY VS. BOLIVIA'S PASSIVE REVOLUTION

To understand Venezuela and Bolivia's contrasting national regimes, and the effects these regimes had on urban participation and left-right relations, it is useful to situate the two countries as cases within the left turn. My account highlights the similar but distinct type of radical left regime that took hold in the two countries early in the left turn, and the way this difference led the regimes to respond differently to the right-wing backlash their rise precipitated. I contend that the regimes' distinct "reactions to the reaction" led to the difference I focus upon, viz. Venezuela's left-populist hegemonic regime versus Bolivia's passive revolutionary regime.

Like Silva (2009) and Roberts (2015), I view the left turn as an instance of Karl Polanyi's (1944) "double movement," which refers to marketization and society's efforts to protect itself from its negative effects. The left turn can specifically be seen as a countermovement for social protection against neoliberal marketization and its untoward effects, like rising poverty and inequality. As Roberts (2015) notes, the countermovement, i.e. anti-neoliberal protest, took different forms in different countries. In some countries (Brazil, Chile, Uruguay) such protest was channeled within existing political institutions, which led to a more moderate left turn. In other countries (Venezuela, Bolivia, Ecuador), anti-neoliberal protest occurred outside of and helped destroy existing political institutions. This resulted in crises of hegemony in which "social classes become detached from their traditional parties" (Gramsci 1971, 210). This cleared the way for radical-left outsider parties to take office and frontally challenge neoliberalism by nationalizing industry, expropriating private firms, implementing heterodox or statist economic policy, progressively redistributing resources, and embracing participatory democracy and socialism, the latter in an uneven and mostly rhetorical way.

Venezuela and Bolivia's radical left turns unfolded differently because the countries experienced contrasting types of hegemonic crisis, roughly corresponding to a distinction made by Gramsci (1971, 210). In Venezuela there was a top-down "involuntary crisis," in which the political order disintegrates from above and within "because the ruling class has failed in some major political undertaking for which it has requested, or forcibly extracted, the consent of the broad masses." Bolivia had a bottom-up "revolutionary crisis," which occurs "because huge masses (especially of peasants and petit-bourgeois intellectuals) have passed suddenly from a state of political passivity to a certain activity and put forward demands which taken together, albeit not organically formulated, add up to a revolution."

Venezuela's involutionary crisis led to it to enter the left turn with a vaguely left-populist party loosely linked to a diffuse civil society. Bolivia's revolutionary crisis led it to enter the left turn with a movement-left ruling party closely linked to a strong and autonomous civil society. This difference proved consequential when Chávez and Morales faced intense right-wing backlash in their initial years in office. Chávez encountered this backlash weakly linked to dispersed popular movements. He sought to build a stronger bulwark against the Right by extensively organizing and mobilizing popular sectors in the name of "popular power." Alongside historically high oil prices and a favorable regional context, this led to a left-populist hegemonic regime. Morales faced right-wing backlash closely linked to a strong, autonomous, and highly mobilized popular movement. Morales thus had an already existing popular bulwark. Fearing civil war (which appeared a real possibility at the time), Morales worked to contain right-wing backlash through limited mobilization and demobilization of popular forces. From 2010 on, demobilization predominated as Morales compromised with lowland elites linked to the Right and clashed with popular movements. This facilitated the consolidation of a passive revolutionary regime.

Scholars continue to debate the distinction between hegemony and passive revolution, and this book will not resolve that debate. I will, however, attempt to be clear in how I am using these terms. By hegemony I mean a form of political rule marked by a ruling bloc that successfully presents its ideas as the ideas of all, thereby achieving moral and intellectual leadership over society as a whole. Gramsci (1971, 181–82) explains this as follows:

A third moment is that in which one becomes aware that one's own corporate interests, in their present and future development, transcend the corporate limits of the purely economic class, and can and must become the interests of other subordinate groups too. This is the most purely political phase, and marks the decisive passage from the structure to the sphere of the complex superstructures; it is the phase in which previously germinated ideologies become "party", come into confrontation and conflict, until only one of them, or at least a single combination of them, tends to prevail, to gain the upper hand, to propagate itself throughout society—bringing about not only a unison of economic and political aims, but also moral and intellectual unity, posing all the questions around which the struggle rages not on a corporate but on a "universal" plane, and thus creating the hegemony of a fundamental social group over a series of subordinate groups.

Two aspects of hegemony are critical. First, it is based on the *active consent of the governed*. The ruling bloc elicits and organizes this consent by establishing strong links between the state and civil society and, relatedly, political elites and nonelites. The material foundation of this active consent is class compromise, whereby the state coordinates (i.e., partially reconciles) the competing interests of dominant and subordinate classes. Second, a ruling bloc is hegemonic only when it is *recognized as such* by its political competitors, who show this recognition by playing the game of politics on the ruling bloc's terrain. If hegemony exists, an opposition political force that fails to "play politics" on this altered terrain risks becoming politically irrelevant. The arguably best illustration of this second point comes from Margaret Thatcher, who in 2002 was asked to name her "greatest accomplishment." She responded, "Tony Blair and New Labour. We forced our opponents to change their minds." Thatcher's answer points to her success making neoliberalism hegemonic in Britain and her awareness that the Labour Party's rightward shift, effectuated by Blair, was the greatest proof of this.

The distinguishing feature of left-populist hegemony is the centrality of populist mobilization as a means of securing the active consent of the governed. As Collier and Collier (1991, 246) argue regarding radical populism (which left populism, as found in Chávez-era Venezuela and elsewhere, can be considered an example of), this "involves a mobilization of the popular sectors into a political movement or party as part of a political strategy that necessitates both augmenting the real power of the popular sectors and controlling and channeling that mobilization." As detailed below, the contradiction between "augmenting the real power of the popular sectors" and "controlling and channeling that mobilization" was key to the dynamic possibilities that Venezuela's left-populist hegemony simultaneously opened and blocked. In the early years of the Bolivarian Revolution these possibilities centered on participatory democracy, which provided the horizon for state- and party-led organization and mobilization of popular classes. In later years, "socialism of the twenty-first century" provided this horizon. As the ubiquity of references to "popular power" shows, participation remained a quite central element within twenty-first-century socialism.

I contend that Venezuela had a left-populist hegemonic regime from roughly 2005 to 2013. The regime's material foundation was the state's distribution of historically high oil revenues between 2003 and 2013, through programs such as the social missions. In addition to Chávez and the ruling party's sustained electoral success in these years, the key indicator of this hegemony is the momentous change in the opposition's stance toward Chávez around 2006, with ruthless and often-violent opposition (visible in the 2002 coup) giving way to mimicking and championing Chavista rhetoric and policies, including those related to participatory democracy. The opposition's strategic shift is particularly notable since it occurred *while Chávez was radicalizing*. This, I contend, provides support for my contention that left-populist hegemony existed in Venezuela at the time. If it hadn't, one might have expected the opposition to engage in the type of right-wing antidemocratic action that has been so common in Latin American history, which the opposition itself had resorted to just a few years before. The opposition's return to fervently rejecting Chavismo in 2014 marks the end of left-populist hegemony. It is not coincidental that oil prices, upon which this hegemony rested, plunged this year.

Passive revolution is a form of rule in which the ruling bloc fails to achieve (or seek) the universalistic moral and intellectual leadership found in hegemony (Gramsci 1971, 106–14). Passive revolution also differs from hegemony (as understood here) in the relationship between "old" and "new" political elites. In hegemony the old elite is forced to adapt to the hegemonic new elite's political agenda, while in passive revolution the old and new elite merge through "transformism" (Gramsci 1971, 109), which involves "molecular" changes that are relatively modest, though not necessarily unimportant.

Passive revolution is not, however, a simple negation of hegemony (and in Gramsci's writings it is unclear if passive revolution can coexist with hegemony in some contexts). The defining feature of passive revolution is the coexistence of two opposing tendencies—revolution, meaning forward-looking change that fundamentally alters the status quo, and restoration, meaning processes that maintain or restore the status quo—with restoration ultimately prevailing. Passive revolution may involve controlled mobilization that partially alters the existing order but leaves prevailing power relations intact. This differs from "active revolution," involving bottom-up mobilization whereby subordinate groups exert unprecedented control over the forces affecting their lives.

Massimo Modonesi (2017) makes a compelling case that passive revolution centers on what he terms *pasivización*. This term, which lacks an adequate English equivalent, refers to the process and project of "making passive." Modonesi's core argument is that "passive revolutions seek to prevent the masses from remaining active and becoming protagonists. . . . The project-program of passive revolution is carried out as a process the purpose of which is to deactivate, pacify [pasivizar] and subalternize" (33). In his view, *passive revolution is most fundamentally a process of demobilizing previously activated popular movements.* Seen in this way, passive revolution appears as radically different from left-populist hegemony, which centers on *mobilizing popular classes*, and subsequent, and not always successful, attempts to channel and control this mobilization.

Following Modonesi, and Webber (2017), who draws on Modonesi, I argue that under Morales Bolivia developed a passive revolutionary regime characterized by the state and ruling party's demobilization of previously activated popular movements. My argument starts with the 2000–2005 protest cycle that preceded and led to Morales's 2005 election. In Gramscian terms this period can be seen as approximating, without equaling, an "active revolution," since it put revolutionary change on Bolivia's agenda but did not result in a wholesale social revolution. Webber (2017) calls the period a "revolutionary epoch," and Hylton and Thomson (2007) a "revolutionary moment." I divide the Morales presidency into two periods. From 2006 to 2009 there was intense left-right conflict and a "mixed" national regime that combined insurgent and passive revolutionary features, with the state engaging in limited mobilization and demobilization. From 2010 to 2019 passive revolution consolidated with escalating demobilization and an alliance with the right-supporting lowland agrarian elite. In the early years of the 2010–2019 period Bolivia had what Modonesi (2017, 47) calls a "progressive" passive revolution, since the state enacted important reforms benefitting popular classes, and political repression was relatively minimal. In later years Bolivia's passive revolution combined progressive and regressive features, with escalating repression and cooptation of movements.[29]

Venezuela's left-populist hegemonic and Bolivia's passive revolutionary regimes are similar in a few ways. In the current Latin American political spectrum both regimes fall on the radical left end. Participation, socialism, decolonization, and anti-imperialism were important features in both, as was populist rhetoric. Yet the weight and institutional expression of these features differed: participation and socialism were more central and more linked to institutions in Venezuela, while decolonization was more so in Bolivia.

For the purposes of this book, three differences between the countries' regimes stand out: how the state and ruling party related to popular classes; how state resources were distributed; and how participation was expressed. In Venezuela the state and ruling party engaged in extensive organization and mobilization of popular classes; resource distribution was linked to popular organization and mobilization (Handlin 2013); and participatory democracy was discursively and institutionally central. In Bolivia the state and ruling party engaged in limited mobilization and significant demobilization of popular sectors; resource distribution was more individual than collective and was not linked to popular organization and mobilization; and, while the ruling party utilized participatory rhetoric it did relatively little to establish new participatory institutions.

Venezuela and Bolivia's contrasting regimes had distinct "general" effects on the operation of politics and meaning of democracy. Venezuela's left-populist hegemonic regime significantly changed politics, in a way that was felt throughout the country and across the political spectrum. Democracy was increasingly understood in substantive and participatory terms. The 1999 constitution committed Venezuela to "participatory and protagonistic democracy." Laws were enacted to actualize this commitment. Participation and "popular power" became central to ruling party *and opposition* political discourse and practice. Relatedly, the state aligned itself with popular sectors—and against elites. Through laws, rhetoric, and state promotion and funding of numerous new participatory and civic institutions, citizens were interpellated as "protagonists" who should actively participate in policies affecting them (Fernandes 2010; Schiller 2018).

In the realm of urban politics Venezuela's left-populist hegemonic regime led to an important, albeit ambiguous, change in which participatory and clientelistic practices were combined in "participatory clientelism" (Goldfrank 2011b, 169). My research on Torres and Sucre supports Goldfrank's and others' contention that something like this was the modal outcome of participatory reform in Venezuelan cities when Chávez was in office (Wilpert 2007, 58; Ellner 2008, 183). I argue, however, that participatory clientelism can lead to participatory democracy under the right conditions. My case studies of Torres and Sucre suggest this is possible, and arguably likely, in electorally competitive cities that have recently flipped from a ruling party to an opposition party of the Left or Right. I contend that this provides an ideal context for refracting left-populist hegemony into participatory democracy. As shown below, by this I mean a process in which an opposition party (or dissident current of the ruling party) uses the ruling party's institutional and rhetorical "toolkit" in ways and for purposes that are notably distinct from how the ruling party itself uses this toolkit.

Bolivia's passive revolutionary regime resulted in more fragmentary change. The most significant change, built on generations of struggle, was the unprecedented political, economic, and cultural incorporation of Indigenous peoples. The meaning of democracy changed but in a more uneven and limited way compared to Venezuela. Bolivia's 2009 constitution recognized participatory, direct, communitarian, and representative forms of democracy. Morales and ruling party officials used participatory rhetoric, though not to the extent found in Venezuela, and, as noted, this rhetoric was largely disconnected from new institutions and practices. In the realm of urban governance, preexisting patterns of clientelism remained largely intact and the Morales administration was unable to get its own supporters, much less the opposition, to accept its rhetoric of "ruling by obeying." I argue that this helps explain the failure of participatory reform in El Alto and Santa Cruz.

LOCAL BALANCE OF CLASS FORCES

If I am correct that the contrast in Venezuela and Bolivia's national political regimes is key to explaining the success of participatory reform in the left- and right-run Venezuelan cities and its failure in the left- and right-run Bolivian cities, the remaining task is to explain why participatory reform was more successful in Torres than Sucre and less unsuccessful in El Alto versus Santa Cruz. This is equivalent to explaining a city's state-society balance, since within the successful and unsuccessful city pairs, the city with a socially controlled regime was more successful (or less unsuccessful) than the city with a state-controlled regime. To wit, Torres's socially controlled democratic regime represents a higher degree of participatory success than Sucre's state-controlled democratic regime, and El Alto's socially controlled clientelistic regime was less of a participatory failure than Santa Cruz's state-controlled clientelistic regime.

I argue that a city's balance of class forces explains its state-society balance. By "balance of class forces" I mean the ability of individuals and associations linked to popular, middle, and dominant classes to shape decision-making within the local state and civil and political society. I use the term popular class to refer to formal and informal workers "whose labour has been commodified in various ways and . . . do not live off [others'] labour" (Webber 2011a, 18). By middle class I mean salaried professionals, midlevel managers, and others with comparatively secure, well-paid employment. Dominant class refers to private entrepreneurs, landowners, and others who "control . . . key power-conferring resources in the capitalist market" (Portes and Hoffman 2003, 44).

The balance of class forces in the study cities fit one of two patterns: "popular power" in which popular classes predominate in political and civil society, and "elite-professional power" in which dominant and middle classes predominate. I contend that a popular power balance of class forces leads to a socially controlled urban regime, while an elite-professional balance of class forces leads to a state-controlled regime. In theoretical terms, this can be understood by thinking about the relationship between class and the state under capitalism. As Block (1977) notes, in capitalist social formations, the state is dependent on dominant classes for tax revenue and business confidence. Social control over political decisions requires breaking this link between the state and dominant classes; this is possible only when popular classes are highly organized and mobilized, as in a popular power balance of class forces.

Torres and El Alto both have a popular power class forces balance, and, accordingly, both have socially controlled urban regimes. Sucre and Santa Cruz have an elite-professional class forces balance, and state-controlled urban regimes. As noted, these differences also account for Torres being more successful than Sucre and El Alto less unsuccessful than Santa Cruz. The book's overall causal argument, that the combination of national political regime type and local balance of class forces explains a city's urban regime type, is represented in table 0.3.

TABLE 0.3 Explaining study outcomes

		LOCAL BALANCE OF CLASS FORCES	
		POPULAR POWER	ELITE-PROFESSIONAL POWER
NATIONAL REGIME	**LEFT-POPULIST HEGEMONY**	Participatory Democracy (Torres)	Administered Democracy (Sucre)
	PASSIVE REVOLUTION	Inverted Clientelism (El Alto)	Technocratic Clientelism (Santa Cruz)

PLAN OF THE BOOK

Democracy on the Ground proceeds in two parts. Each part comprises three chapters: a first on national context, followed by case studies of the left- and right-governed case studies for each country. Part I covers Venezuela. Chapter 1 examines the succession of four national periods: neoliberal reform and the crisis of the old order in the 1980s and 1990s; the conflict-laden rise of a new left-populist regime between 1998 and 2005; the consolidation of left-populist hegemony from approximately 2005 to 2013; and the crisis of left-populist hegemony between 2014 and 2018. The chapter focuses on explaining left-populist hegemony's rise and the Right's reaction. Chapter 2 examines Torres, where a left-opposition local incumbent party, with strong links to mobilized popular classes, refracted left-populist hegemony into participatory democracy. The chapter details the rare degree of decision-making power Torres's residents possessed, the attempt to extend this power from the political to the economic realm, and the partial erosion of Torres's participatory democracy from 2013 on. Chapter 3 examines Sucre, in which a right-opposition local incumbent party, with a middle- and upper-class core base, refracted left-populist hegemony into adminis-tered democracy. The chapter seeks to show that the unexpected success of participatory reform in Sucre is an artifact of national-level left-populist hegemony and competitive local elections. The chapter also details the limits and contradictions of administered democracy, in which the local state gives ordinary citizens "some but not too much" power over local political decisions.

Part II covers Bolivia. Chapter 4 examines Bolivia's strikingly similar but not identical succession of national political periods: neoliberal reform and the crisis and collapse of the old order from the 1980s to 2005; the conflict-laden rise of a new left regime between 2005 and 2009; the consolidation of passive revolution between 2010 and 2015; and crisis from 2016 to 2020. The chapter aims to explain Bolivia's similarities and differences to Venezuela, focusing on the post-2010 turn to passive revolution and the Right's reac-tion. Chapter 5 examines Santa Cruz, in which a right-opposition local incumbent party, with an upper- and middle-class core base, refracted passive revolution into technocratic clientelism. The chapter details the resolutely antidemocratic nature of this urban regime, with attention to its difference from Torres's participatory democracy and, more surprisingly, Sucre's administered democracy. I explain the latter as partly due to the Morales administration's failure to establish leftist hegemony. Chapter 6 examines El Alto, where a left-ruling-party-affiliate local incumbent party, with patronage-based links to highly organized popular classes, refracted passive revolution into inverted clientelism. The chapter details the regime's surprising similarities to Santa Cruz's technocratic clientelism and unexpected differences from Torres's participatory democracy, arguing that both relate to Bolivia's passive revolutionary national regime.

The conclusion reviews the book's four major contributions. The first shows that leftist hegemony can reshape the Right such that it will not only tolerate but even embrace and promote a more real form of democracy. The second advances a framework for understanding participatory urban governance that endeavors to provide a more conceptual and multidimensional way to think about outcomes, showing how national political processes matter to such outcomes, thus avoiding explanatory localism. The third advances a relational framework for understanding the dynamics of leftist regimes, with particular attention to how such regimes change over time based on the regimes' responses to right-wing backlash. The fourth rethinks Venezuela and Bolivia as cases within Latin America's left turn. The conclusion also discusses the generalizability of the findings and analysis presented. I ask if leftist hegemony can exist outside the left turn and how different forms of leftist hegemony compare.

PART I

VENEZUELA

Refracting Left-Populist Hegemony Into
Participatory Urban Governance

1

VENEZUELA

From Crisis to Left-Populist Hegemony

On December 6, 1998, Venezuelans elected Hugo Chávez president; a career army officer who had led a 1992 coup against a highly unpopular regime, his election led to the establishment of a left-populist regime that transformed Venezuela by making popular sectors central to national politics in a way not seen since the 1945–1948 "trienio." Chávez enjoyed broad support in his first two years in office, but when he started to radicalize in 2001 socioeconomic and displaced political elites reacted with fury to the threat he posed to their interests, repeatedly seeking to remove him from office between 2001 and 2005. Chávez survived this reactionary onslaught, and until his March 2013 death he pursued an increasingly radical reform program that continued to significantly threaten elite interests. From 2006 to 2013 Venezuela's right-led opposition reacted to this threat in a surprising manner—by increasingly seeking to copy Chávez rather than oust him by any means. The reason was the establishment of left-populist hegemony. This chapter tells the story of how and why this occurred, and of the regime's contradictions and post-2014 implosion.

To tell this story I compare Venezuela and Bolivia. Both countries went through a strikingly similar sequence of periods between the 1980s and

2000s: neoliberal reform and the crisis and collapse of the old regime; the rise of a new left regime; and right-wing backlash. The new left regimes' contrasting responses to this backlash set Venezuela and Bolivia on distinct paths, leading to left-populist hegemony in Venezuela and passive revolution in Bolivia. Here and in chapter 4 I seek to show that Chávez and Morales's distinct "reactions to the reaction" stem from the different type of crisis of hegemony by which the old regime fell and the left turn commenced in the two countries.

NEOLIBERAL REFORM AND THE CRISIS AND COLLAPSE OF THE OLD REGIME

Chávez's election ended Venezuela's Punto Fijo system of pacted democracy. Established by the 1958 Punto Fijo Pact, the system revolved around center-left Acción Democrática (AD) and center-right COPEI (Committee of Independent Electoral Political Organization or Comité de Organización Política Electoral Independiente). Yet it is complicated to view Punto Fijo-era Venezuela through a classic left-right lens, as Alejandro Velasco (2015, 158) and others have shown, since AD and COPEI both had left and right wings, with the 1979–1984 presidency of COPEI's Luis Herrera Campíns arguably the most leftist of the era. The Punto Fijo pact excluded the Communist Party, despite the central role the party played in the 1958 restoration of democracy. In conjunction with the Cuban Revolution, this exclusion helped fuel leftist guerilla insurgency in the 1960s, which the state responded to with brutal repression (Ciccariello-Maher 2013; Velasco 2015).

The late-1960s "pacification" of this insurgency and the 1973 oil boom facilitated the consolidation of Venezuela's "model democracy" (Ellner and Tinker Salas 2007).[1] This system rested on robust oil-fueled growth and state-led development. Key industries, including iron, steel, and oil, were nationalized, and there were major public investments in iron, steel, hydroelectric power, petrochemicals, aluminum, telecommunications, infrastructure, and air transport. Social spending significantly increased, and the state established price controls, subsidized food, cooking oil, and gasoline, and took actions supportive of workers' rights. Workers and the poor saw rising incomes, and during the 1970s were effectively linked to AD and COPEI through benefits, patronage, and clientelism (Morgan 2011; Silva 2009, 196–98). This system collapsed in the 1980s due to falling oil prices and the government's inability to pay its debt. On February 28, 1983, known in Venezuela as "Black Friday," the government devalued the currency. Declining revenues led to steep spending cuts in health, education, and social services (Dunning 2008, 163, 167, 187). Poverty also started to climb, after declining during the 1970s.

MARKETIZATION

Venezuela's neoliberal turn started relatively quietly in 1980 when COPEI's Herrera Campíns—who won the presidency in 1978 calling for participatory democracy (Velasco 2015; López Maya 2014)—leased trash collection routes to private contractors in Caracas's famously contentious 23 de Enero neighborhood in what was "the first effort toward privatizing public services in Venezuela" (Velasco 2015,167). In subsequent years he went further by privatizing public housing in 23 de Enero (187–93). Velasco (2015, 193) notes the mixed meanings this act held. To some it was "an expression of democratic maturity through popular empowerment," while others saw it "a sign of . . . a fissuring of the social pact between a state no longer able to meet its responsibilities and popular sectors suddenly forced to fend for themselves."

Marketization took off following the 1988 victory of AD's Carlos Andrés Pérez. This was unexpected, as Pérez had campaigned on a promise to avoid austerity and return Venezuela to the prosperity found during his first presidency, 1974–1979, when he nationalized oil amid a historic oil boom. Within days of returning to office in 1989, he commenced his "great turnaround." He signed a secret IMF agreement agreeing to deep spending cuts, price and interest rate deregulation, currency devaluation, privatizing banking, air, telecommunications and ports, and liberalizing trade (Silva 2009, 200–201). Pérez implemented these policies in an exclusionary, technocratic way with little input from the public or even his own party. Promarket business leaders and intellectuals of the "Grupo Roraima" designed policies behind closed doors, as Pérez "planned to push as many reforms as possible (mainly fiscal and monetary policy) through by decree" (200–201).

Neoliberal reform devastated popular and middle classes. Prices rose, incomes fell, and working conditions deteriorated. By the mid-1990s per capita GDP had declined 20 percent from its late-1970s peak (Roberts 2003, 59). Between the 1980s and late 1990s, per capita public sector spending fell 40 percent, minimum wages fell 60 percent, and state spending declined 40 percent in education, 70 percent in housing and urban development, 37 percent in health care, and 56 percent in social development and participation (Silva 2009, 201). From 1984 to 1995 poverty rose from 36 to 66 percent, and extreme poverty tripled from 11 to 36 percent (Roberts 2003, 59). In 1989 the economy contracted 10 percent and poverty rose from 46 to 62 percent. From 1980 to the late 1990s unemployment rose from 6.6 to 15.4 percent, and informal employment from 35 to 50 percent, with wages 30 percent less than in the formal sector (Silva 2009, 202–203).

AN INVOLUTIONARY CRISIS OF HEGEMONY

The devastating consequences of marketization generated significant resistance. The signal instance of this was the February 1989 Caracazo, a week of largely spontaneous looting and protest in Caracas and cities nationwide. Reprising his 1960s role in antiguerilla counterinsurgency, Pérez sent 10,000 troops to working-class and central Caracas neighborhoods leading to between 300 and 1500 civilian deaths (Velasco 2015, 120–21, 194–226).[2] Looting centered on small businesses that hoarded goods anticipating that Perez's market reforms would soon drive prices up. Police often stood by while looting occurred and in some instances joined in (Silva 2009, 204; Velasco 2015, 207–8).

Repression did not quell protest. In the three years after the Caracazo there were five thousand protests over hunger, rising prices, and exclusionary policy-making (204–5). These concerns also led to two 1992 military coups, with Hugo Chávez, then a junior officer, leading the first in February. Both coups failed and led to a short-term decline in protest. The coups also destabilized the political system and were a factor in Pérez's May 1993 impeachment and the December 1993 presidential election. Former president Rafael Caldera left COPEI—the party he cofounded in 1946—and won the election on an anti-neoliberal campaign, though many felt La Causa R, a small radical left party in second place, had actually prevailed.

Caldera implemented heterodox policies in his first two years in office, instituting price controls and reversing privatizations. In 1996 fiscal problems and a banking crisis led him to enact market reform. In exchange for a 3.3 billion USD loan from the IMF, Caldera raised gas prices 500 percent, deregulated interest rates and prices, established a unitary free-floating exchange rate, increased sales taxes, and privatized aluminum, airlines, and oil. This sparked a second protest wave of around five hundred protests a year from 1996 to 1998. Public-sector unions, teachers, students, transport workers, and popular- and middle-class neighborhood associations led this wave, like the 1989–1992 protest cycle. Both waves were similarly "defensive." Protesters demanded delayed pay raises, improved pensions, and payment of bonuses promised but canceled, and expressed concerns over increasing crime and police violence, the low quality and deterioration of public services, the high cost of living, rising transportation fees, and market reform generally (Silva 2009, 221–22).

Pérez and Caldera's bait-and-switch tactics (campaigning against and then enacting market reform) fueled rising discontent with AD, COPEI, and parties generally. By the end of the 1990s this discontent resulted in an involutionary crisis of hegemony, with Venezuela's political order crumbling from the top down as the neoliberal project, foisted upon an unwilling public by the bipartisan ruling class, spectacularly failed. Table 1.1 shows how this occurred. Support for AD and COPEI plunged between the 1970s and 1980s, when the two parties garnered 85–93 percent of the presidential vote in every election, and the 1990s, with the parties together winning 46 percent of the 1993 presidential vote and 3 percent in 1998. Turnout also plunged in these years, partly since compulsory voting ended in 1993.

TABLE 1.1 Support for traditional parties and turnout in Venezuela, 1973–1998

	VOTE % (AD + COPEI)	TURNOUT %
1973	85	97
1978	90	88
1983	92	87
1988	93	82
1993	46	60
1998	3	64

The involutionary nature of Venezuela's crisis of hegemony can be seen in two features. The first is the fact that anti-neoliberal protest was decentralized, uncoordinated, and not linked to a new political alternative. A key reason for this is that the Confederation of Venezuelan Workers (Confederación de Trabajadores Venezeula, CTV) did not offer sustained leadership of anti-neoliberal protest due to its close ties to AD, the party leading market reform. Pérez exploited the CTV's links to AD to limit worker protest by, e.g., engaging the CTV in on-and-off negotiations. The second key feature of the crisis is the formal and temporal disconnect between the most intense instances of anti-neoliberal protest—the Caracazo and the 1989–1992 protest wave—and the collapse of the party system, which took place gradually and was finalized only in 1998 with Chávez's election.

THE EMERGENCE OF A NEW LEFT-POPULIST REGIME, 1999–2001

Chávez went to prison for two years for the February 1992 coup. After Caldera pardoned him in 1994, Chávez spent several years traveling, learning, and organizing. In 1998 he launched an outsider presidential campaign with his "anti-party" Fifth Republic Movement (MVR). Chávez's promise of greater social and political inclusion led to a landslide victory. After taking office, Chávez sought to make good on this promise by convoking a National Constituent Assembly (Asamblea Nacional Constituyente, ANC). The process by which delegates were elected garnered criticism, but the assembly itself was highly participatory, with civil society associations actively taking part. "Human rights organizations, women's, neighborhood, environmental, and educational groups organized citizen assemblies and drafted proposals to present to the 1999 National Constitutional Assembly. Their efforts resulted in the submission of 624 proposals to the ANC; of these, 321 were partially or completely adopted by the assembly" (Mallen and García-Guadilla 2017, 43).

The new constitution declared Venezuela a "participatory and protagonistic democracy." In his August 1999 speech inaugurating the ANC, Chávez proclaimed, "We have to give the people diverse mechanisms such as plebiscites, referenda, popular assemblies, the power to initiate laws, all these instruments must remain inserted, in my opinion delegates, in the new fundamental charter, so that participation may be binding, so that it is not simply participation for participation's sake, but an instrument to construct, of protagonism and a true democracy, of effective participation, vital to construct a new country, a direction, a project" (35).

Many articles in the constitution, which 72 percent of voters approved in a December 1999 referendum, sought to give flesh to the idea of participatory and protagonistic democracy. Participation was understood to involve more than voting. Citizens were constitutionally endowed with power to propose legislation and recall elected officials. Citizen assemblies became a legally binding form of decision-making. In subsequent years new laws concretized the constitution's commitment to participation. The 2002 Law of Local Public Planning Councils mandated nationwide municipal participatory budgeting (though this did not lead to successful nationwide implementation of local PB). As noted above, leaders before Chávez, like Herrera Campíns, had championed participation, with limited and mixed results (Velasco 2015, 158–59; López Maya 2014). But under Chávez participatory democracy became politically and institutionally central within

Venezuela to an unprecedented extent (Mallen and García-Guadilla 2017; López Maya and Lander 2011, 59).

Chávez's MVR dominated voting for the ANC and the July 2000 "mega" elections that put nearly every elected post in the country up for a vote. This thoroughly displaced traditional parties and generated resentment. However, opposition to Chávez was initially muted due to his moderation in 1999 and 2000, when he courted domestic and foreign capital, supported free-trade zones, and advocated "Third Way" policies to create "neoliberalism with a human face" (Webber 2010, 22–25; Ellner 2008, 110–12).

RIGHT-WING BACKLASH, 2001–2005

The first clear sign Chávez was not a Venezuelan version of Tony Blair came in November 2001 when he issued forty-nine decrees. Three of them, regarding fishing, farmland, and oil, modestly challenged property rights. Chávez's willingness to take such a step, which was quite radical for the times, was partly due to the low price of oil, which severely hampered the state's ability to fulfill pent-up social demands. In conjunction with Chávez's displacement of the traditional political class, the decrees helped spark a cycle of backlash that lasted until 2005. Opposition to Chávez was politically and socially heterogeneous, but the revanchist Right was predominant during this period.[3] Private media, the Federation of Chambers of Commerce and Production (Fedecámaras), opposition parties, and the CTV, which retained close ties to AD, led the antigovernment forces, which included some small leftist parties, like Bandera Roja.

On December 10, 2001, Fedecámaras called a general strike to oppose Chávez's forty-nine decrees. This was the first of a series of strikes and mobilizations against Chávez in coming months. Chávez's February 2002 appointment of new leadership to PDVSA, Venezuela's national oil company, sparked more protest. Things came to a head with the April

2002 coup, which Fedecámaras, private media, and the CTV led. After the military removed Chávez from office, Fedecámaras president Pedro Carmona declared himself president and moved to install a right-wing dictatorship. Carmona "abolished democratic institutions, abrogated the forty-nine laws of 2001, and pledged to hold elections only within one year" (Ellner 2008, 115). He appointed pro-neoliberal far-right figures to top interim posts, and sidelined the CTV and opposition parties (115–16). Yet "throughout the coup attempt, opposition leaders who had misgivings about Carmona's dictatorial and antipopular measures failed to assert themselves by assuming a critical stand towards the provisional government" (116–17). In a stunning turn of events with no parallel in modern Latin American history, Chávez was brought back to office forty-seven hours later due to mobilization by his supporters, who surrounded Miraflores Palace demanding his return, the actions of midlevel officers loyal to him, and opposition infighting.

The coup revealed and helped accentuate the stark class divide between Chavistas and oppositionists. Opposition to Chávez was multiclass, as the CTV's actions show, but led and dominated by the upper and middle classes with the popular classes forming Chávez's core base.[4] Racism and the threat of redistribution fueled the predominantly white elite's disdain for Chávez, who had dark skin and strongly identified with Venezuela's multiracial majority. As Dunning (2008, 175) notes, "[A]ctual redistributive measures remained relatively muted at the time . . . [but t]he threat of redistribution played an important role in shaping elite support for an attempted coup against Chávez." Low oil prices made Chávez's mildly redistributive policies appear more threatening, since redistribution in this context would touch directly on elites' interests. The U.S. government supported the coup and gave millions to the opposition in coming years (Golinger 2006; Gill 2022).

The opposition continued its all-out effort to remove Chávez through 2005. From December 2002 to February 2003 Fedecámaras, the CTV, opposition parties, and PDVSA's top brass fomented an oil lockout. In conjunction with the damage caused by the April 2002 coup, the lockout decimated Venezuela's economy, which contracted 17 percent in 2002 and

2003. But Chávez did not fall, partly due to his continued popular-sector support. The opposition next tried to remove Chávez through a 2004 recall referendum. Chávez survived by delaying the referendum (generating sharp critiques, as Handlin [2017] notes), and launching a series of popular social missions, detailed later in the chapter. The opposition's final move against Chávez in this time was boycotting the 2005 National Assembly elections. The chief result of this was to give pro-Chávez parties near-total legislative control from 2005 to 2010.

TOWARD LEFT-POPULIST HEGEMONY, 2005–2013

Chávez faced the backlash loosely linked to a diffuse and divided civil society.[5] His support was dispersed due to the MVR's loose structure, the historical weakness of Venezuelan civil society, which neoliberalism had exacerbated, and the CTV's opposition. To counter ongoing elite intransigence Chávez sought to build a sturdier popular bulwark by adopting a left-populist governance strategy with three main features.

First, the state extensively organized and mobilized popular classes. This took many forms, the first being Bolivarian Circles, which brought together neighbors for mutual aid work and local activism supporting the government, in 2001. From 2002 on state organization and mobilization of popular classes intensified. The state helped to organize urban land, water, and health committees in 2002 and 2003, communal councils in 2006, and communes from 2007 on, to mention just some forms this took (Azzellini 2017). In 2007 Chávez created the United Socialist Party of Venezuela (PSUV) in response to concerns about the MVR's electoralism, distance from social movements, and perceptions of rampant internal corruption (Ellner 2008, 127). The PSUV established links to Chavista popular associations. Through the PSUV and state-sponsored civic associations Chávez mobilized his supporters regularly for elections and in opposition to the "oligarchy" and "Empire."

Second, state spending on popular sectors significantly increased, and it was linked to popular organization and mobilization, which the state incentivized (Handlin 2013). This occurred, in large part, through social missions, like Barrio Adentro, which provided the poor free health care (Cooper 2019). Other missions provided access to literacy training, higher education, and subsidized food and basic goods (Ellner 2008, 122–23). Social missions fostered, incentivized, and often required collective organization.

Third, participatory democracy became increasingly important. As noted, the 1999 constitution championed participatory and protagonistic democracy, and many laws aimed to concretize this: the 2002 Law of Local Public Planning Councils, 2006 Law of Communal Councils, and 2010 Law of Communes. Chávez spoke of an "explosion of popular power" in 2007, and renamed ministries as such: the Ministry of *Popular Power* for Health, Defense, Electricity, for example. And Chavista and a growing number of opposition politicians extolled participation and popular power in their political speeches.

The argument made here, that Chávez embraced a left-populist strategy to build a sturdier popular bulwark to counter elite intransigence, is consistent with other work on this period. Goldfrank (2011b, 167–68) contends that Chávez's contentious relationship to organized labor and the weak links between Chávez's "Patriotic Pole" (comprising the MVR and smaller left parties) and civil society led him to a "radical democratic approach emphasizing broad-based individual participation" in his early years. Ellner (2008) makes a related argument that Chávez survived the 2002 coup not because of the strength of popular forces, as Ciccariello-Maher (2013) holds, but despite their weakness. Ellner (2008) writes, "Had it not been for the blunders of the provisional government, headed by Pedro Carmona, in failing to call for immediate elections, Chávez may very well have not returned to power. In this case, one of the main explanations for the coup's success would undoubtedly have been Chávez's failure to galvanize mass support for his socioeconomic reforms." (115).

I contend that Chávez's left-populist strategy facilitated the consolidation of left-populist hegemony between approximately 2005 and 2013.

Chávez's charisma, the high price of oil, alongside Chávez's reassertion of state control over PDVSA, and a favorable regional context (due to the left turn), were also important to this outcome. I turn now to the material basis, indicators, and contradictions of Venezuela's left-populist hegemony.

MATERIAL BASIS

Without the 2003–2014 oil boom it is hard to imagine that Chávez could have achieved anything resembling left-populist hegemony, which rested on state redistribution of robust growth literally and fiscally fueled by oil. As already noted, in Chávez's first years in office the low price of oil hindered his ability to meet long-standing popular demands and underlay elite anger toward his relatively modest redistributive measures. From 1999 to 2001 growth averaged just 0.37 percent, and in the conflict years of 2002 and 2003 the economy contracted 16.7 percent. The end of acute government-opposition conflict in 2005, and rising oil prices from 2003 on, helped spur an economic rebound, with annual growth averaging 4.5 percent between 2005 and 2013.[6] Other economic indicators were also positive in this period: foreign reserves increased substantially,[7] growth was higher in the private versus public sector, and in the non-oil versus oil sector, and inflation was low by domestic standards.[8]

While oil provided the revenue, the materialist key to Venezuela's left-populist hegemony was increased state spending on the poor. From 1998 to 2011 social spending as a percentage of the GDP doubled from 11.3 to 22.8 percent. Through subsidies, price controls, and direct state provisioning (e.g., the missions), the government partially decommodified key sectors, including health care, education, social services, food, housing, utilities, and basic goods. This led to major social gains. From 2003 to 2011 poverty fell from 62 to 32 percent, and extreme poverty declined 71 percent. The number of university graduates more than doubled. School enrollments steadily increased. Unemployment was halved. Child malnutrition declined almost 40 percent. The number of pensioners quadrupled. Inequality declined steeply, with the Gini coefficient dropping from 0.5 to 0.4 between 2001 and 2003 and 2009 to 2011. From 2012 to 2015 Venezuela was Latin America's most equal country (ECLAC 2017, 14).

INDICATORS

The key indicator of left-populist hegemony is the opposition's remarkable strategic shift before and after 2005. The opposition frontally opposed Chávez from 2001 to 2005, repeatedly seeking to oust him, including by unconstitutional and violent means. In these years the opposition (which, as noted, was heterogeneous) refused to recognize Chávez, the 1999 constitution, or its electoral losses as legitimate. The 2006 election shows a clear change. Dunning (2008, 198) notes the "striking . . . extent to which the [opposition] Rosales campaign appeared to lift pages out of Chávez's political-economic book. Rosales advocated the creation of a banking card that he baptized "*Mi Negra*"—loosely, "my dark-skinned woman" or, alternately, "my dear"—that would transfer oil rents directly to the poor." His immediate concession of his loss to Chávez was also striking. "This was the first time since 2000 that the opposition recognized Chávez as the legitimately elected president and thus opened the path toward the normalization of Venezuelan politics in the Chávez era" (Wilpert 2007, 28).[9]

As evidence presented in chapter 3 shows, the opposition's shift continued and deepened in coming years. Leading opposition figures, like Carlos Ocariz, Sucre's mayor and cofounder of the center-right party Primero Justicia, used rhetoric and institutional forms indelibly associated with Chavismo. This would have been nearly unthinkable in the 2001–2005 period. A thought experiment suggests that an opposition party or leader who gave even the appearance of mimicking Chavismo in these years would have been quickly marginalized within the antigovernment forces. But Primero Justicia was *rewarded* for "playing politics" on Chavista terrain, with the party rising to become the opposition's indisputably leading force by 2012. The party won the February 2012 opposition primary by a landslide, with its candidate, Henrique Capriles, besting the second-place finisher by a Chávez-like margin of 64 to 30 percent. This pitted Capriles against Chávez in the 2012 presidential election. Capriles was also the opposition candidate in the 2013 special presidential election against Nicolás Maduro. In both elections Capriles drew on Chávez's playbook: he made frequent references to Simón Bolívar and promised to *increase* social spending and "dramatically increase salaries and pensions" (Grandin 2013). Capriles immediately recognized Chávez's 2012 victory but notably did not recognize his 2013 loss to Maduro. In addition to showing Chávez's political importance, this also provided an early sign of the coming demise of left-populist hegemony.

It is important to note that the MVR and PSUV absorbed more than a few members of the two main parties they displaced, AD and COPEI, during the Chávez era. In popular parlance this was referred to as someone "putting on the red shirt" regardless of whether they believed in Chavismo's ideals. This shows that transformismo was not absent from Chávez-era Venezuela, but it does not invalidate my argument that the establishment of left-populist hegemony had a critical impact on the opposition's strategy, namely forcing it to move left. It is also important to note that hard-line opposition to Chávez did not end during the period of left-populist hegemony. My argument is that the hard-line position was marginalized within the opposition, and thus within Venezuelan politics generally, because opposition leaders and base-level activists (the three million voters in the February 2012 opposition primary) saw it as politically unviable in a context marked by left-populist hegemony. This context demanded (and certainly privileged) opposition non-hard-liners, like Primero Justicia, willing to engage on Chavismo's terms.

Electoral and public opinion data help show why this was the case and constitute additional evidence indicating left-populist hegemony in the 2005–2013 period. Chávez enjoyed a honeymoon after his 1998 election, but his public approval plummeted in 2002 and 2003. Things started to turn around with his convincing victory in the 2004 recall referendum. By 2006 Chávez was at the peak of his popularity, winning that year's presidential election with 63 percent of the vote, 26 percent more than his main opponent. In his last election in 2012, when he was dying of cancer, Chávez prevailed with an 11-point margin of victory, a significant achievement after almost fourteen years in office. Chávez led the ruling party to

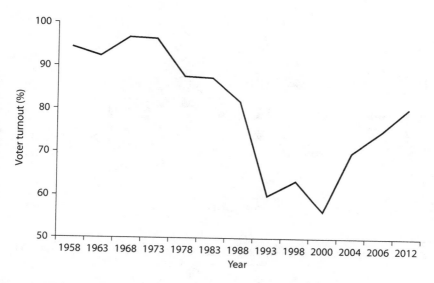

FIGURE 1.1 Turnout, presidential elections, 1958–2012.

Source: Venezuelan National Electoral Council.

victory in twelve of the fourteen major elections held during his time as president. He can also be credited with a dramatic increase in voter turnout. As figure 1.1 shows, turnout plunged in the 1980s and 1990s and then dramatically rose from 2000 on. However, rising turnout alone does not constitute evidence of left-populist hegemony. Part of the reason turnout rose under Chávez was increased polarization, with many turning out to vote against Chávez and his party. But the combination of rising turnout and Chávez's significant margins of victory (in 2006 and to a lesser extent 2012) offers evidence of quite widespread popular support for Chávez and his left-populist project.

Public opinion data also indicate widespread popular consent to this project. Figures 1.2 and 1.3 use Latinobarómetro data in all years available from 1995 to 2018 to compare Venezuela to three other Latin American countries and the Latin America country average on citizens' views of the state of democracy in their country. The three countries are Uruguay, often seen as the region's highest-quality democracy, Chile, which many

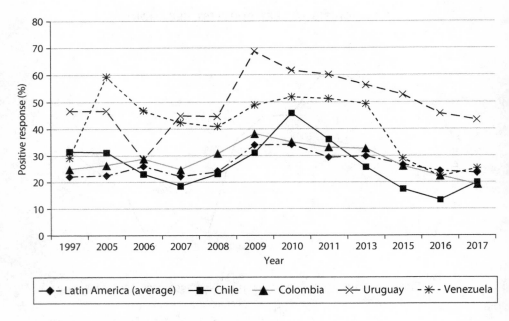

FIGURE 1.2 How democratic is [country], 1997–2017.

Source: Latinobarómetro 1995–2018.

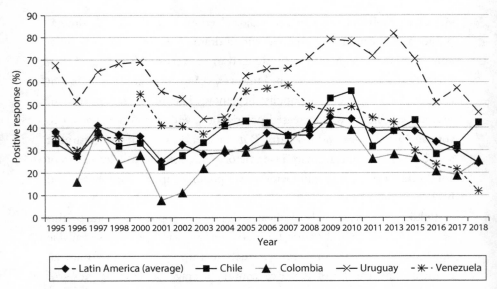

FIGURE 1.3 Satisfaction with how democracy works in [country], 1995–2018.

Source: Latinobarómetro 1995–2018.

scholars view as much more democratic than Venezuela under Chávez, and Colombia, considered one of the region's lowest-quality democracies in these years.

Figure 1.2 shows responses to the question "How democratic is [country]?" Data shown are the aggregate of scores 8, 9, and 10, the three most positive responses to the question. The data show clearly that Venezuelans' view that their country was democratic increased significantly after Chávez took office and remained high throughout his period as president. From 2005 to 2013 Venezuela had the highest or second-highest score on this question, second only to Uruguay (from 2007 to 2013) and far above the Latin American average. Venezuela's score on this question declined significantly and sharply in 2015 and remained near or below the Latin America average through 2017.

Figure 1.3 shows responses to the question "How satisfied are you with how democracy works in [country]?" Data shown are the aggregate of "very satisfied" and "rather satisfied" from all years from 1995 to 2018 except 1999, 2012, and 2014. This provides a more granular level of detail versus figure 1.1 (with many fewer years) for Venezuelans' and others' view on the quality of democracy in their countries. In the four years prior to Chávez's election, 1995–1998, Venezuela was near or below the Latin America average. Venezuela's score had risen considerably by 2000 and remained higher than average through 2013, when Chávez died in office. Venezuela's score was second, to Uruguay, for the entire 2000–2013 period, except 2009 and 2010, when it was third, behind Chile.

These data show that Venezuelans saw their country as becoming more democratic under Chávez, a strong indicator that Chávez governed with a high level of popular consent. Figures 1.2 and 1.3 also show that this was not true of Chávez's successor, Nicolás Maduro. From 2013 on Venezuelans' sense that their country was democratic and their satisfaction with the quality of their democracy fell precipitously. This is consistent with my argument that left-populist hegemony started to erode after 2013.

The increased link between the state and (subaltern) civil society that occurred from (roughly) 2003 to the end of Chávez's presidency is also indicative of left-populist hegemony. During this time, the state facilitated the creation of, and funded, tens of thousands of grassroots organizations. Goldfrank (2011a, 263) argued, "Venezuela is undergoing the largest experiment in direct citizen participation in the region (and perhaps the world), with roughly a third of its total population, over eight million people, participating in 33,549 Communal Councils." Millions also participated in tens of thousands of urban land, health, and water committees, communes, and other Chavista organizations. As scholars have noted, Chávez and Chavista officials used these associations and ruling party cells to mobilize millions of supporters for electoral and nonelectoral purposes. I turn now to the contradictions this involved.

CONTRADICTIONS

These contradictions stem from the dynamic inherent to populist mobilization in which, as noted, the state attempts to enhance popular sectors' power and then control it (Collier and Collier 1991, 246). Scholarship critical of Chavismo has tended to emphasize the second part of this dynamic, portraying Chávez as a demagogue who ran roughshod over opponents, stifled civil society, and eroded democracy, while duping the masses with empty rhetoric and unsustainable spending (Brewer-Carías 2010; Sánchez-Uribarri 2008; Hawkins 2010; Corrales and Penfold 2011; Weyland 2013). Observers with a more favorable view of Chavismo have emphasized the first part of the dynamic and portrayed Chávez as a democratically elected leader who empowered the poor and made their lives immeasurably better. To his most ardent supporters, Chávez appears as an outright hero.

A number of rich ethnographies seek to avoid these either/or views and instead explore the messiness and contradictions of Chavismo (Fernandes 2010; García-Guadilla 2011; Ciccariello-Maher 2013; Velasco 2015; Valencia 2015; Azzellini 2017; Schiller 2018; Kingsbury 2018; Cooper 2019). These works attend to "the paradoxes of state-sponsored participatory democracy" (Smilde 2011, 25), which concern issues such as state funding and organizational support for civic associations, civic autonomy, and electoral politics. Fernandes (2010) and García-Guadilla (2011) discuss how associations supportive of Chavismo strategically related to the government, muting critiques in electoral periods, but strongly criticizing and challenging the government in nonelectoral times. Fernandes (2010, 185–94) also shows that popular movements' relations to, and autonomy from, the government varied due to interrelated differences in organizational structure and funding.

Goldfrank's (2011b, 168) concept of participatory clientelism is particularly useful for understanding participatory democracy in the Chávez era. The concept refers to the way Chavismo combined features associated with participatory democracy, such as collective mobilization and deliberation, and clientelism, i.e., making access to state resources contingent on political support. Goldfrank and others (Ellner 2008, 183; Wilpert 2007, 65) argue that the Chávez government's support for participation tended to result in (what Goldfrank calls) participatory clientelism rather than participatory democracy. My research on Torres and Sucre, presented in chapters 2 and 3, supports but also complicates this idea. I show that attempts to implement participatory reform led to participatory clientelism in both cases, but I also demonstrate that this generated a political backlash that facilitated a subsequent successful attempt to create participatory decision-making, which was led by local opposition incumbent parties of the Left and Right that utilized the rhetoric and institutional forms of Chavismo.

THE CRISIS AND COLLAPSE OF LEFT-POPULIST HEGEMONY, 2014–2021

Venezuela's left-populist hegemony rested on three pillars: Chávez's charisma, historically high oil prices, and the favorable regional context created by the left turn. After 2013 each of these pillars disappeared and left-populist hegemony eroded and then collapsed. Chávez's March 2013 death set the stage for the April 2013 election of Nicolás Maduro, who is near-universally seen as significantly less charismatic than Chávez. This was likely a reason (among others) for Maduro's slim 1.5 percent margin of victory, and for

Capriles's refusal to recognize his loss. But the PSUV's decisive victory in the December 2013 local elections suggests Maduro's lack of charisma alone may not have ended left-populist hegemony. The PSUV triumph helped convince Capriles to engage in talks with Maduro in January 2014, which raised hopes Venezuela could return to political stability.

These hopes were shattered weeks later when the hard-line opposition launched the #LaSalida protests seeking Maduro's immediate removal. From February–April 2014 Venezuela was engulfed in an often-violent opposition-government conflict, which left a reported forty-three dead (and harkened back to the 2001–2005 period of conflict). Investigations indicate opposition protesters and state security forces were each responsible for roughly half the deaths. Maduro's lack of charisma appears as a partial cause of this protest wave, with the hard-line opposition sensing and seeking to exploit Maduro's political fragility to further their agenda and in the process gain the upper hand over opposition moderates.

Maduro faced a new challenge starting in July 2014, when oil prices plummeted. Prices fell through 2016 and stayed low until 2021. This contrasts with the 2004–2014 period, when prices consistently topped $80–100 a barrel (apart from a dip in 2008 and 2009). For most of the 2014–2021 period prices hovered in the $60-a-barrel range (with a plunge to just over $20 a barrel in April 2020 at the start of the COVID-19 pandemic). The fall in oil prices led to a steep and prolonged decline in state revenue, revealing Venezuela's continuing hyperdependence on oil. This long-standing problem had worsened on Chávez's watch, with 69 percent of Venezuela's export earnings coming from oil in 1998, when Chávez was first elected, and 96 percent in the years after his 2013 death (Lander 2016).

Falling oil prices were one of several factors that led Venezuela to experience "the worst economic depression ever recorded in Latin America" (Monaldi 2018, 2) from 2014 on. Velasco (2022, 67) reports a stunning 86 percent fall in Venezuela's GDP "from $323 billion in 2015 to an astonishingly low $45 billion in 2021." Inflation, "which had averaged 24 percent between 2003 and 2012, exploded into the third-worst and longest hyperinflation in history, reaching an astonishing 350,000 percent in 2019" (66). This decimated the social gains achieved in Chavismo's "golden years" (2005–2013).

Real wages collapsed, infant mortality grew, undernourishment increased by a factor of twelve from 2011 to 2018, and poverty skyrocketed to an estimated 96 percent by 2019 (66). This situation led six million Venezuelans to leave the country from 2014 on, in what the United Nations called "the second-largest external displacement crisis in the world."[10]

Two other factors, beyond falling oil prices, are key to explaining the economic crisis. The first was Maduro's continuation of a dysfunctional currency policy. In 2003 Chávez established currency controls to prevent capital flight, but he did not end them several years later when this threat had passed. The system involved multiple exchange rates, which created a parallel ("black") market for currency exchange. The gap between different official rates and between these rates and the black-market rate created immense opportunities for corruption. Roland Denis (2015) estimates that corruption related to this had reached 300 billion USD by 2015, with this figure continuing to grow until Maduro finally modified the system in 2019. Currency mismanagement also contributed to inflation, plunging domestic production, and immense shortages of dollars and goods.

The second factor is the increasingly brazen efforts of domestic elites and the U.S. government to disrupt the economy with what the government calls "the economic war." This took multiple forms—one being the direct and indirect economic damages caused by the 2014 and 2017 protest waves, which disrupted daily life and involved protesters directly targeting government infrastructure. In a 2017 *New York Times* op-ed Maduro estimated that protests that year, which claimed an estimated 150 lives due to both opposition and government actions, resulted in at least 1 billion USD in economic damage. As it had for years, Washington cheered, funded, and otherwise supported the opposition (Gill 2022).

The United States also imposed debilitating economic sanctions on Venezuela. This started in 2015 under President Obama, who declared Venezuela an "extraordinary security threat" to the United States, and imposed sanctions on select government officials. Trump went far beyond this. In 2017 he implemented financial sanctions preventing the issuance of new debt, which impacted oil by preventing Venezuela from forming joint ventures with private companies. In 2019 Trump levied sanctions directly on

Venezuelan oil, and in 2020 secondary oil sanctions were levied that prevented foreign companies from doing business with PDVSA.[11]

The direct and indirect damage from sanctions (with indirect damage due to business "overcompliance," a refusal to do business with Venezuela due to fears of being punished by the U.S. government; see Weisbrot 2017) has been immense, and from at least 2017 on may be considered the leading factor behind Venezuela's crisis. It is challenging, however, to separate the internal and external causes of the crisis since the two are closely intertwined. For instance, Venezuela's damaging currency policy was established due to the threat of capital flight in 2003. And U.S. sanctions are a leading cause of the immense fall in Venezuelan oil production since 2017, which (alongside falling oil prices) led to the tremendous decline in state revenue already noted.

The third pillar supporting Venezuela's left-populist hegemony was the favorable regional context created by the left turn. Critically, this meant Chávez had like-minded allies across Latin America throughout his time in office. The 2003 commodity boom and intra–South American bodies such as Mercosur and the Union of South American Nations (UNASUR, created in 2008) gave Latin American governments unprecedented autonomy from the United States. In 2015 Latin America began a "right turn," with pro-U.S. right-wing regimes winning elections in Argentina in 2015, Peru in 2016, and Chile in 2018, and coming to office through a parliamentary coup in Brazil in 2016 and a bait-and-switch election in Ecuador in 2017. The Right remained in office in Colombia, Honduras (following its 2008 military coup), and Paraguay (after a 2012 parliamentary coup) as well. As its domestic situation deteriorated, Venezuela was thus increasingly regionally isolated.

Economic and social crises led to political crisis. In 2015 the PSUV suffered its worst defeat ever, with voters punishing the party for rampant shortages, rising poverty and hunger, and long lines at grocery stores, banks, and elsewhere. The opposition gained a two-thirds supermajority in the National Assembly, with the government conceding its loss but wrangling over three seats for months. Polarization increased throughout 2016, as the opposition mounted a recall campaign against Maduro and sought to use its newfound political power to remove him from office (with some in the opposition frustrated by their colleagues' lack of focus on improving ordinary Venezuelans' lives).

The government responded to its loss of political support and the hard-line opposition's intransigence with a turn toward repression. The Supreme Court, which Maduro controlled, blocked the National Assembly from passing major legislation.[12] In October 2016 Maduro abruptly halted the recall referendum and delayed gubernatorial elections scheduled for December. Further moves toward authoritarian rule followed. In March 2017 the Supreme Court dissolved the National Assembly, prompting a public rebuke from the attorney general, who condemned this as "a rupture in the constitutional order." This was later reversed but not before it sparked the 2017 protest wave. In April the government banned Henrique Capriles from participating in electoral politics for fifteen years on politically motivated corruption charges. In July Maduro held a highly controversial election for a new constituent assembly. The company that ran the election reported that it could not vouch for the government's claim that over eight million people had voted. Later that year the government held delayed elections for governors. Evidence indicates the government committed outright fraud in Bolívar state (Kurmanaev 2017). In conjunction with the government's false claim on turnout in the constituent assembly election this further eroded public confidence in Venezuela's electoral authorities. Maduro won reelection in May 2018, but the three leading opposition parties were banned from participating since they had boycotted the December 2017 municipal elections. The government was also accused of manipulating the media to the disadvantage of the main opposition candidate, Henri Falcón. Maduro won by a substantial margin, but the vote was roundly seen as illegitimate and served to cement Maduro's authoritarian rule.

The most significant challenge to Maduro's rule came in 2019 when Juan Guaidó—an opposition backbencher and protégé of far-right leader Leopoldo López who had just assumed the National Assembly's rotating presidency—declared himself Venezuela's legitimate president. This was carefully coordinated with the U.S. government, which immediately recognized Guaidó's claim, as did Canada and many Latin American and European countries. Guaidó appears to have thought Maduro would fall quickly. When he didn't, Guaidó and his backers engaged in a series of tragicomic actions: a botched humanitarian incursion into Venezuela from Colombia in February; a failed coup attempt in April; and supporting a May 2020 maritime invasion "headed by several dozen opposition-hired mercenaries" (Velasco 2022, 72), which Maduro easily discovered and put down. Guaidó initially enjoyed significant domestic support, but this evaporated as each of his ever more desperate attempts to bring Maduro down failed. In January 2021 Guaidó's presidency of the National Assembly ended, and with it the purported basis of his claim to be Venezuela's president. Yet Guaidó's claim continued, leading to jokes that neither of Venezuela's two presidents (Maduro and Guaidó) would ever step down.

Maduro's approach to Guaidó was relatively restrained, with Guaidó largely free to move about Venezuela and enter and exit the country. This contrasts with the increasingly harsh and lethal state repression unleashed on popular sectors from 2015 on. This repression is documented in the Office of the United Nations High Commissioner for Human Rights' July 2019 report on human rights in Venezuela. As I wrote in *The Nation*, the report "paints a devastating picture of the country's economic, social, and political situation: 7 million Venezuelans, a quarter of the population, are in need of humanitarian assistance; more than 4 million have recently fled the country; between January 2014 and May 2019, more than 15,000 people were detained for political reasons; between January and May 2019, there were 66 documented deaths of political demonstrators; and, according to the government's own numbers, 5,287 people were killed in 2018 while 'resisting authority' in poor neighborhoods" (Hetland 2019). The report also notes accounts of people who say they were denied access to government food boxes "because they refused to support the government" (Hetland 2019). All of this is indicative of the collapse of left-populist hegemony, or any other type, within Venezuela, with the Maduro administration sustaining its rule through force rather than consent.

2

TORRES

Participatory Democracy in "Venezuela's First Socialist City"

From 2005 to 2016 Torres municipality, in the central-western Venezuelan state of Lara, may have been the world's most democratic city.[1] During this time ordinary citizens exercised a remarkable degree of popular control over local political decision-making. This occurred in several ways, the most important being Torres's Participatory Budget, which gave citizens binding control over 100 percent of municipal investment funds. Decision-making in Torres's PB was highly deliberative, with agricultural laborers, students, domestic caregivers, teachers, small farmers, and others engaging in thoughtful discussions of the merits of spending limited budget money on this versus that project. The process was highly inclusive, with no formal or de facto restrictions in terms of class, race and ethnicity, gender, religion, or political views. Most participants came from the popular classes, and there were more women than men, and more non-whites than whites. Chavistas predominated, but there were many non-Chavistas and some oppositionists. Thousands and likely tens of thousands of people, comprising between 8 and 25 percent of Torres's population of 185,000, participated in the process each year. Decisions were effectively linked to outcomes: upward of 85 percent of projects were implemented in a timely manner, with citizens directly implementing more than three-fourths of these projects.

This chapter tells the story of how Torres's PB, and the participatory democratic urban regime it anchored, came about. At first glance the story seems to fit with existing thought. The key event that led to Torres's participatory democracy was the 2004 election of a movement-left mayor closely linked to popular movements. If there is a formula for successful urban participation, this is it. But a closer look shows that Torres's participatory success followed a "crooked" path due to the multifaceted relationship between Torres's movement-left mayor, Julio Chávez, and the ruling MVR (Fifth Republic Movement). Julio (as he is universally called) defeated the MVR in 2004, in part due to support from Chavistas disappointed with the MVR's unfulfilled promises. Julio faced significant opposition from the MVR in his first years as mayor, but he identified strongly with the Bolivarian Revolution. Drawing heavily on Chavista discourse, laws, and institutional forms, he saw his actions as fulfilling Chavismo's promise to build participatory and protagonistic democracy and twenty-first-century socialism. Using the language of this book, Julio refracted left-populist hegemony into participatory democracy; his administration's links to mobilized popular classes were critical to achieving this outcome.

The chapter begins with a brief overview of Torres's socioeconomic structure and history. I then discuss the transition from clientelism to participatory clientelism and then to participatory democracy. The bulk of the chapter assesses Torres's participatory democracy. I close by discussing how Julio and others linked participatory democracy to a broader struggle to construct a new form of socialism and examining the internal tensions within Torres's participatory democratic regime, which increased from 2013 on.

GODOS CONTRA CHIVEROS: A BRIEF HISTORY OF TORRES

Torres is an unequal, agrarian-based municipality of poor goat farmers, urban service workers, affluent cattle ranchers, and sugar barons. With a third (37 percent) of its population in rural areas, Torres is six times more rural than Venezuela as a whole. Most of Torres's urban residents live in Carora, population 89,417 (Alcaldía de Torres 2011, 27–28). During the twentieth century Torres's economy was based on cattle ranching, sugar production, and small-scale goat farming. In the early 2000s there were 8,600 cane cutters and 1,000 workers in two sugar-processing plants.[2] Goat farmers, derisively called *chiveros*, derive meager income selling goat cheese, milk, and *suero* (fermented milk) at ramshackle stands on local highways. Milk processing, small-scale fruit and vegetable production, an industrial slaughterhouse, an emergent wine industry, and retail, service, and public-sector work in Carora provide additional sources of income and employment.

The scarcity of industry in Torres has generated various problems, including high unemployment and underemployment, and a limited local tax base, resulting in fiscal dependence on central government transfers. Like all of Venezuela, Torres experienced rising poverty, unemployment, and crime in the 1980s and 1990s (Harnecker 2008). A 2001 study found over a third of Torres residents living in poverty, with 53 percent of houses categorized as "needing improvement," and 40 percent of residents lacking sewage treatment and garbage collection (FUDECO 2010, 50–52). As of 2003, Lara state had 20 percent unemployment (50–52).

RULE OF THE *GODARRIA*

From the sixteenth through the middle of the twentieth century a small group of interlocking landowning families, known as the *godarria* or *los godos*, ruled Torres. The term references Spain's Gothic region from whence these *familias de apellido* ("named families") came (Cortés Riera 2007). Per historical scholarship and local lore, the godarria considered itself a separate caste and married largely within its own ranks, eschewing relations not only with "mixed-raced" *pardos*, *mestizos*, and *morenos*, but also with "white creoles" (García Ponce 1986, 17; Cortés Riera 2007).

The godarria's domination was consolidated between the 1870s and 1930s, a period of intense accumulation by dispossession when rising landowners used violence, bribery, trickery, and control of local and regional state institutions to defraud thousands of peasant smallholders of public "wastelands" (*baldíos*) they had occupied for years or generations (García Ponce 1986; Cortés Riera 1997; Salazar 2007). Wealth concentration proceeded apace. In 1922 nine families owned half the wealth of Torres's cattle industry (García Ponce 1986, 14). By the 1940s, "astonishing crosslinking" led just four families to control nearly all this wealth (50–52). The godarria also monopolized local political power. In 1940 the opposition weekly *Cantaclaro* characterized the godarria's political control as follows: "They hold all three powers here, the legislative, executive and judicial. And more: all other offices, from the simplest bureaucratic position, remain trapped between their hairy hooves" (quoted in Salazar 2007, 227–28).

Sugar surpassed cattle as Torres's leading source of wealth in the middle of the twentieth century. As of 2010 sugar covered 77 percent of Torres's agricultural land, with Torres contributing 11.2 percent of national sugar production (FUDECO 2010, 78). The godarria's economic dominance continued, with named families owning or controlling Torres's two sugar-processing plants, cattle lands (which remained important), local private schools, a hospital, baseball team, bank, and slaughterhouse (Cortés Riera 2007).

Accounts indicate that feudal class relations prevailed in Torres's countryside from the early to mid-twentieth century. Debt peonage (bonded labor) and police patrols kept peasants bound to large estates; peasants were required to carry identity cards at all times listing their personal effects, land occupied, rental agreement, debts, and specific crops farmed. These cards stipulated tenants' "strict submission to the provisions of the present regulation" and had to be produced on demand (García Ponce 1986, 35). Tenants were required to provide unpaid labor for landlords' maintenance, supervision, and security, and needed landlords' permission to hunt, build, and sublet their homes (35). Eladio "Lalo" Paez, a social movement leader who held several key posts under Julio Chávez, recalls his youth in the 1950s as follows: "The oligarchs owned the houses, they gave permission about who could move where, [and] they even owned the families. When a peasant couple got married in any of the towns in these zones, and it was on one of the haciendas, the bride was given to the hacienda owner on her wedding night" (Harnecker 2008, 21).

RESISTANCE MOVEMENTS

The godarria's rule was contested. In the late nineteenth and early twentieth century peasants refused to vacate land, withheld "illegitimate" rent, and took claims to court, often with little success (Salazar 2007, 205–31). The 1935 death of Venezuelan dictator Juan Vicente Gómez led to nationwide mobilization. Peasants in Torres and neighboring municipalities organized unions and direct actions to take back land (Powell 1971, 56; Yarrington 1997, 181–85). Future president Rómulo Betancourt noted "the serious disturbances of the peasants of Carora and Quíbor, which began in early 1936" (Powell 1971, 55). The Union of Small Agricultural Producers of Montes de Oca Municipality (now a parish of Torres) boasted a thousand members in 1936 and compelled landlords to sign an agreement stating that "peasants may cultivate their plots, build their houses and use the forest and water while the Nation proceeds to definitively resolve the property relationship of these lands" (García Ponce 1986, 51–52). Torres and nearby municipalities were foci of leftist organizing in the 1930s (Cortés Riera 2007). Radical intellectuals, such as Cecilio "Chío" Zubillaga, supported this by founding the radical weekly *Cantaclaro*. The paper's support for land reform led to its editors' imprisonment for "advocating the abolition of private property" (Salazar 2007, 229). There is scant information on Torres during the 1945–1948 trienio, though Salazar (2007, 181–182) reports that peasant leaders were beaten, threatened, and fired from jobs after mobilizing in 1945.

The 1958 restoration of democracy led to more mobilization. Torres and nearby areas were centers of guerilla activity and brutal state repression in the 1960s (Linárez 2004, 2006). Víctor García, a lifelong leftist who moved to Torres in the 1960s with his wife Myriam Giménez to organize cooperatives, told me about a 1968–1973 wave of peasant organizing in Torres led by Jesús Morillo Gómez, who, like Luis Herrera Campíns, belonged to COPEI's left wing. In one of many conversations we had driving around town, and in his and Myriam's modest but comfortable home in Carora's working-class neighborhood of La Guzmana, where I stayed on many of my trips to Torres, Víctor said Morillo Gómez organized 'over 100 land committees.' Herrera Campíns spoke of this in a July 8, 1970, radio interview for the program *Buenos Días*:

> Carora's cattle industry and those who have developed it are the pride of Venezuela. . . . In Torres District there are also thousands of landless families, traditionally humiliated by the prestige and power of the Caroreño landowners. This is why Jesús Morillo Gómez's work in Torres District has been profoundly popular. He doesn't have moderation in his words, but he has energy, charisma, and a vocation to struggle for the people, a popular appeal and an honesty that not even his worst enemies can deny. This is what Acción Democrática can't forgive. It's because of Morillo Gómez, with his efforts and expositions, that the peasants of Torres District and their demands are taken into account and considered a national problem. Naturally, these peasants thank COPEI for this, given that Morillo Gómez is our Secretary General in the zone, and this brings despair to Acción Democrática, which has now lost the hegemony it had in Lara.[3]

Morillo Gómez's crowning achievement was leading two hundred landless families in their 1972 takeover of the fertile Hacienda Sicarigua, with the land farmed cooperatively since.[4]

With support from the Communist Party and the progressive Catholic organization Centro Gumilla, Víctor and Myriam helped make Torres a center of radical cooperative organizing in the 1960s and 1970s. According to Myriam, the cooperatives led "massive mobilizations of the people against increases in the price of water and gas" (Giménez 2008, 81). Torres was also a site of radical cultural organizing in the 1970s and 1980s. Lalo Paez and Miguel "Chicho" Medina (who would both go on to hold top posts in Julio Chávez's movement-left administration) founded the *movimiento cultural* (cultural movement) in their hometown of Los Arangues. Over a multiday interview in his family home during the 2009 Christmas holiday, Lalo told me that 'dozens and dozens' of activists, including Myriam and Víctor, were active in the cultural movement, which in the 1980s comprised '22 organizations . . . sports associations, crafts, music, coops, and the [peasant] union.' Local meetings and international exchanges provided a space for 'discussion and debate, including political discussion and debate.'

As the rest of this chapter shows, the history just recounted was very much alive for people like Víctor, Myriam, Lalo, and Julio Chávez, who referred to their efforts to build participatory democracy, and socialism, as continuing the long struggle against the godarria. This history also illustrates the social movement roots of Torres's participatory democracy. I turn now to the more proximate processes that helped lead to this outcome.

CLIENTELISM (1980s-1990s)

To establish a baseline for understanding subsequent developments, I begin by examining politics in Torres in the 1980s and 1990s, the end of Venezuela's Punto Fijo era of pacted democracy. Available evidence indicates Torres had a clientelistic urban regime during this period, with citizens' and civic associations' access to public resources and decision-making fora linked to political support. A 2011 report by the *alcaldía* (the mayor's office, run by Julio Chávez's successor, Edgar Carrasco) characterizes this system as follows: "Citizen participation through these social organizations [neighborhood associations] is described as geared towards activism and protest, with citizens having no access to decision-making. Decisions were made through written or verbal requests, aimed at solving problems of access to basic services such as water, electricity and roads, among others. *Solutions had a strong discretionary bias in accord with the political-party interests of the government then in office*" (Alcaldía de Torres 2011, 47, emphasis added). This report is not neutral, as it comes from an administration that prided itself on having ended this clientelism. But the report is consistent with other accounts, such as that given by Myriam Giménez, who at the time was not part of, and often criticized, the *alcaldía*.

Myriam told me of her years as a neighborhood association leader during one of many conversations we had in her airy kitchen. Neighbors often interrupted to gossip or confirm the time of the next community meeting, which Myriam unfailingly knew. Except during not-infrequent blackouts, state-run radio or television blared in the background. (Myriam religiously watched Mario Silva's *La Hojilla* and Diosdado Cabello's *Con El Mazo Dando*, while Víctor preferred "Dr. House" with Hugh Laurie.) Myriam recounted her and her fellow leftists' efforts to keep neighborhood associations—which numbered a hundred at their height in the 1980s and 1990s (Alcaldía de Torres 2011, 46)—autonomous from parties and the local government. She said this allowed the associations to pressure local authorities. Speaking of her neighborhood, La Guzmana's association, Myriam said, 'We worked for the whole community. . . . Many of us were leftists, and with leftist political parties . . . but it was never the case that any of these parties decided things in our neighborhood association.' Myriam said this was not how things worked generally. 'The neighborhood associations became very politicized. . . . They basically just followed the orders of political parties, who ruled them. . . . The Adecos had their neighborhood associations . . . the Copeyanos had theirs. . . . When the Adecos ruled, everything went to the Adecos. When the Copeyanos ruled, everything went to the Copeyanos.'

As AD-COPEI hegemony crumbled in the 1990s, Myriam and other leftists tried and failed to transform Torres's politics. Myriam ran for mayor in 1995 for the movement-left party, La Causa R. Her memory of the outcome is hazy. 'I think we came in fourth or fifth place, and I don't remember how many votes we got, but very few,' she laughingly recalled. Julio Chávez, a student and labor leader, launched a similar radical-left mayoral campaign in 2000. He was trounced, receiving just eight hundred votes (Harnecker 2008, 13). At the regional level, however, change was afoot, as the success of Orlando Fernandez Medina's outsider campaign for governor of Lara state in 1995 showed. This victory prefigured the sweeping, but highly contradictory, changes of the coming Bolivarian Revolution.

PARTICIPATORY CLIENTELISM (2000–2004)

The Revolution came to Torres in 2000 in all its contradictory glory when Javier Oropeza, a rising media baron from one of Torres's leading families, was elected mayor with support from Hugo Chávez's MVR and Fernandez Medina's eponymous OFM party, which allied with the MVR. To local leftists, like Julio Chávez's uncle, Hermes Chávez Crespo (2010, 18), Oropeza's win marked the restoration of godarria rule:

> Javier Oropeza is so *godo*, so genetically *godo*, his grandfather, his mother's father, was Ramón Herrera, whose father was Epímaco Álvarez, and his other grandfather was Chico Juan Oropeza, who owned lands from Los Bucares . . . to Empedrado, on the border with Trujillo State. . . . The peasants couldn't go see Chico Juan. Ramón Herrera grabbed the whole valley from what's now La Balonchera through Bucare, Morere, Papelon. Javier's other grandfather, on the Álvarez side, took half of El Empedrado, everything that was El Empedrado, so I mean they were three vultures, so he's the sonny boy of a vulture, he has vulture blood.

Chávez Crespo reports that Oropeza appointed the head of the Cattle Ranchers' Society his director of government, with this man's cousin heading the conservative local Catholic hierarchy. This marked a continuation of the godarria's long-standing control of the church. According to Julio Chávez, "The command of the Catholic Church's hierarchy in our municipality was comprised of the region's powerful families" (Harnecker 2008, 20). Oropeza was known for being a lifelong Copeyano before 2000. His election can thus be seen as helping to prolong traditional party rule within Torres.

But Oropeza's administration was not a simple restoration or continuation of the past. The administration instead reflected the class and ideological contradictions of the MVR, which included an unwieldy mix of revolutionaries, reformers, and politically promiscuous and ambitious members of the landed elite. To staff his cabinet, Oropeza had to negotiate with local and regional MVR leaders, including Luis Reyes Reyes, the Lara governor, and Carlos Miguel Álvarez, a progressive doctor who had run participatory health councils in the 1990s with help from none other than Myriam Giménez. When the doctor told Oropeza to make Myriam his director of social development, Oropeza agreed.

In this capacity, Myriam was tasked with forming Torres's Local Public Planning Council (CLPP) in conformance with a 2002 national law mandating the creation of such councils in all Venezuelan municipalities. One of the CLPP's tasks was to implement a local participatory budget. Myriam recounted the mayor's instructions. 'Javier called a meeting and told us, "Look we have to form a planning council. If you don't I'll be fined fourteen thousand *bolívares* and I don't have the funds, so just go ahead and do it. But *make sure you put our people in there*" ' (emphasis added). Using a truck and resources provided by the mayor, Myriam assembled a team to form Torres's CLPP.

Zoila Vásquez, a social worker who a few years later became secretary-general of Torres's CLPP, was part of this team. In 2009 I accompanied Zoila to CLPP-run participatory budget assemblies throughout Torres. On one of many dusty, bumpy, and long drives across Torres's vast and varied territory of scorched desert valleys and lush mountains, Zoila spoke of her 2002 work under Myriam. 'We traveled to every corner of the municipality' to hold popular assemblies where residents elected CLPP delegates and discussed proposals for Torres's first-ever participatory budget. Myriam said she ignored the mayor's command to 'put our people in there' and worked to ensure that CLPP delegates were democratically chosen in conformity with the law, which mandated that community members outnumber current or former elected officials on the CLPP. Myriam said Oropeza continued to interfere by, e.g., 'having people from his former party, COPEI, attend assemblies and try to make sure they ran things.' Myriam also said the mayor 'refused to recognize the participatory budget' after the process was completed.

Over time Oropeza's relationship with the MVR became increasingly tense. Myriam said 'there were rumors [Javier and his friends] celebrated Chávez's fall' in the 2002 coup. Myriam had felt 'uncomfortable for some time with how close Javier was to the opposition.' When he joined the opposition in 2003, Myriam resigned. 'I couldn't stay. I was part of the mayor's office and he'd declared himself in opposition to Chávez.'

Oropeza's defection opened up the 2004 mayoral election. It was a closely fought race between Oropeza, now backed by opposition parties, commercial media, the church, and the landed elite; Walter Cattivelli, a local contractor backed by the MVR; and Julio Chávez, who was supported by social movements and several radical left parties, Julio's own party, Patria Para Todos (Fatherland for All), an outgrowth of La Causa R, the Communist Party, the Socialist League, and the People's Electoral Movement. To the surprise of many, Julio won by a razor-thin margin, taking just over 16,000 votes (35.6 percent of the total) to Oropeza's 15,000-plus votes, and Cattivelli's 14,000 votes (Harnecker 2008, 20). Leftist activists say Julio's election was possible because of support from many disaffected Chavistas who felt betrayed by Oropeza's defection and were unimpressed with Cattivelli, who was known for being 'an Adeco his whole life.'

PARTICIPATORY DEMOCRACY (2005–2016)

Julio's election facilitated a sustained process of collective organization and mobilization that undergirded the establishment and maintenance of a participatory democratic regime in Torres from 2005 through 2016 (with important changes occurring from 2013 on). The mayor's refraction of MVR and PSUV rhetoric and institutional forms and his administration's strong links to mobilized popular classes help explain this result.

The MVR strongly opposed Julio's candidacy and vigorously opposed him in his first years as mayor. According to Chicho Medina, one of many social movement leaders who worked under Julio and Edgar Carrasco, 'Reyes Reyes [the governor of Lara] never forgave Julio for defeating his candidate.' Chicho says Reyes Reyes sought to thwart Julio by "establishing a parallel city hall," in which Reyes Reyes provided significant state funds to a Torres municipal councillor allied with him while denying Julio's requests for funds. Julio corroborates this. 'The state government provided a lot of resources to other municipalities and they didn't approve resources for us during the first two years.' The MVR used its municipal council majority to block Julio's signature policies, including participatory budgeting, in his first year as mayor. Julio commented, 'My own party [meaning the MVR] was against me. They thought I was crazy for giving up my power.'

Julio's comment requires unpacking. He was never a member of the MVR. But he considered himself a stalwart supporter of Hugo Chávez and the Bolivarian Revolution. Julio was a member, and leader, of the United Socialist Party of Venezuela (PSUV), which he immediately joined when the party was formed in 2007, reportedly at the president's own behest. Julio saw his actions as fully consistent with the Chavista project of participatory democracy and socialism of the twenty-first century, and he regularly used Chavista language, laws, and institutional forms. In discussing

FIGURE 2.1 Sign on back of municipal bus: "Julio Chávez Is Popular Power."

Source: Photo by author.

his 2004 mayoral campaign, Julio said, 'My only promise was to build popular power.' He elaborated:

> We say all expressions of socialism should be based on the people's participation, a participation that impedes bureaucratism. . . . This socialism should start with the idea of constructing popular power . . . [and be based on] projects that make visible the process of governing *with* the people, *not for* the people, so that decisions are taken by the people, in a pedagogic and liberating process, that the people take on big decisions . . . We say the people should make all the decisions. . . . We'd rather err with the people than be right without the people.

As mayor, Julio worked to enact this vision. His considerable success was due to his administration's robust and sustained link to organized and mobilized popular classes. Julio never wasted an opportunity to distinguish himself from Oropeza, whom he called "the oligarchy's mayor, who responded to the dominant classes' interests" (Harnecker 2008, 19). Julio relished his antagonistic relationship to Torres's landowning elite, whom he referred to as "the oligarchy," "godarria," and "los godos." His view was that "the oligarchs and the godos de 'apellidos' had 40 years ruling here and always controlled the local authority" (19). Julio says the enmity was mutual, recounting that the day after his election as mayor: 'My head appeared in a frying pan on the front page of *El Caroreño*,' Torres's only daily, which Oropeza edited and his family owned.

Julio proudly implemented policies favoring popular over dominant classes. In one of the interviews I conducted with him in the years after he was mayor, Julio said one of his first mayoral acts was to eliminate a lifetime pension paid to the head of the local church and reallocate the funds to indigent seniors. 'To us, it seemed unchristian and immoral to give this pension to [the church head].' In coordination with the National Land Institute, Julio's administration expropriated five large haciendas, totaling over fifteen thousand hectares. He said, "We hope to return [land] to the hands of those who've always owned it, peasants of the zone. . . . We've undertaken a war against latifundios, the struggle

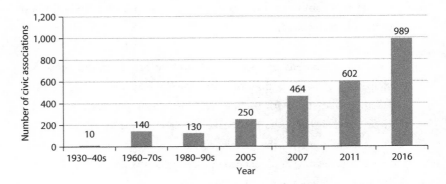

FIGURE 2.2 Approximate number of civic associations in Torres, 1930s to 2016. Note that figures prior to 2005 are rough estimates, with figures from the 1930s and 1940s particularly limited due to a lack of available data. Estimates are likely conservative for each period, including the post-2005 era, since figures are primarily for communal councils and do not include many other civic associational forms, such as health committees, urban land committees, and sports, cultural, and educational committees (Harnecker 2008, 51).

*Source*s: García Ponce (1986, 51); Salazar (2007, 181); Powell (1971, 55); Alcaldía de Torres (2011, 47, 49); Harnecker (2008, 58); Giménez (2008); and interviews with Myriam Giménez, Lalo Paez, Chicho Medina, and Rodney Crespo.

for the land" (Harnecker 2008, 37). Julio spoke proudly of "municipalizing the fairgrounds," which he said only "the oligarchy [had previously] utilized. . . . Small peasants can now go and display their goats with pride, the same peasants and goat breeders who [cattle ranchers] have always contemptuously called 'chiveros'" (38). Edgar Carrasco, Julio's successor as mayor, pledged "unconditional support for small and medium producers" (Alcaldía de Torres 2011, 9).

Julio's administration led a major effort to organize and mobilize residents. The Office of Citizenship Participation (which replaced the Office of Social Development) spearheaded this. Lalo Paez headed the office, which was located in a building in the recently municipalized fairgrounds that I visited often. Lalo and his team first organized communal boards and later organized and registered communal councils and communes (Harnecker 2008, 51). This facilitated a boom in civic associationalism, as shown in figure 2.2.

The resistance Julio faced from the MVR resulted in a stronger link between his administration and popular classes since he sought to counter the MVR's obstruction by regularly mobilizing his popular-class base. This occurred frequently in Julio's first year as mayor. In June 2005 Torres's MVR-controlled municipal council refused to approve an ordinance recognizing the results of Torres's municipal constituent assembly. Julio mobilized hundreds of his supporters to occupy city hall and pressure the council to reverse its decision. This was unsuccessful but the ordinance was approved in late 2005, after an election in which councillors more favorable to Julio gained a majority. The mayor also mobilized supporters in December 2005 when the council refused to support the participatory budget. In May 2008 Julio sought to gain ballot access for the PSUV primary for governor of Lara. Regional party leaders blocked this move. Julio responded by bringing hundreds of his supporters to the PSUV's regional office. This worked, and the party let Julio run against Barquisimeto's mayor, Henri Falcón, who beat Julio in a landslide.

These examples show that popular organization and mobilization literally undergirded Torres's participatory democratic regime; in turn it strengthened popular classes' power. Torres's popular power balance of class forces helps account for the socially controlled character of its democratic regime, which can be seen in officials' movement trajectories and institutional mechanisms facilitating social control of the state.

Julio's path to office was through social movements. As a teenager he was a student organizer, and in the 1980s and 1990s he was involved in radical organizing against Carlos Andrés Pérez and semiclandestine revolutionary activity, including Hugo Chávez's MBR-200 movement in a civilian capacity (Harnecker 2008, 6–7). As noted, Julio placed movement leaders such as Lalo Paez and Chicho Medina in top positions. After years directing the Office of Citizen Participation, Lalo became chief of staff for Julio's successor, Edgar Carrasco. Chicho was an elected delegate to Torres's municipal constituent assembly and held various important posts under Julio and Edgar Carrasco. Julio's first chief of staff, Johnny Murphy, was an anarchist exile from Argentina with Irish ancestry and a member of the radical Colectivo Alexis Vive in Barquisimeto. Murphy, as he was known, also had an entrepreneurial spirit. After Julio's mayoral term ended in 2008, Murphy opened a bar on the highway leading out of Carora, where I spent many afternoons hearing of his years working with Julio and other leftist activists.

Torres's participatory democratic regime had robust institutional mechanisms facilitating social control over the state. This can be seen in the participatory budget and the municipal constituent assembly that Julio convoked just after taking office. In an interview with Marta Harnecker (2008, 28), Julio explained, "There was a very clear provision of the decree indicating that anyone who had been elected to public office through popular vote could not participate in the Municipal Constituent Assembly. This served to guarantee that the *vocero* [spokesperson] would be a person from the community and that it would be this person who would bring proposals from the neighborhood assemblies into the heart of the Municipal Constituent Assembly."

Establishing and maintaining social control of the state involved conflict. This occurred in two main ways. The first pitted Julio and other top officials against the MVR, PSUV, and national state bureaucracy. Lalo, for instance, recounted resistance he faced from Fundacomunal, the national agency in charge of registering communal councils and communes. 'They think that City Hall shouldn't have anything to do with popular power [and] they don't want to recognize [communes set up in Torres as of 2009] because they weren't organizing them from the beginning.' Conflict also occurred within city hall. During a December 2009 interview in his childhood home in Los Arangues, Lalo told me of tension he faced after being appointed director of Citizenship Participation in 2005. Lalo said there were five social promoters in the office who were holdovers from the Oropeza administration. Lalo said other officials 'told me "get rid of these people." ' He ignored this but said, 'I had trouble with them at first. They wanted to do everything in strict accordance with the laws, for instance, in strict accordance to work hours. [They'd say] "We aren't paid to be here after hours." I had to break with all of this.' Lalo said that he told these promoters, ' "This is all going to fail unless we adapt ourselves to the community's needs. We have to figure out when the community is going to meet." So we'd ask them and they would say 6 or 7 and so we'd have to be

FIGURE 2.3 Lalo Paez during a June 2008 visit to a rural community in Torres.

Source: Photo by author.

there.' Lalo said it was a struggle but all five of the holdover social promoters eventually adapted.

ASSESSING TORRES'S PARTICIPATORY DEMOCRATIC REGIME

Torres's participatory democratic regime scores higher or equal to the other study cities' regimes on the extent and quality of popular control and institutional and political effectiveness. Torres does show a commonality with other cities, with officials in all the cases sometimes (or often) taking a "we know best" attitude. A key difference is that in Torres there were robust institutional mechanisms allowing citizens to override officials.

EXTENT OF POPULAR CONTROL

Consistent with "the people making all the decisions," Julio Chávez established a participatory budget giving residents binding control over 100 percent of Torres's investment budget (6.8 million USD in 2006). As of 2009–2011, when most of my fieldwork occurred, the process worked as follows. The first step was a "participatory diagnosis" in which residents in each of Torres's 560-plus communal councils collectively mapped their community's resources and needs. This occurred through household surveys to determine such things as the number of homes with electricity, running

FIGURE 2.4 Participatory diagnosis in La Guzmana communal council, June 2008. (Myriam Giménez is second from right.)

Source: Photo by author.

FIGURE 2.5 Participatory diagnosis in La Guzmana communal council, June 2008.

Source: Photo by author.

water, etc., and broader meetings to discuss collective needs. Next, in community assemblies, residents discussed and voted on their priorities and elected a delegate (and backup) to be the community's *vocero/a* (spokesperson) in the parish assembly. Two rounds of parish assemblies then met, in Torres's seventeen parishes, with voceros discussing and—in the second round—making binding decisions on projects, including specifications of budget allocations. When speaking publicly of Torres's PB, as I heard him do on a number of occasions including my first trip to Torres in 2007, Julio would regularly say, 'The mayor can't even veto these decisions.' As proof of citizens' binding decision-making control, Julio points to the fact that in the PB's first year 13 percent of funds went to evangelical churches; Julio was unhappy but (proudly) unable to change this (Harnecker 2008, 45). The PB's final step is approval by Torres's local planning council (CLPP). Interviews with residents, civic leaders, and municipal officials, and direct observation of the 2010 CLPP year-end assembly, indicate the CLPP at this time did not alter citizen decisions in any major way.

The smoothness of Torres's PB, and its ability to generate popular control over decision-making, depended upon behind-the-scenes political work. In a December 2009 interview, Lalo Paez told me that the *alcaldía* had to provide favors for most of Torres's nine municipal councillors to ensure their support for moving the PB forward. Eight of the councillors were part of the government's "revolutionary alliance" with six belonging to the ruling PSUV and two with the Communist Party. Lalo said most of these councillors were formerly with COPEI or AD and had switched parties solely to stay close to power. He said the mayor, Edgar Carrasco, had to meet with the councillors shortly before the December 16, 2009, CLPP meeting to approve the PB. In this meeting the mayor had to agree to provide certain favors to the municipal councillors in return for their agreement to not delay the vote on the PB. Lalo said if the councillors were not given favors they would refuse to support the PB by, at the very least, delaying the vote on it.

Turnout for Torres's PB appeared consistently high. Hard data are unavailable but a conservative estimate is that over fifteen thousand people (8 percent of Torres's population) participated in PB annually from 2009 to 2011, and likely from 2005 to 2013.[5] This high turnout is related to officials' commitment to popular empowerment. This commitment helps explain the sharp rise in the number of communal boards and councils, from 250 in 2005 to 560 in 2009, an increase largely due to the Office of Citizen Participation (Harnecker 2008, 58; Alcaldía de Torres 2011, 48), which had fifteen full-time organizers as of 2009.

In addition to very high turnout in a PB covering 100 percent of the investment budget, Torres stands out for having extensive popular control over nonbudgetary matters. The municipal constituent assembly is a key example. The *constituyente*, as it was called, was modeled on Venezuela's

1999 national constituent assembly. In March 2005 thirty political and social leaders—the mayor, trade unionists, peasant and other social movement leaders, and members and leaders of radical left parties, including Patria Para Todos, the Communist Party, and the Socialist League, with one of the party's founders, ex-guerilla Fernando Soto Rojas, attending—elaborated an initial proposal (Harnecker 2008, 29). The constituyente, comprised of delegates elected in fifty-five zonal assemblies, then discussed and voted on this proposal. As noted, elected officials were prohibited from being delegates. Citizens participated in the process through barrio assemblies held twice a week, with all-day sessions on Saturdays and Sundays. Julio says, "What the people discussed in barrio assemblies was what the voceros and voceras brought to the heart of the Municipal Constituent Assembly, and at the same time what they discussed in that assembly was carried by them to their respective communities" (Harnecker 2008, 29). "In a great popular act" on June 19, 2005, the constituyente's delegates approved the ordinance this process generated (32). Torres's municipal council initially refused but later also approved this ordinance. To Julio's consternation, Venezuela's National Electoral Council rejected his request to allow Torres's population to directly vote on the ordinance.

Two examples show the more mundane, but still significant, ways citizens exercised control over nonbudget political decisions. The first is a March 2010 public assembly to discuss bus fares in Torres's largest parish, Trinidad Samuel, where the city of Carora is. The Trinidad Samuel Parish Council convened the assembly, which like many meetings I attended in Carora was held in an open-air space in the fairgrounds. Parish officials faced the assembly of half a dozen union leaders and around sixty residents. The first act was electing a director of debate. Then there was discussion on a union proposal to raise bus fares 100 percent. Union leaders said this was needed since city residents had not funded road paving via PB for years, generating potholes 'big enough to swallow a car.' (I can confirm that car and bus rides in Carora in this time were very bumpy. Victor García, with whom I drove around regularly, took quite circuitous routes to his and Myriam's home to avoid potholes and swore vociferously whenever he hit one.) A resident replied, '100 percent is too much. . . . We're a socialist country, not a capitalist one,' and suggested a 50–60 percent fare increase. A union official responded by enumerating rising vehicle, labor, and imported auto parts costs. He attributed the latter to the government's currency policy. The assembly moved to approve a 50 percent fare increase for regular buses and a 60 percent increase for express routes. Parish leaders advised the union leaders to accept this without a vote, reminding them that an earlier community proposal had been made to raise fares just 25 percent. A union official, seeming to speak for all unions present, accepted the 50 percent fare increase, noting, 'We are clearly a minority and you are the majority here.'

Another example comes from La Guzmana's communal council, of which Myriam was a member. In the months I stayed in Myriam and Victor's house I regularly tagged along when Myriam attended her council's meetings. In early 2010 the council was involved in selecting a new director for the local school, located a few blocks from Victor and Myriam's house. The council held meetings and a few assemblies with other local communal councils, with a February 2010 assembly including the state education director and teachers and workers from the school. In March the council held an education committee meeting discussing qualifications the new director should have. All agreed the director should be open to democratic decisions, know and be willing to work with the community, and have five to seven years of administrative experience. There was vigorous deliberation by the committee of mostly working-class women, who produced a nonbinding proposal to submit to the school's interim director and other relevant parties.

QUALITY OF POPULAR CONTROL

Decisions in Torres's PB were usually made through deliberation, with participants airing contrasting views and offering reasons to justify their views. This claim is based primarily on observation of twelve (of seventeen) second-round parish assemblies (in which binding decisions were made) in November and December 2009. To illustrate the pattern found in most of the assemblies I discuss the November 23, 2009, Antonio Diaz parish

FIGURE 2.6 Sandry Gil (left) and Zoila Vasquez (right) during a November 2009 participatory budget parish assembly in Cecilio Zubillaga.

Source: Photo by author.

FIGURE 2.7 Cecilio Zubillaga participatory budget parish assembly, with Sandry Gil in background, November 2009.

Source: Photo by author.

FIGURE 2.8 Camacara participatory budget parish assembly, December 2009.

Source: Photo by author.

assembly. It was held in a pretty courtyard next to a library in the *Casa de Cultura* (cultural center) in the town of Curarigua. As with most of the parish assemblies I attended, I traveled from Carora in a municipal pickup truck with Zoila Vásquez, the CLPP's general secretary, Sandry Gil, Torres's director of engineering, and several lower-level city officials. The drive took about an hour on a very twisty road through arid mountains, with the road much improved compared to my first very rough trip on it in the summer of 2008.

Before the meeting started, I chatted with a few voceros. A man named Francisco told me about the hamlet of Ira, where he was from, a three-hour walk or forty-minute drive from Curarigua on 'a very poor road.' Francisco said Curarigua had once been a booming town, with ten small factories that made sweets from sugarcane grown in nearby fields. He said it started to decline in the 1970s when the sweets industry collapsed, leading to 'social dislocation' as residents left to find work. Another vocero told me 'one extremely rich family' living in the parish's "upper part" owned all the sugarcane fields. He said, 'There's a lot of exploitation up there. The workers' salaries are truly miserable.' This vocero said small agriculture accounted for most of the parish's other economic activity. Francisco said that many local families subsisted on very small plots of lands.

Another vocero told me how wonderful the PB was. Using a line I heard regularly across Torres, he said, 'This is the only municipality in the country that gives 100 percent of the budget to the communal councils. We're pioneers. In the past we had neighborhood associations, but the governments never trusted us. They didn't think we could possibly manage resources. But look what we've done. We've done marvelous things with the resources they've given us. In my community they gave us ten thousand [bolívares] for a Catholic chapel and we managed to use the money to get twice as much done versus what was projected.'

By the time the assembly started over thirty people were present. Everyone clustered in two tight rows in a partially shaded part of the courtyard to avoid the blistering sun. For several hours the participants discussed how to spend 520,961 *bolívares* (approximately 243,440 USD). There was an initial discussion about managing resources. Some voceros criticized the *alcaldía* for unfinished projects. Zoila pushed back against this idea. Discussion later turned to specific projects, including a pedestrian walkway. A vocero said, 'The pedestrian walkway should be done because everyone will benefit from this.' Another agreed but argued the cost was too high. 'This bridge will benefit everyone, but if we use the resources [for this] nothing will be left for anything else.' A few other unfinished projects were discussed, including a seniors' center (*Casa de Abuelos*). As with other parish assemblies I attended, this example highlights the back-and-forth character of discussion about projects, with voceros speaking for and against specific projects and providing reasons to justify their views. This parish assembly was also typical in that it featured regular input from state officials, which I will discuss further.

Nondeliberative decision-making was the norm in only one of the twelve parish assemblies I attended—Trinidad Samuel—which not coincidentally includes the city of Carora. Like many large meetings there, the assembly was held in the open-air meeting space in the fairgrounds. The assembly was split into a small rural and a much larger urban section. The urban section included over 150 voceros, making it by far the largest discussion of all I attended. It was also the most chaotic, resembling a rugby match more than an ideal-typical Habermasian public sphere. When this urban assembly was in full swing, voceros were elbowing each other aside to get to the facilitator, who was writing down which communities would get what in a manner that was unclear to me, and, by the look of things, to many others. The rural discussion was notably calmer. Each participant had a chance to speak, and the group debated and voted on which projects to approve in an orderly way. Local state officials were aware of and upset about the more chaotic nature of decision-making found in Carora and (in their view) Torres's urban civic spaces generally. Julio Chávez and Lalo Paez blamed this on the greater "individualism" of urban versus rural residents. My fieldwork suggests the urban assembly's size and facilitation also contributed to its nondeliberative character.

The (generally) deliberative character of decision-making in Torres's PB appears to be largely by design. Officials who played a key role in designing and supporting the process saw deliberation as key to citizens learning to govern themselves. Lalo spoke of his goal of 'the people being government.' He felt widespread discussion in meetings was critical to this. It was how citizens learned to change their minds, persuade others, and accept losing arguments, skills Lalo saw as critical to *autogobierno* (self-governance). He lamented that Torres fell short of this goal. He noted and sought to change the fact that 'sometimes only four or five people [in a meeting] will speak . . . and then people raise their hands and vote, but just for what one of these [four or five] people has put forward.' Lalo wanted 'to make sure that there is input from every family [attending a meeting] at least.' Parish assemblies I attended were mostly in between what Lalo worried about and wanted: there was significant participation (e.g. more than four to five people) but it wasn't universal.

Julio and other local officials were fond of noting that Torres's PB gave citizens binding control over decisions. Observational and interview data show this claim to be true in that citizens had the final word on decisions and officials did not—and by design could not—alter decisions they disagreed with. But officials regularly sought and often managed to influence citizens' decisions. In parish assemblies I attended I regularly observed such interventions from three officials: Zoila, the CLPP's general secretary, Sandry Gil, Torres's director of engineering, and the parish president.

These officials regularly gave both general and specific advice to voceros in parish assemblies. In nearly every parish assembly I attended, Sandry advised voceros to 'think about the future' and choose 'projects that benefit the whole community.' In the Las Mercedes parish assembly (described in the opening pages of this book), Sandry remarked, 'Think about the future. For example, a sports field that can be used for social events, and meetings, and missions, and that can hold two to three hundred people [is better than] a cultural center that might serve four or five people who stay inside in the air conditioning, with everyone else outside.' In this and other assemblies, Sandry and Zoila regularly admonished voceros to 'stick with the priorities' that voceros had themselves established (e.g., water and transportation) in their first parish assembly. When the Las Mercedes assembly moved to discuss funding new projects, Sandry commented, 'We'll do what's left according to the priorities laid out.' At several points in the assembly voceros brought up projects that were not one of the parish's two priorities, water and roads. Each time this occurred, Sandry said, 'We need to focus on the priorities." At one point the parish board president followed up by saying, 'These are the priorities we ourselves came up with. This isn't something the engineer [i.e., Sandry] is trying to impose upon us.'

Sandry and Zoila's remarks were often more specific. For instance, later in the Las Mercedes assembly, discussion turned to funding health centers. Sandry advised the assembly to think carefully before funding a particular health clinic: 'An observation: if you do this medical center but don't have supplies or a doctor, it's a lost investment.' The assembly listened to Sandry but decided to fund the clinic, albeit with a lower amount. This allowed the assembly to also provide some funds to Torres's fire department, which sent two firefighters to each parish PB assembly throughout Torres to ask for funding.

In the Montes de Oca parish assembly, Sandry engaged in a lengthy back-and-forth with voceros about the importance of supplying water to

San Francisco, the parish's main town, which is in an arid valley and was where we were meeting. Sandry asked voceros where their children went to high school, knowing San Francisco was the answer. A few said their children were not in high school, and their communities had other needs they viewed as more pressing than water for San Francisco. Sandry asked, 'Where will your children go when they leave [their current school]?' 'The high school' in San Francisco, replied the voceros. Sandry then asked everyone, 'So if there's no water available in San Francisco and the school has to close for the day, who suffers?' The assembly replied, 'Everyone.' Sandry repeated the question. 'Who suffers?' The assembly responded, 'Everyone.' 'So who benefits from having water in San Francisco?' Sandry asked. The assembly again replied, 'Everyone.' Sandry didactically concluded, 'So water here is not just for San Francisco but is a benefit for the entire community.'

In Antonio Diaz parish, Zoila made a sustained case that voceros should vote against a proposal for an ambulance, which seemed likely to pass. Her main argument was that the parish already had an ambulance, which just needed new tires. Zoila felt it would be cheaper to repair the tires than purchase a new ambulance. This, in turn, would allow the parish more funds for completing unfinished projects, which Zoila also felt was very important. One of the many comments she made about the ambulance was, 'Since many of the roads in this area are very bad, you'll definitely need to have an ambulance with double traction, and you need to realize that. This is your decision, you'll have to decide, but I want to make sure you take this all into account. You need to think about who will drive the ambulance and how you'll find money for maintenance.' After a very long discussion the voceros voted against the new ambulance. Zoila was clearly relieved. On the long drive back to Carora she animatedly remarked, 'I could've sworn they were going to fund the ambulance.'

Officials did not always get their way, however. I learned this in the November 18, 2009, Espinoza de los Monteros parish PB assembly, the first I attended. This assembly had a subdiscussion for a group of communal councils organized as a commune. Voceros in this discussion wanted to fund a series of small projects. One vocero said, 'I can do a lot with twenty thousand *bolivares*.' Zoila was adamantly opposed and said, 'The problem is when everyone wants to do their own project.' She insisted that this was *not* what communes were designed to do. After a long discussion, the group voted to fund five relatively small projects, one for each council in the commune. I asked Zoila about this on the ride home. She was clearly still upset and said, 'This isn't what the communes are for.'

These examples illustrate several important points concerning the relationship between citizens (i.e. voceros) and officials with respect to the issue of popular control over decision-making in Torres's PB. It is clear officials regularly sought to influence voceros' decisions. It is also clear that officials had success doing so, at times. Yet it is important to note the *manner* in which officials sought to influence decisions and the *limits* of officials' influence due to institutional features of Torres's PB. In seeking to influence voceros' decisions, officials engaged in deliberative discussion, presenting general reasons why certain types of projects should be funded or not (e.g., Sandry admonishing voceros to 'think about the future' and choose projects benefitting 'the whole community') and specific reasons for or against particular projects (e.g., Zoila's arguments against funding the ambulance). In no instance did officials impose decisions on voceros in a command-and-control fashion.[6] It is also important to note that officials most often sought to get voceros to approve projects that fit within the parish's priority list. It was voceros, not officials, who established these priorities, as the Las Mercedes parish board president noted: 'These are priorities we came up with ourselves. This isn't something the engineer is trying to impose upon us.' And most importantly, voceros had final say on decisions, as officials acknowledged and often noted (e.g., saying 'This is your decision'). In addition to the Espinoza de los Monteros parish example, I observed voceros in a number of assemblies choose projects officials opposed. In Las Mercedes voceros funded a health clinic Sandry opposed. In Montes de Oca they approved a project both Sandry and Zoila opposed.[7] Zoila's exasperation when voceros opposed her and relief when they agreed with her (as in Antonio Diaz) clearly indicates that at the end of the day voceros, not officials, controlled decisions.

Torres's PB appears highly inclusive vis-à-vis class, gender, race and ethnicity, and political views. As with so much else, this reflects officials' commitment to self-rule and their view that inclusivity is crucial to attaining it. Lalo said most participants in Torres's PB were 'the people,' specifically 'the humble people.' In the rural sector, comprising the majority of Torres's parishes, Lalo said most participants were agricultural workers or 'farmhands' on medium-sized private farms producing cattle and vegetable crops, with small-holding goat farmers (which Lalo estimated at around three thousand in Torres) also participating. In the urban sector, participants included private hospital workers, unionized public employees, teachers, street vendors, service workers, and domestic caregivers and students. In parish assemblies I attended most participants came from the popular classes, but middle and upper classes were not excluded nor entirely absent. I met some middle-class professionals in assemblies. Lalo told me, 'The godarria has its own communal council,' referring to a communal council in central Carora led by members of the named families, who participated in the PB and received a streetlight project to spruce up Carora's colonial center. Women outnumbered men in parish assemblies, often by a significant margin, with the exception of a small handful of rural parishes, where men outnumbered women. Most voceros in assemblies were categorized (through self-identification or according to others)[8] as morenos (roughly 'brown-skinned people'), with light-skinned whites and Blacks present in lower numbers.[9]

In a 2016 interview, Rodney Crespo, a CLPP staffer (and Zoila's husband), gave estimates on PB participants' racial, gender, and political composition. He estimated that women comprised 70 percent of participants in community assemblies and said 80 percent of PB participants were mestizo, a category roughly equivalent to moreno (with the terms used more or less interchangeably in Torres). This category, as Rodney used it, included an estimate of 10 percent Black participants. Rodney said 20 percent of participants were white. He estimated oppositionists to comprise 6–10 percent of PB participants, with a larger number of ni-nis, those not supporting the government or opposition, and a clear majority of Chavistas. Rodney said he did not know of any instance of oppositionists facing discrimination in the PB, adding, 'To the contrary, I know of a communal council run by the opposition that managed to convince an assembly that was almost completely Chavista to approve their proposal for a sewer.'

Interview and observational data from 2009 to 2011 indicate that Torres's PB and civil society generally was politically pluralistic. Top officials were strongly committed to pluralism. Lalo regularly spoke of the importance of political and religious inclusivity. In several communal council assemblies I heard him say, 'You can't divide councils by politics or religion. It won't work unless everyone's welcome.' Torres's engineering director, Sandry, also expressed similar ideas. When I asked him about pluralism, he said, 'The municipality's resources are for everyone. They aren't for any party.' I pressed him, asking if opposition supporters should have the same access to resources as Chavistas. Sandry replied, 'If someone comes here [to city hall], and perhaps they have to ride a bicycle, walk for miles, ride on a mule, and there might be economic resources involved [i.e. money spent to travel]. It's not always easy for them to come to Carora. Considering all this, should we not help them, after all the sacrifice they have made to come here, just because they are from the opposition?'

Mid- and lower-level officials showed significant but less universal support for pluralism. A few lower-level officials openly favored giving preference to Chavistas and, in one case, excluding oppositionists from some public fora. Most mid- and lower-level officials, however, expressed views resembling those of Lalo and Sandry. Citizens who participated in PB and communal councils also showed significant support for pluralism, at times in a "colorful" manner. In nearly every PB and other event I attended I asked participants if participation was only open to Chavistas or PSUVistas (these terms were often though not always used interchangeably). I was universally told, 'No, anyone can participate.' On many occasions in communal council meetings I was told, 'We don't discuss politics in communal councils.' I also heard this phrasing used about Torres's PB. In both cases "politics" referred to party politics. During the Espinoza de los Monteros parish assembly I asked a vocera if non-PSUVistas participated in her communal council. She said they did and recounted that many people in her community had recently left the PSUV, 'possibly because of something crazy that President Chávez said, or because they think he's starting to make war with other countries [this referenced recent statements of Chávez toward Colombia], or because this is all tending towards

communism.' She said all those who had left the PSUV still felt comfortable in her communal council. Like others she said there was 'no discussion
of politics [in the communal council]. . . . It doesn't matter what party or
color you have, if you're blue or green or what.' During the Las Mercedes
PB parish assembly I asked a group of voceras, 'Do you need to be Chavista
or with the PSUV to participate in the PB?' One responded, 'No, no, no!
In fact, we have a lot of *escualidos* who participate.' Her use of that term,
meaning the squalid ones, was a common, and pejorative, way of referring
to oppositionists. Her statement shows the pluralism of Torres's PB and
reveals the "impurity" of this pluralism, specifically the symbolic violence
(some) oppositionists faced in predominantly Chavista/PSUVista spaces
that were also de jure and de facto inclusive.

An important test of political pluralism was whether these predominantly Chavista venues were ever sites for discussion of internal PSUV
party matters. I was repeatedly told that this did not occur, and I did not
observe such discussions in any of the PB or communal council meetings
I attended. I was, however, told that there was sometimes internal discussion of PSUV matters in a few extremely rural districts of Torres where
'over 95 percent of the population' purportedly belonged to the PSUV.

Before closing this discussion, two final points are worth making.
The first is to simply note that while party politics was rarely discussed,
"politics" in a more general sense was far from absent in Torres's PB,
communal council, and other civic participatory spaces. Voceros often
used words associated with politics, generally, and Chavismo, specifically, such as socialism and revolution. Second, on relatively rare occasions I heard base-level participants make exclusionary comments. For
instance, in a January 2010 meeting of the Pan-Americana commune-in-
formation a woman said, 'We get rid of people in the communal council
who aren't with the PSUV.' She justified this by saying, 'Things are a
bit difficult,' in her town of Los Aranagues. Another woman who over-
heard this shook her head and said, 'That's wrong. You shouldn't do that.'
This shows that exclusion was not entirely absent in Torres, but also that
there was at least some possibility others would counter this exclusion if
and when it surfaced.

INSTITUTIONAL EFFECTIVENESS

Torres's participatory democratic regime was institutionally effective, with participatory inputs effectively linked to policy outputs. Official data on rates of project implementation (the percentage of approved projects implemented in a given timeframe) and budgetary execution (the percentage of an approved budget spent) are unavailable. Unofficial data suggest Torres's project implementation rate for 2009–2012 was above 86 percent. This estimate is based on a 2012 report listing 1,204 executed projects between 2009 and 2012, and interviews with top Torres officials who told me that 300 to 350 projects were approved annually in Torres's PB in this period. This provides a project implementation rate of 86–100 percent, depending on whether the figure of 300 or 350 projects is used.[10] This report also states that communal councils directly executed 76 percent of these 1,204 projects. By 2016 officials reported that communities directly executed 90 percent of projects, indicating that citizens in Torres were central not only in deciding but also executing PB projects.

FIGURE 2.9 Engineers and local public planning committee staff carrying out a participatory budget project inspection in Reyes Vargas parish, December 2009.

Source: Photo by author.

Subjective measures also support the claim that Torres's regime was institutionally effective. During my fieldwork I traveled throughout the municipality with officials to attend PB and communal council meetings and visit project sites. I asked residents everywhere I went what they thought of PB and the mayor (both Julio Chávez and then-current mayor, Edgar Carrasco). Unlike what residents in the Bolivian cities included in this study (particularly Santa Cruz) told me, I never heard Torres residents complain of projects marked as executed when they were not. Torres residents generally expressed a high level of confidence that projects approved through PB were being completed. On a number of occasions residents said they had initially been skeptical that PB would produce results but that these doubts had disappeared after they saw concrete results.

POLITICAL EFFECTIVENESS

Torres's participatory democratic regime appears highly effective politically, with the incumbent party's core policies, such as participatory budgeting, seeming to generate significant and rising consent from residents. Electoral returns are consistent with this view. Julio Chávez won the 2004 mayoral election with 35.6 percent of the vote, with turnout of 49 percent. In 2008 Julio's chief of staff, the engineer Edgar Carrasco (known by his last name) won as the PSUV's mayoral candidate with 48.8 percent of the vote on 52 percent turnout. In 2013, Carrasco was reelected with 54.7 percent of the vote. Turnout was 60 percent. Since Carrasco is notably less charismatic than Julio his increasing support is impressive, particularly given the competitive nature of elections in Torres, which differs from districts, like parts of Sucre (see chapter 3), where Chavismo dominates. Torres is notably the only study city where the incumbent party won reelection with a new candidate.

Julio's post-mayoral career also suggests Torres's participatory democracy was politically effective. Julio won 51.1 percent of the vote for a state assembly seat in 2008. In 2010 he was elected to the National Assembly with 55.6 percent of the vote. He was reelected in 2015 with the most support of any candidate in his district. Consistent with the view that Torres has a popular power class force balance, Julio and Carrasco performed best in poorer rural parishes.

State-society relations were generally cooperative in Torres under Julio and Carrasco. I asked voceros in all parish assemblies I attended if they felt satisfied with Torres's PB, often being provocative by asking how anyone could support a process that gave out low sums of money and left many needs unaddressed. Everyone I asked said they were satisfied with PB, and only a few delegates I observed in parish assemblies seemed disgruntled. Voceros regularly said things like "we get to decide" and "we're the ones who decide" as reasons they were satisfied. I occasionally asked, "Why not just leave the budget to the mayor?" A teacher in the Manuel Murillo November 2009 parish assembly responded, 'Why not? I'm equal to the president of the United States; if he can make decisions why can't I?' Another vocero then chimed in: 'In the past, government officials would stay all day in their air conditioned offices and make decisions there. They never even set foot in our communities. So who do you think can make a better decision about what we need, an official in his air conditioned office who has never even come to our community, or someone who is from the community?' These responses are indicative of the generally high level of popular consent Torres's PB appeared to produce.

TOWARDS SOCIALISM, "A NEW AND BETTER FORM OF DEMOCRACY"

Julio Chávez and his allies saw participatory democracy as part of a larger struggle to construct socialism. In an interview I did with him in November 2010, Julio discussed this as follows,

> We aspire to construct a model of organization that overcomes the contradictions of [the] bourgeois [system], that overcomes the logic of accumulation . . . [and] is a higher state where we introduce a new institutionality, where we introduce fundamental concepts like protagonistic,

participatory, direct democracy of the street. From this perspective we introduce the idea that everything should be discussed. . . . [Socialism] converts popular power into the historic subject of the revolution. . . . This establishes a project that develops the productive forces, and is based on new forms of property, on social property, new modes of production, a mode of production that establishes new relations, between men and nature, and between men and men, which aren't based on exploitation but on solidarity and complementarity, which achieves a new distribution of the oil rent, more social investment, harmony with nature, a new model, based on [putting] men and women . . . at the center of politics and making the big decisions. Not like capitalism, which is based on exploitation, on the accumulation of capital, which is an expression of exclusion that impeded the construction of a new and better form of democracy, which is what socialism is.

Socialism was a common term in Torres, and throughout Venezuela, at this time, but it was usually used in a more colloquial manner. Torres's PB parish assemblies show this. In the November 2009 Las Mercedes assembly, for instance, a vocero rhetorically asked, 'If we're not doing socialism, then what are we doing?' The facilitator had earlier asked, 'What is socialism? Socialism is working together. Socialism is society working.' Later, a vocera prefaced her remarks by saying, 'As a socialist . . .' This prompted another vocero to say, 'We're all revolutionaries here, but the truth is there are few socialists among us.' Torres's engineering director at one point told the assembly, 'Socialism doesn't consist of bringing a little piece of the pie to your community. Socialism means helping those who really need the resources most . . . so let's think as socialists and give to those who are most in need.' In a different meeting, Lalo Paez said this of socialism: 'It means not being selfish, but putting collective interests ahead of your own. It means that if there is a resource, you let others take it before you take any yourself.' These examples show that socialism was a common, and contested, touchstone that citizens and officials constantly used to discuss and justify their choices with respect to PB and much else.

Torres's PB was one of several institutions widely viewed as an embryonic form of socialism, akin to Erik Olin Wright's "real utopias" (2010), which are concrete attempts to build the world-as-it-should-be amid the imperfections of the world-as-it-is. The success of Torres's PB led Lara's governor to call Torres "Venezuela's first socialist city." Socialism was also used to refer to the institutional forms through which PB, and Torres's participatory democracy generally, was enacted. In a 2010 assembly to form a commune, a young man said,

[Socialism] is putting the human side, the social side before the material side. . . . It's equality, justice and peace . . . [and] the three go together. . . . If you don't have equality you can't have justice, and if you don't have justice you can't have peace. . . . It's not having a market vision . . . it's having equality of condition. . . . We're all equal before the law, but some treat you equally and some people don't. . . . There isn't equality in everyday life, and socialism would make everyone equal in their conditions. . . . Socialism isn't an abstract theory of Leninism, or Marxism, it's the practice. . . . It's what you see here.

Many viewed socialism as extending popular control from the political to the economic realm. One notable local effort to do this was the 2009 creation of a socialist electric meter factory.[11] This elicited a fierce struggle between the factory's workers and local communal councils seeking to have the factory designated a "social property" and the Ministry of Popular Power for Electrical Energy, which sought to maintain it as a "state property." The distinction was crucial: if the factory were a social property then workers' and communal councils would decide how it ran and, crucially, how to use its profits. Keeping it a state property meant the ministry would control all this. This struggle was ongoing when I visited the factory in December 2010. The workers had, however, established a degree of worker control over production through a workers' assembly, which managed daily operations, and a workers' council, comprising eighteen workers elected by the full assembly, who made decisions on health and disciplinary matters. Workers proudly told me they were chosen in assemblies, which took the person's situation into account, meaning what their economic situation was, if they really needed this job, if they had kids, etc.. A supervisor noted this was unlike 'capitalist [firms] where they don't care who you are.'

In addition to serving as an ultimate horizon, common touchstone, and real utopia, socialism was also used in a narrower, partisan sense, to refer to members of the ruling PSUV. In my six months of fieldwork I saw this occur regularly among Torres residents, though the vast majority of residents I met insisted that partisan affiliation should not and did not affect participation in PB and other fora. I observed only a few officials, out of dozens I interacted with regularly, acting in a partisan manner. Almost all officials were very careful to support nonpartisanship. Officials regularly spoke of the imperative of being "impartial" when interacting with citizens. One spoke of 'the need to avoid going too much to one side or the other.' A social promoter from the Office of Citizen Participation said oppositionists 'will give it to us hard but we can't give it back to them.'

PARTICIPATORY DEMOCRACY UNDER STRESS (2014–2016)

Torres was affected by the crisis that ravaged Venezuela from 2014 on. In contrast to Sucre (see chapter 3), Torres did not experience a clear change in its urban regime type as a result of the crisis. Torres's participatory democratic regime, and its core institution of PB, survived but came under increasing strain in two main ways. First, there was high inflation, which made it hard to do medium- and long-term planning. In a 2016 interview a CLPP official said, 'We've responded [to inflation] by lowering the number of projects done each year.' Second, pluralism appeared to be fraying. Speaking in 2016, Myriam Giménez said, 'The PSUV seems to be confusing itself with popular power. The PSUV is trying to dominate communal councils, but [they] are the community. . . . My critique is that the party is trying to substitute itself for popular power. The communal councils cannot be an appendix of the party; they have to be the community.' Myriam said,

'We have to live with the opposition.' She felt the PSUV's attempts to substitute itself for popular power 'creates a distortion of what the communal councils should be.'

In fieldwork in Torres in 2016 I heard more reports of political exclusion than I had on trips from 2007 to 2011. Lalo Paez, however, said oppositionists still participated in institutions as they had in the past, though he acknowledged that he had heard growing complaints of exclusion. A promoter in the Office of Citizen Participation was concerned that 'not a single vocero on the CLPP is someone who isn't a member of the PSUV.' As of mid-2016 it appeared Torres's participatory democracy was still functioning, but it was clearly under stress and people were unsure how long it would last.

Between 2005 and 2016 Torres had a remarkably democratic form of governance. Torres's participatory democracy gave citizens extensive and high-quality popular control over local political decision-making and was institutionally and politically effective. Citizens enjoyed full control over decisions about the local investment budget and had significant influence over nonbudgetary political decisions. The process was socially and politically inclusive. Most participatory budget participants were mestizos and morenos from the popular classes, although there were middle- and (in smaller numbers) upper-class participants. Women outnumbered men. The process was politically pluralistic: Chavistas identified with competing political factions made up the majority of participants, and many non-Chavistas and some oppositionists participated as well. City hall respected residents' decisions. And projects were generally implemented in a timely and satisfactory manner, with residents directly implementing over three-fourths of them.

Torres's radical left political leaders and grassroots activists within its robust civil society worked to extend popular control over decision-making from the political to the economic realm as part of a collective effort to build a participatory form of "twenty-first century socialism." This effort bore fruit. As the example of Torres's electric meter factory shows, workers and community members succeeded in establishing an impressive degree of control over decisions about working hours and conditions, and at the time of my research they were seeking control over decisions about the factory's output.

All of this was highly contested by la godarria, the landowning class that ruled Torres from the late nineteenth through the late twentieth centuries, and the ruling party, in its MVR and PSUV forms, which also sought to block popular control in Torres. As the chapter has shown, Torres's MVR mayor from 2000 to 2003 implemented a form of participatory clientelism, and local and regional party leaders repeatedly sought to thwart Torres's first movement-left mayor, Julio Chávez. On the surface, there seems to be a straightforward explanation for why Torres achieved participatory success in the face of this resistance: having a movement-left incumbent party closely aligned with highly organized and mobilized popular classes. This explanation fits with existing thought about participatory urban governance, which holds that it is most likely in cities with "the right combination of a capacitated civil society and a committed executive branch" (Baiocchi et al. 2011, 9). The explanation also fits existing thinking about left-populist parties, like the MVR and PSUV, which urban participation scholars have viewed as an obstacle to participation.

Existing thought falls short, however, in fully explaining Torres's participatory success since it misses the complex ways Torres's movement-left incumbent party related to the left-populist MVR and PSUV. As this chapter has shown, Julio strongly identified with the Bolivarian Revolution, considered himself a stalwart Chavista, and used language and institutional forms associated with Chavismo to build Torres's participatory democratic regime, which he viewed as an instance of popular power and twenty-first-century socialism. (Hugo Chávez recognized this and put Julio on a presidential task force on popular power in 2006.) The chapter has shown that Julio's (and others') refraction of Chavismo's left-populist hegemony was critical to the construction of participatory democracy and the struggle for socialism in Torres. This points to the need to reconstruct thinking about left populism, participatory democracy, and socialism to better account for the ways left-populist parties can simultaneously inhibit and facilitate efforts to build participatory and socialist institutions.

The next chapter shows that left-populist hegemony can be refracted into participatory success in other contexts, even ones that might seem quite unpropitious.

3

SUCRE

Administered Democracy in a Right-Governed "Chavista City"

If Torres from 2005 to 2016 provides a seemingly ideal setup for successful participatory urban governance—a proparticipation movement-left mayor aligned with highly organized and mobilized popular classes—this was decidedly not the case for Sucre between 2009 and 2017, when it was governed by Primero Justicia, a center-right party with a middle- and upper-class core base. Based on existing research, one would expect this type of party to govern in an antidemocratic or "safely democratic" way that protects elite interests. This can be done through technocratic governance that minimizes popular input into decision-making or by implementing (legally mandated) participatory reform in a pseudoparticipatory way that provides a semblance of participation but prevents genuine popular control over decision-making. This combination of technocratic rule and pseudoparticipation is found in the other right-governed city examined in this book, Santa Cruz, which as shown in chapter 5 can be seen as Torres's mirror image, a nearly ideal-typical case of antidemocratic right-wing urban governance.

But Sucre does not conform to this expectation. After taking office as mayor, Primero Justicia's Carlos Ocariz embraced participatory rule in an unexpectedly robust way. From 2009 to 2012 Ocariz made participatory budgeting a centerpiece of his administration. The percent of the budget given to PB doubled in this period, from 20 percent in 2009 to 40 percent in 2011 and 2012, when Sucre's PB covered an impressive 35.3 million USD (Giusti and De Viveiros 2012, 56). At its peak, the process involved nearly a thousand meetings a year, with thousands of citizens and dozens of municipal employees attending. As this chapter shows, it is impossible to dismiss this experience as a case of pseudoparticipation. Sucre's PB provided residents, most from the popular classes (and many Chavistas), a significant degree of popular control over political decisions.

This outcome would be surprising under any circumstances. It appears particularly surprising given Venezuela's political context, namely the increasingly radical left-populist, and nominally socialist, Hugo Chávez administration. What explains why Primero Justicia reacted to this challenge not by seeking to end democracy or make it safer but by embracing participatory governance in a relatively robust way? This chapter seeks to show that the combination of Venezuela's national and Sucre's local political context—specifically national left-populist hegemony and competitive local elections—pushed Ocariz to refract, not reject, the left-populist ruling party's participatory toolkit. In conjunction with Sucre's elite-professional balance of class forces, this generated administered democracy, a state-controlled democratic urban political regime. When the ruling party's left-populist hegemony eroded from 2013 on, Sucre's administered democracy entered into a terminal crisis. This supports a main argument of the book: the presence or absence of leftist hegemony shapes right-wing action vis-à-vis democracy.

In addition to explaining how Sucre's administered democracy rose and fell, the chapter also examines how this regime compares to the urban regimes found in the other three cases and also in Sucre before 2009 and after 2013. Evidence presented shows that Sucre's administered democracy provided residents a real, albeit limited, degree of control over political decisions. This evidence suggests Ocariz administration officials sought to give citizens *some but not too much power*. A reason for this, I suggest, is the tension between administered democracy's two dimensions: its democratic form of rule pushed in the direction of giving citizens more power over decisions but the state-controlled character of this democratic rule pushed in the direction of limiting citizens' decision-making power. Comparison with the other cases helps illuminate the surprisingly impressive yet limited degree of popular control that Sucre's administered democracy allowed for. Sucre's administered democracy appears limited, in the extent of popular control it provides, compared to Torres's participatory democracy but still impressive compared to the regimes found in right-governed Santa Cruz *and* left-governed El Alto.

The chapter begins with a brief overview of Sucre's history and socioeconomic structure. I then trace the succession of urban regimes found in Sucre between the 1980s and 2010s. In the 1980s and 1990s Sucre, like each of the other three study cities, had a clientelistic regime. This was followed by participatory clientelism from 2000 to 2008, just like Torres. Sucre's subsequent path paralleled Torres's with an opposition local incumbent party refracting left-populist hegemony into democratic rule. In Sucre this was combined with an elite-professional balance of class forces, which led to administered democracy. The heart of the chapter provides a systematic assessment of this regime. The chapter closes by examining how the erosion of left-populist hegemony from 2013 on led to the demise of Sucre's administered democracy, with its center-right mayor governing in a more "typically right-wing" nonparticipatory manner in his second term, 2013–2017.

SUCRE: A DIVIDED CITY

Sucre is the easternmost of the five municipalities comprising greater Caracas (the other four are Libertador, Chacao, Baruta, and El Hatillo). As of 2011, Sucre's official population was 600,351, though local officials estimate it to be twice this or more.[1] Sucre was a district within Caracas until 1989, when it was designated an autonomous municipality. Like the rest of Caracas, Sucre's population expanded in the twentieth century through repeated waves of urban migration. This was connected to Venezuela's transformation into a petro (oil) state and the related decline of agriculture

FIGURE 3.1 La Urbina and Petare.

Source: Photo by Jonathan Quintap.

from the 1930s on. Through the mid-1940s, Sucre was a sparsely populated agricultural zone of small subsistence farms and larger sugar and coffee plantations (Baptista et al. 1993, 35). Between the 1940s and 1960s Sucre became an important center of industry and commerce. New textile, auto parts, and clothing factories, along with banking and shopping centers, led to an explosion of Sucre's population, which doubled in the 1940s, tripled in the 1950s, and doubled again in the 1960s (Baptista et al. 1993, 41–42; Ellner and Myers 2002, 108).

In the 1960s Sucre residents (like residents across Caracas) formed Juntas Pro-Mejoras, (Improvement Councils). According to Baptista et al. (1993, 49), leftist parties and COPEI played a key role organizing Juntas in parts of Sucre. This was the case in Alto Lebrún, a working-class Petare neighborhood settled in the 1940s and 1950s, known as a "red zone" due to left parties' influence. COPEI's ability to establish early roots may help explain its later success in Sucre. Baptista et al.'s account of politics in Alto Lebrún in this era suggests that Sucre was subject to the clientelistic political logic found throughout Caracas at this time (cf. Fernandes 2010, 47): "As time passed, and with the resulting deepening of the process of community consolidation, the inhabitants of Lebrún channeled their struggles to improve their conditions of life through specific organizations of various types: political-protest, religious, sports, cultural, etc., thus *these same organizations were converted into a propitious terrain for clientelism and the demagogy of the parties*" (Baptista et al. 1993, 49, emphasis added).

As in Torres, more contentious forms of social and political organizing also existed in Sucre in these years. I learned some of this history from Fernando Giuliani, a longtime Sucre resident and staff member of the Catholic social justice organization Centro Gumilla, which was founded in 1968 and has supported grassroots organizing throughout Venezuela, including in Torres and Sucre. In a December 2010 interview in his office, Fernando said Christian base organizations, linked to liberation theology, were formed in Petare in the 1970s. Bruno Renaud, a Belgian worker-priest, moved to Petare at this time and established a popular education school, the Escuela de Formación Popular de Petare, to foster popular organization.[2] Fernando noted other initiatives that 'provided a base for future popular organization,' including popular libraries, a cultural movement, and environmental, popular health, and popular pharmacy organizations.

Notwithstanding this history, Sucre is a divided and unequal municipality, as the photograph shown in figure 3.1 indicates. On the left is La Urbina, a middle-class sector where more affluent, predominantly lighter-skinned white residents live in relatively orderly and secure high-rise apartment complexes, or *urbanizaciones*. On the right is Petare, often called "the largest barrio in Latin America." Petare's residents are overwhelming poor and working class, and most are darker-skinned morenos (or mestizos) or Black Afro-Venezuelans who live in much more precarious conditions.

Statistics give some sense of the differences between Sucre's more and less affluent areas. More affluent residents are known for being obsessed with crime, but Sucre's poorer residents are much more likely to face violence—from gangs involved in a thriving drug trade and also from the police, who are viewed as highly corrupt and violent. Per newspaper accounts, which must be viewed with caution, there were nearly four thousand murders in Sucre between 2000 and 2007, with 90 percent occurring in the barrios of Petare.[3] Housing quality also varies tremendously in Sucre's more and less affluent areas.[4] In Venezuela's 2011 census over a quarter of the houses in Sucre's poorest parish, Files de Mariches, were categorized as inadequate due to a lack of at least one basic service such as running water, electricity, or sewage. In Leoncio Martínez, Sucre's wealthiest parish, less than 0.1 percent of housing was categorized as inadequate. Sucre's other three parishes were in between, with 5–10 percent of housing categorized as inadequate in the second- and third-poorest parishes of Caucagüita and La Dolorita. A 1998 study in the Petare Norte barrio found 40 percent of residents worked in the informal sector and the bottom 20 percent of families earned an average of 125 USD a month (World Bank 1998, 11–12).

Sucre is similar to Torres in its striking inequality, but the two municipalities differ in many notable ways. Sucre is highly urbanized, with much greater population and density. It is also much more industrialized, with the municipality containing seven industrial sectors, several of which are so large they are divided into subsectors. Through the early 2010s a number of major domestic and foreign companies, including Coca-Cola, Polar, Bigot, Parmalat, and Primrose, had factories in Sucre. There were also many smaller factories, as well as numerous commercial and agroprocessing firms located in the municipality. This accounts for a third major difference compared to Torres. Due to its lack of industry, Torres has a very weak local tax base, with central government transfers accounting for up to 90 percent of its budget as of the mid-2000s. In Sucre, by contrast, local tax revenue provided 86 percent of the annual budget as of 2011, according to Silvia Dohnart, Sucre's then-director of economic development. The final, political difference has been noted: the backlash against Chavista rule in the early 2000s led to a movement-left opposition mayor in Torres and a center-right opposition mayor in Sucre. These differences make the similarity of Torres and Sucre's political trajectories from the 1980s to 2010s striking.

CLIENTELISM (1980s–1990s)

As was the case in Torres, and throughout Venezuela, political parties played a central role in Sucre from the 1960s through 1990s. According to Fernando Giuliani, 'In the 1950s and 1960s political parties played an important part in what was a new democracy, and they occupied all the spaces, neighborhood organizing, [and] unions. People believed in them.' Fernando said parties enjoyed prestige because of the leading role some parties, particularly Acción Democrática and the Communist Party of Venezuela, played in the underground struggle against Marcos Pérez Jiménez's dictatorship.

Accounts suggest that Sucre was subject to the increasingly clientelistic political logic that prevailed across Venezuela in the 1980s and 1990s. A key way this worked was through new neighborhood associations formed in middle- and popular-class zones in these decades. Fernando said the neighborhood associations 'were a great advance' when they first formed, but subsequently 'they were taken over by the political parties' and merely advanced party interests and not communities' true needs. This accords with the account of Jesus "Chuo" Alazar, a municipal employee and longtime Sucre resident, who served as president of his neighborhood association, in Petare's San Miguel barrio, in the 1980s and 1990s. Chuo told me the neighborhood associations were highly politicized and dominated by Acción Democrática and COPEI, which controlled Sucre's mayor's office from 1989 (its first mayoral election) through 2000. Chuo was a Copeyano, which meant his neighborhood association received 'lots of help from city hall.' Like Fernando, Chuo said the neighborhood associations often served the needs of leaders rather than the community as a whole: 'The [neighborhood association] presidents were like little Fidel Castros. . . . Some of them were there for forty years and no one could do anything to displace them. They were the boss.' Chuo recounts that presidents would take funds given to their association and use them for their personal benefit, such as building a house for their families. He said that any funds 'left over' might be given to others in the community.

By the 1990s the prestige that political parties had formerly enjoyed in Sucre, and elsewhere, had evaporated. According to Fernando, 'The problem was that the parties didn't open up. . . . The parties didn't give space to the base. There was bad administration, and there was corruption. . . . The worst sin of all was elitization,' parties increasingly catering only to elites. Like Torres, Sucre was primed for change by the end of the 1990s.

PARTICIPATORY CLIENTELISM (2000–2008)

Change came in 2000, when Hugo Chávez's Fifth Republic Movement (MVR) swept COPEI out of the mayor's office. Sucre's new mayor was José Vicente Rangel Ávalos, the son of José Vicente Rangel. One of Venezuela's most prominent leftist journalists, Rangel served as Venezuela's vice president from 2002 to 2007 and held other important posts in the Chávez administration. The administration of José Vicente, as the mayor was known, was plagued by the same contradictions found nationally in the Chávez era, such as the coexistence of participatory rhetoric and policies and ruling party leaders' efforts to maintain their own power. He also faced credible accusations of rampant corruption. One rumor held that the mayor's wife and other family members controlled construction companies that did business with city hall during his tenure.

Like Torres's Javier Oropeza, José Vicente established a participatory clientelistic urban regime. He appointed a proparticipation radical leftist, Carlos "Pitufo" Molina, to a top social development post in his administration. In a September 2010 interview that started at Caracas's Parque Carabobo metro station and ended in his twenty-seventh-floor Ombudsman's office, Pitufo recounted his experience. Like Torres's Myriam Giménez, Pitufo had worked to foster popular participation in the 1990s when he headed a project in the Vargas state government establishing participatory planning councils. Vargas's governor was from the same movement-left party that Julio Chávez belonged to until 2007, Patria Para Todos (PPT). Pitufo told me he had worked in the Vargas state government just six months when MVR leaders who felt threatened by his participatory work forced him out. In 2000 two leftist MVR city councillors in Sucre recruited Pitufo and convinced José Vicente to appoint him president of Fundasucre, a foundation in charge of social development work in Sucre's municipal government.

Pitufo's two years as Fundasucre's president are strikingly similar to Myriam Giménez's time as Torres's director of social development. Like Myriam, Pitufo worked to foster participatory planning. One of the main ways he did this was by establishing approximately fifteen community development councils (CDCs) in Sucre's barrios. Pitufo explained that at the time 'Petare was very fragmented, and there were lots of spaces that were privatized, sometimes by communities themselves, by drug dealers' and by others. Pitufo saw the CDCs as a way 'to foster integration, . . . strengthen the sense of community identity, and overcome social fragmentation.' He said the CDCs 'were similar to communal councils, but much more horizontal. . . . They [the CDCs] were essentially tools of self-government.' According to Pitufo, the CDCs succeeded in fostering a more horizontal and autonomous relationship between communities and the state: 'We were the intermediaries between the communities and many institutions in the national government, which we would help the communities to approach to get resources. . . . And this generated a process among the people that was not directed from above, but was horizontal. . . . This was not a tutelage process, but generated communities' self-capacity. . . . We respected the [CDCs'] autonomy.'

José Vicente initially supported Pitufo, just as Oropeza had initially supported Myriam. Yet like Oropeza, José Vicente sought to maintain control over the participatory institutions his administration was creating; one way was by seeking to prevent political pluralism. Pitufo said, 'When I arrived, I presented the [CDC] proposal to the whole municipality and they supported it.' However, this support did not last long. Pitufo felt this was 'because government functionaries don't work with the people, they decree [what the people should do]. . . . Mayors aren't interested in the process, but just in the product. . . . Our political culture is based on the accumulation of power, it's very Machiavellian, and a process like this doesn't allow for the accumulation of power.' Pitufo said José Vicente was particularly threatened by the CDCs' political pluralism: 'In the barrios there were Copeyanos, Adecos, and we worked with all of them. But José Vicente didn't accept having them there. He said of me, "Carlos Molina is putting Copeyanos into the CDCs." He wanted to have only people from the MVR in the CDCs.'

In 2001, Pitufo and CDC leaders sought to create a new municipal ordinance that would institutionalize the CDCs and expand the program to all of Sucre. Pitufo said this effort failed due to 'an alliance between the MVR, supposedly on the left, and COPEI, from the right, [which] defeated the ordinance' in Sucre's municipal council. Pitufo incurred additional enmity from José Vicente when President Chávez filmed an episode of *Aló Presidente* in a community where Pitufo was working. Chávez praised Pitufo and the CDCs, which Pitufo said 'brought difficulties with the mayor, who was constantly afraid of being displaced. . . . Eventually they brought a lot of pressure and the mayor asked for my letter of resignation.' In 2002, Pitufo agreed to resign, and the CDCs came to an end.

In 2004 José Vicente won reelection, surviving a strong campaign from Carlos Ocariz, who lost by less than six thousand votes out of a total of 148,325. During his final two years in office, 2006–2008, José Vicente implemented participatory budgeting. The process had four phases, according to officials involved. First, the mayor held a workshop with technical staff, leaders of Sucre's five parish boards, the Local Public Planning Council (which accounts indicate was never particularly functional or important, unlike Torres's CLPP), and communal council delegates. Second, communal councils met to determine three priorities per council, with the top one made into a project proposal. Third, there were parish assemblies, with two assemblies held in Petare, Sucre's largest parish. An official who had attended such assemblies showed me photos to back up her claim that hundreds, if not thousands, of people had attended. The PB's fourth and final phase was project implementation. This same official said the Department of Public Works handled this phase, 'and after [giving them the projects] we had no idea what happened.'

Nor, it seems, did anyone else. During my initial fieldwork in Sucre, in mid-2010, I spent weeks trying to divine what happened to projects approved in "José Vicente's PB," as some officials called the process. I never succeeded. After multiple dead ends, I found myself face-to-face with two public works administrators, Alba and Yelitza, who had worked under José Vicente and had knowledge of his administration's PB. To my surprise, Alba told me, 'There was no participatory budget like there is now,' meaning under Ocariz. Yelitza said the same thing. 'They had assemblies with the communities [but] there was no participatory budget with José Vicente.'[5] I also asked grassroots Chavistas who had been active when José Vicente was mayor if they had knowledge of PB under his watch. In an interview, Griselda, an experienced Chavista whose first organizing work was the CDCs with Pitufo (an experience she recounted with great pride), said, 'There was no participatory budget in which we could decide on projects' under José Vicente. Griselda said his administration distributed benefits clientelistically: 'Some through familial networks [familiarismo], or through old boys' networks, [and] some through fraud. . . . This led to an explosion of problems in the communal councils.'

Some Chavistas I spoke with had a positive view of José Vicente, but a majority of the many Chavistas I asked viewed his administration as highly flawed. Residents of Sucre from across the political spectrum said the ex-mayor had governed in a clientelistic and corrupt manner. International watchdog groups, like Transparency International, backed up such claims. A Transparency Venezuela (the organization's national affiliate) report discussed actions Ocariz took against José Vicente: "On April 29, 2009, Carlos Ocariz arrived to the Contraloría General de la República with fourteen boxes filled with documents of alleged irregularities committed during the period of his predecessor" (Poliszuk 2016). Among other things, José Vicente was accused of funneling hundreds of municipal contracts, totaling millions of bolívares, to companies controlled by his wife, cousin, and other family members. The report alleged, "Contracts that remained in City Hall, commercial records of contractors, as well as the names of managers and directors who signed on their behalf, made it very clear that a group of [the mayor's family members and friends] took more than 60 percent of the municipal budget" (Poliszuk 2016). The report also alleged that in July 2009 a company owned by José Vicente's cousin returned nearly 400,000 USD to Sucre municipality for a project awarded the previous year (when José Vicente was mayor) that was never finished and seemingly never started (Poliszuk 2016).

My fieldwork does not allow me to evaluate the veracity of these claims. It is important to note Transparency International's close ties to Venezuela's opposition and the obvious political rationale behind Ocariz's accusations against his predecessor. It is also important to note that José Vicente was not convicted of corruption. Yet there are reasons for taking the allegations against him seriously. Notably, even Chavistas with a positive view of José Vicente felt he was corrupt. For instance, Rafael Blanco, a Chavista communal council leader from Guaicoco, a barrio in the parish of La Dolorita, said, 'José Vicente did a good job. [But] there were acts of corruption. We have to recognize that.'

In addition to the charges of clientelism and corruption, José Vicente was also criticized, including by many Chavistas, for his alleged "populism." This term was used to describe the former mayor's practice of directly giving low-income residents material goods, such as refrigerators. Some Chavistas said this showed that José Vicente was "helping the poorest sectors." But others thought it was just a form of electioneering that allowed the mayor to win votes without tackling more difficult, long-term problems.

Term limits prevented José Vicente from running for a third term, but many Chavistas blamed him for the PSUV's shocking loss in Sucre's 2008 mayoral election. Ocariz was again the opposition's candidate and this time he prevailed, defeating the PSUV's Jesse Chacón by a comfortable margin of 56–44 percent. Ocariz's win, what Chavistas call "the day we lost Petare," was deeply surprising to many since Sucre had been considered a stalwart "Chavista territory," as graffiti and PSUV campaign posters continued to proclaim several years into Ocariz's term. Echoing a line I heard from many Chavistas in Sucre, in October 2010 Ruben Pereira, the secretary general of Sucre's pro-Chavista municipal health-care union, said José Vicente's 'poor management is the main factor responsible for the loss of the Greater Caracas mayoralty, Sucre municipality, and Miranda state' in 2008. Another Chavista declared Ocariz's victory 'the price we pay for [José Vicente's] mistakes.' Chavistas also cited Jesse Chacón's allegedly lackluster campaign as a reason for Ocariz's victory. During a Chavista community meeting in Maca, a barrio in Petare, a group of women complained, 'He [Chacón] didn't come to the barrios.' Electoral data suggest Chavista abstention played a key role in facilitating Ocariz's victory. The opposition won nine thousand more votes in the 2008 election compared to the 2006 presidential election, while the Chavista vote decreased by forty-one thousand, which was also the difference in Ocariz and Chacón's vote totals in 2008. Interviews suggest that Chavista abstention in 2008—and thus Ocariz's victory—was likely due to grassroots Chavistas's frustration with José Vicente and a lack of excitement for Chacón.[6]

ADMINISTERED DEMOCRACY (2009–2013)

On December 10, 2008, Ocariz was sworn in as Sucre's mayor. With this act Sucre (and Venezuela) entered into uncharted waters. How would an anti-Chavista, center-right party with a predominantly white, middle- and upper-class core base govern a municipality in which 80 percent of residents were from the predominantly Black and Brown popular classes and had historically strongly favored Chavismo? Electoral data show that the notion that Sucre was *Territorio Chavista* was far from being a thing of the past. In each election between 2006 and 2013, the ruling MVR and PSUV (created in 2007) decisively won in Sucre's three poorest parishes of Filas de Mariches, La Dolorita, and Caucagüita. The ruling party's vote exceeded 60 percent in these parishes in all but one of these elections and regularly exceeded 70 percent.[7] The ruling party also won by similar margins in the poorer districts of Petare, which includes a mix of more and less affluent electoral districts. Primero Justicia officials were aware of this electoral map. In discussing Ocariz's 2008 victory, a party official commented that Ocariz 'lost in the popular zones and won on the basis of high turnout in middle-class communities' in Sucre's wealthiest parish, Leoncio Martínez, and Petare's affluent parts.

As he began his term as mayor, Ocariz thus had a clear political need to increase his support among the popular classes. Conservative parties have often sought to do this by emphasizing "non-class" issues such as family, religion, and crime (Przeworski 1985). Brazil's Jair Bolsonaro's 2018 presidential campaign is a recent example of the success this strategy has borne for right-wing parties in Latin America (Richmond 2018). Ocariz did not follow this path but instead made participation central to his governance strategy, most notably by devoting tens of millions of dollars and many hundreds of staff hours to participatory budgeting. In so doing, Ocariz ignored advice from some of his own top officials, who, like some middle- and upper-class oppositionists, disparaged participatory budgeting, and participation generally, as foolish, and worse, "populist" and "Chavista."

The notion that Ocariz governed "like a Chavista" is, I argue, apt. The reason he did so is twofold: he needed to increase his popular-sector support, and governing "like a Chavista" was the best, and arguably only viable, way for him to do so because Chávez's left-populism was nationally hegemonic. Multiple pieces of evidence support my claim that the presence of left-populist hegemony pushed Ocariz to embrace participation in an unexpectedly robust manner. First, as already noted and detailed further in the chapter, Ocariz devoted quite significant resources to participatory budgeting, spending beyond what was constitutionally mandated. Second, Ocariz symbolically linked his participatory policies to Chavismo in an explicit way. For instance, he deliberately used language widely understood as being "Chavista." One example of this occurred in the participatory budget assembly described in the opening paragraph of this book, with Ocariz telling assembly participants, 'We don't just believe in popular power, we're doing popular power.' This comment was also an oblique dig at Ocariz's predecessor, José Vicente, who Ocariz could credibly accuse of merely "believing in" but not "doing" popular power.

Third, Ocariz administration officials acknowledged that Venezuela's (as well as) Sucre's) political context was part of the reason why Ocariz made participation a priority. When I asked why Ocariz was doing participatory budgeting, one official gave me a look suggesting the answer was obvious and said, 'because of the context.' I asked Alexander González, the second in command at Fundasucre, the municipal agency that ran PB under Ocariz, the question. He replied by noting several factors, including 'the political aspect':

> In this municipality, an important percentage of the people support the national government. And they talk about participation, and empowering the communities, but usually it's just a discourse, and they don't actually do anything concrete in terms of participation or empowerment. So we look for ways to bring together this discourse with concrete actions. [He then describes how Sucre's PB works.] On Saturdays [in Community Encounters] we discuss ideas and proposals and then from Monday to Thursday [in Technical Assistance sessions] we take this information and put it into projects. This shows that we're not against the organization of the people, or discussion with the people, or transferring responsibilities to the people.[8]

One way to interpret this comment is that the presence of left-populist hegemony, of which participatory democracy was a central element (as discussed in chapter 1), compelled the Ocariz administration to take actions, such as robustly implementing PB, that 'show that we're not against the organization of the people, or discussion with the people, or transferring responsibilities to the people.' Another piece of evidence supporting the view that left-populist hegemony pushed Ocariz to robustly implement participation is the fact that he implemented PB in his first term, 2009–2013, when left-populist hegemony was present, but not during his second, 2014–2017, when this hegemony crumbled.

It is important to note that Ocariz may have been more inclined to support participation compared to other opposition figures due to his political history. Primero Justicia is historically linked to COPEI, which as discussed in chapter 1 had a left wing that supported participation in the 1970s and early 1980s. Ocariz worked for Miranda's Copeyano governor, Enrique Mendoza (who it should be noted was not linked to the party's left wing), in the 1990s, and helped support the state' government's participatory initiatives. This history may help explain Ocariz's willingness to embrace participation during his time as Sucre's mayor, but it does not explain several key details just highlighted: the robust degree to which Ocariz embraced participation; the manner in which he did so, namely by using language and institutional forms associated with Chavismo; and the fact that he did so only during his first term. My argument about left-populist hegemony, by contrast, is able to explain these details.

Like Torres's Julio Chávez, Sucre's Ocariz refracted left-populist hegemony into democratic rule. This was combined with a professional-elite balance of class forces, which led to administered democracy, a state-controlled democratic regime. Electoral data show that upper and middle classes form Primero Justicia's core support. In Sucre's wealthiest parish, Leonicio Martínez, Primero Justicia won over 70 percent (and often over 80 percent) of the vote in every election from 2006 to 2013. In Sucre's three poorest parishes Primero Justicia only topped 40 percent once in this time, with the party's vote still well below 50 percent. The way Ocariz administration officials spoke of and related to dominant classes is also telling. Silvia Dohnert, the director of economic planning, told me, in English, 'We support the private sector and we have no complex about this, and we're not ashamed to say this.' The contrast with Julio's denunciations of "the oligarchy" is obvious. Silvia proudly told me of Ocariz's sponsorship of business fairs but noted 'businesses have been careful to not openly support the municipal government' to avoid antagonizing the national government. It is also worth noting Primero Justicia's direct ties to the business sector. Henrique Capriles, the party's leader and one of its founders (alongside Ocariz and others), is from one of Venezuela's leading business families, with major stakes in the communications, industrial, entertainment, service, and real estate sectors.

Sucre's elite-professional balance of class forces accounts for the regime's state-controlled character, which manifests in two ways. The first is top officials' professional trajectories. Officials hold degrees from prestigious foreign and domestic universities, such as Harvard, MIT, Columbia, American University, Universidad Central de Venezuela, Universidad

Católica Andrés Bello, and Universidad Metropolitana, and they have prior experience in government, the private sector, and prestigious international financial institutions. For instance, Ocariz worked for the Inter-American Development Bank and held a cabinet-level post in the Miranda state government under the COPEI governor Enrique Mendoza. Second, Sucre's administered democracy contains institutional mechanisms providing for state control over decision-making, as detailed in the next section.

ASSESSING SUCRE'S ADMINISTERED DEMOCRATIC REGIME

The distinguishing feature of Sucre's administered democratic regime is a local state that gives citizens "some but not too much power." The reason for this is the tension between the regime's democratic form of rule and state-controlled character. This tension can be seen in various ways: the institutional design of Sucre's Participatory Budget, which facilitated a real-but-limited extent and quality of popular control over decision-making; officials' uneven commitment to fostering citizen control over decision-making; the contradictory, and at-times convoluted, ways in which officials spoke about participation and its limits; and citizens' attempts to push beyond these limits.

As this section shows, Sucre's administered democracy scores below Torres's participatory democracy but above Santa Cruz's technocratic clientelistic and El Alto's inverted clientelistic regimes on the extent and quality of popular control and political effectiveness. Sucre ties Torres and exceeds the other cases in institutional effectiveness.

EXTENT OF POPULAR CONTROL

Ocariz made participation in decision-making a central theme of his first mayoral term. He and many top officials regularly spoke about participation and its importance to the administration. A 2012 book promoting Ocariz's administration vividly illustrates this, beginning with its title, *Carlos Ocariz: El mandato de la calle* (The Mandate of the Street). The book features interviews with top officials, including Ocariz, who says "having better educated citizens who make decisions . . . is the key to everything" (Giusti and De Viveiros 2012, 29). José Luis "Chispiao" López Noriega, Fundasucre's president and Sucre's director of government after 2017, speaks of Ocariz's commitment to "the ideal of participatory democracy" and calls "participatory budgeting . . . a banner of Carlos Ocariz from his first campaign" (51). Participation is highlighted in the titles of many of the book's sections, for instance: "The community as protagonist" (29), "The people decide" (30), "My office is the street" (35), and "The power in the people" (55).

FIGURE 3.2 Carlos Ocariz (seated) at a community event with Maribel Piñango speaking, 2011.

Source: Photo by author.

FIGURE 3.3 Participatory budget zonal assembly, May 2011.

Source: Photo by author.

Ocariz put his money where his mouth was to an extent that appears impressive (versus most mayors, and particularly most right-of-center mayors) and limited (versus movement-left mayors like Julio Chávez). In 2009, Ocariz's first year as mayor, Sucre's PB covered a relatively modest 20 percent of an investment budget exceeding 100 million USD. This percent doubled over the next two years: PB covered 30 percent of the investment budget in 2010 and 40 percent in 2011 and 2012. Fundasucre oversaw Sucre's PB process, which comprised three phases. The first was zonal assemblies held on Saturday mornings in forty-one zones.[9] These assemblies brought together officials and the zone's residents and civic leaders. Assemblies I attended always started with a PowerPoint presentation, by Fundasucre's president or another official, laying out the process. After this, residents split into working groups covering themes such as security, culture, sports, and infrastructure. Each working group was charged with producing a list of ten to twenty proposals. The second phase was technical assistance sessions on the following Monday through Thursday evenings. In these meetings officials from Fundasucre or NGOs contracted by Fundasucre worked with residents to produce refined lists of projects including estimated costs, technical specifications, and social benefits. Fundasucre officially had the final say over project approval. The third stage was project implementation, usually the following year; officials said citizens implemented 70 percent of PB projects (Giusti and De Viveiros 2012, 57), with the municipality and private companies implementing the rest.

In mid-2010, when I conducted my initial fieldwork in Sucre, Fundasucre officials were considering having PB cover 50 percent of the investment budget. My conversations with officials about the idea, which never came to fruition, reveals the real but limited degree of popular control Sucre's PB gave residents. Alexander Gonzalez was one of the officials who favored PB covering 50 percent. I told him Torres's PB covered 100 percent of its investment budget and asked if Sucre might consider doing the same. He dismissed the idea: 'The mayor has certain strategic priorities [and] giving 100 percent would tie his hands.' Alexander distinguished PB projects, which he saw as 'very specific and focused,' from larger projects that happened via Sucre's "normal" budgetary process and benefitted everyone in the municipality and not just one sector. Alexander felt PB was important, but viewed it as clearly secondary to nonparticipatory governance projects. I also asked Maribel Piñango, Fundasucre's coordinator of training and a highly skilled PB facilitator, if Sucre's PB should cover 50 percent of the budget. Since Maribel was a strong proponent of participation I expected her to fully support this plan. To my surprise, she opposed it: 'People aren't ready . . . [so] it makes sense to go slowly, giving a little this year and seeing how it goes, seeing if the people are capable, before increasing the amount.' Despite their differences, Alexander and Maribel both supported giving citizens a real but limited degree of decision-making power. This position differs from views of officials in more "traditional" right-governed cities, like Santa Cruz, where officials were almost completely opposed to citizen input in decision-making. The position also differs from Torres, where officials in Julio Chávez's movement-left administration strongly supported "the people making all the decisions."

It is worth noting that Alexander and Maribel were among the Ocariz administration officials who showed the most support for popular control over decision-making. A number of key officials showed much less enthusiasm. I asked Mauro de Palma, director of the (important) Department of Works and Urban Maintenance, his thoughts on PB. He dutifully replied, 'We all support the Participatory Budget.' But when pressed he showed his support was quite limited, saying, 'Rather than a solution, the participatory budget is a symptom of the problems of public administration in this country. I'll speak clearly with you. . . . There's a need for professionals to run things. If we were in a normal municipality, who would run the railway, the Metro, the schools?' When I replied probably not the community, Mauro folded his arms as if to rest his case.

Turnout for Sucre's PB was modest but increased over time. Available evidence indicates around 1,200 residents participated in PB in 2009. By 2011, this had doubled to 2,500 participants.[10] There was a significant increase in turnout in PB zonal assemblies I attended in late 2010, when there were twenty to thirty people per assembly, and 2011, when there were seventy to eighty. The main reason for this appears to have been a major increase in Chavista participation in Sucre's PB in 2011. There seem to be two main reasons Sucre's PB attracted fewer participants than Torres's PB. Sucre officials appeared less committed to participatory decision-making, and the Ocariz administration had a contentious relationship with Chavista organizations, particularly in its first two years.

Sucre's administered democracy differs clearly from Torres's participatory democracy in its very limited degree of popular control over nonbudgetary decision-making. Ocariz implemented two modest participatory programs besides PB. One was a project giving communities control over twenty-two outpatient health clinics, with Sucre's PB providing funding (Giusti and De Viveiros 2012, 70). The second was a controversial program, Uno+Uno, in which the Ocariz administration pledged to match parents' contributions, of 60–200 *bolívares*, to public schools (67). This was envisioned as a form of "community co-responsibility" whereby parents would participate in "managing the school's physical plant, endowment, and recreation and entertainment" (67). In its first incarnation this program was critiqued by Chavistas as a form of privatization, since it included a request to parents to contribute to school registration costs (56). Fundasucre's president, Chispiao, said, "The revulsion was so great that we had to cancel [the request]" (56).[11]

QUALITY OF POPULAR CONTROL

The quality of popular control over decision-making in Sucre's administered democratic regime was moderate. A key reason for this was the unevenness of officials' commitment to participation. This can be seen in, and helps explain, the variety of decision-making forms in Sucre's PB. Some officials used deliberative decision-making while others operated in a command-and-control way. The distinct way two working groups were facilitated in the April 30, 2011, PB zonal assembly in Caucagüita illustrates this unevenness.

I drove up to the assembly with Fundasucre officials in a caravan of cars through the steep, winding, and often narrow streets of Petare to a school in Caucagüita. Around eighty mostly Black and Brown residents and several dozen officials, many but not all white, attended. I was surprised to see a significant presence of Chavistas, visible in their red hats and communal council vests. My rough count suggested at least half the participants were Chavistas. The mayor arrived around noon and addressed the assembly as follows:

> This is the third year of the participatory budget. . . . When we started the participatory budget two years ago people didn't believe it. They didn't believe the community could execute [projects] and monitor receipts. . . . This is popular power. We don't just believe in popular power. We're doing popular power. . . . And we don't exclude. You can see that we have lots of, how do you call them, lots of *compañeros* here. . . . Before nobody even knew how much the budget was, or who decided it. . . . You know how airplanes have a black box that remains intact even if there's a crash

[with] all the information sealed inside. Well, that's what the budget used to be like here. It was a black box. . . . Well, we've opened the black box up so that communities could participate and execute projects. . . . But it hasn't been us who've done this. It's been you who've done this.

These comments illustrate several things: the importance participation had for Ocariz; his self-evident pride in supporting it and doing so in an inclusive way, with *compañeros*, i.e., Chavistas, welcomed with open arms; and his self-conscious appropriation of language associated with Chavismo, namely the "we're doing popular power" in his opening remarks.

After Ocariz's and a few other officials' comments, the assembly broke into three working groups, with twenty-five to forty participants in each. I observed two of the three groups. The first was for "social equipment" (*equipamiento social*). Oscar, a mid-level Fundasucre official, facilitated this working group. From interactions in Fundasucre's office I knew Oscar had little experience or apparent interest in facilitating participatory decision-making.

This lack of experience and interest was clear in the bumbling way Oscar facilitated his working group. After I entered the classroom it was held in, Tacho, a young Black man and a Chavista, objected that a representative of a civic association from Tacho's barrio was present. Tacho referenced comments Fundasucre's top two officials, Chispiao and Alexander, had made that if a barrio had both a communal council and a civic association, the communal council had precedence in presenting a PB proposal. Tacho then said, 'There's already a communal council here and they [the civic association] didn't have an assembly or anything.' This second comment was a reference to why communal councils had precedence in making PB proposals: councils had regular public assemblies to vet proposals while civic associations usually did not.

Oscar dismissed Tacho. 'That's not relevant to what we're doing here.' Tacho left to complain to Chispiao (Fundasucre's president). The working group proceeded to its main task: selecting ten of twenty-one proposals. It was soon clear Oscar was unable to keep order over the process. This prompted another official present, Tibisay, from Sucre's Department of Works, to take over. Tibisay quickly wrote down a list of communities whose proposals would advance beyond the working groups. As she wrote communities' names down, Tibisay said, 'I was here last year and I know these communities didn't receive anything.' As this happened, participants rushed forward, trying to get their communities on the list. After a few chaotic minutes, Tibisay finalized a list of ten communities. Many participants, presumably from communities not listed, appeared upset. Tacho, who was now back at the working group, shook his head and said, 'I don't agree with this.'

Throughout this time, periodic applause could be heard from the working group in the adjacent classroom. After Tibisay finished, I moved to this other group, which Maribel Piñango facilitated. I knew Maribel to be one of Fundasucre's most experienced meeting facilitators. As described in the introduction to this book, Maribel's process at her working group was smooth and deliberative. She gave all participants a chance to present a proposal. She and other participants then asked questions about what each proposal was for and the number of beneficiaries. Applause followed each participant's presentation. Maribel then guided the participants through the task of selecting five of the eleven proposals presented, explaining the criteria for evaluating proposals. Each proposal was considered. Several were quickly approved. A few involved lengthier deliberation, with Maribel and the participants engaging in back-and-forth questions about the proposals. Once the final list of five proposals was determined, Maribel read each of the selected proposals. The full group applauded as each proposal was read. As the room emptied I asked participants how they felt. Nearly everyone indicated they were happy.

The contrast between these two working groups is indicative of the tensions, unevenness, and contradictions of Sucre's administered democracy. Oscar and Maribel represent the extremes of Sucre officials in terms of commitment to popular empowerment, with most officials falling in between the two. My fieldwork does not permit precise comparison, but it suggests that Sucre officials were generally more committed to popular empowerment than officials in Santa Cruz and El Alto and less than those in Torres. It is important to note, however, that even the most pro-empowerment Sucre officials, like Maribel, demonstrated paternalism and distrust of popular classes. An anecdote from the Caucagüita assembly just discussed illustrates this behavior. After the assembly ended I briefly chatted with some Chavista participants about their work and experience with the Ocariz administration. Fundasucre officials told me it was time to go, with one saying, 'The taxi you came up in is ready to leave.' I said, 'I'd prefer to stay and can find my way home.' This seemed to make the officials uncomfortable. At one point Maribel grabbed my wrist and dragged me out, saying, 'We're not leaving you here. If we do you won't have your bag anymore.' I replied, 'I'll be fine,' and mentioned that I had gotten home on my own from many places. But Maribel and others were so insistent that I complied and left with them.

Sucre is also an intermediate case in terms of residents' degree of control over decisions, which was lower than Torres but higher than Santa Cruz and El Alto. Sucre residents had near-binding control over PB decisions. Fundasucre officials had final say over accepting or rejecting projects approved in zonal assemblies and technical assistance sessions, but residents and officials said officials almost never rejected or altered projects residents chose. Sucre's PB did differ markedly from Torres's PB in who determined how much money specific projects and project areas received. In Torres residents decided this, while in Sucre officials did. In an August 2010 technical assistance session in Guaicoco, I asked the facilitator, Victoria—from the NGO Centro al Servicio de la Acción Popular (Popular Action Service Center), which Fundasucre had contracted to help run PB—if citizens could make these decisions, like in Torres. She said, 'It's dangerous to give this job to the people. . . . There's not maturity to assume these great responsibilities. . . . We've always had a very paternalistic political [culture] in Venezuela. . . . This comes from years and years of paternalism, which has prevented people from having more maturity. . . . In my opinion we haven't reached this level of maturity, [so] it would be very dangerous.' Victoria did not seem aware that her answer displayed the very paternalism she was decrying. She also said residents were too selfish for 'these great responsibilities': 'If you let the people decide the amounts, it's just me, me, me . . . [and] they don't look at others' needs. . . . An example of this is the woman at the security table, who felt security is the most important thing, without thinking about everything else.' I pressed the point. 'What would happen if people were given the right to decide specific amounts?' Victoria responded, 'Total anarchy. . . . There's no maturity in the Venezuelan people.'

Victoria's comments illustrate a view common to Ocariz administration officials: the people can be trusted with *some but not too much* responsibility. There is a striking difference between this and Julio Chávez's view: "It's better to err with the people than be right without them." This highlights the difference between Torres's participatory and Sucre's administered democracies. Officials in both cases displayed a "the state knows best" attitude (as did officials in Santa Cruz and El Alto). But the import of this attitude differed due to the distinct institutional mechanisms embedded in Torres and Sucre's contrasting urban regimes. In Torres's socially controlled participatory democratic regime, institutional mechanisms ensured citizens had final say on decisions and could override officials, who were not shy about voicing their views (usually in a deliberative way, as chapter 2 shows). In Sucre's state-controlled administered democratic regime, institutional mechanisms ensured officials had final say over decisions and could override citizens' views (though this rarely happened) or make decisions without citizen input (e.g., determining monetary allocations for specific projects and project areas).

Sucre's PB was moderately inclusive in 2009, its first year, and highly inclusive by 2011 in terms of partisanship, class, and race and ethnicity. (In terms of gender it was always highly inclusive.) In a 2016 interview, Fundasucre's then-president Juan Vicente Mijares said at its height, circa 2011, over 80 percent of Sucre's PB participants were from the popular classes, working in the service, construction, banking, and informal sectors. The other nearly 20 percent of participants were middle-class professionals. Juan Vicente estimated that 60 percent of participants were mestizo, 30 percent Afro-Venezuelan, and 5–10 percent white. He said women accounted for 70 percent of participants in PB events and 70 percent of zonal coordinators.

The main reason Sucre's PB became much more inclusive from 2009 to 2011 was the dramatic shift in how Chavistas related to it. In 2009,

TABLE 3.1 Chavista participation in PB zonal assemblies, 2009–2011

		2009	2010	2011
ZONE	Barrio Union II & III	Sabotage	Boycott	>50% Chavista
	Barrio Union I & IV	Sabotage	Very Low (< 5%)	Low (10%)
	Caucagüita I & III	No Data	Moderate	75–80% Chavista
	Caucagüita II	Boycott	Very Low (< 5%)	20–25% Chavista
	Caucagüita IV	Boycott	Boycott	15% Chavista
	Maca I & II	Sabotage	No Data	25–40% Chavista

there was virtually no (open) Chavista participation: Chavistas boycotted two-thirds and sabotaged the other third (twelve of thirty-eight) of the zonal assemblies, with sabotage consisting of activists physically blocking or loudly and repeatedly disrupting assemblies to the point that they had to be rescheduled or relocated. Chavista participation in the PB modestly increased in 2010. An official who facilitated fourteen assemblies that year told me Chavistas were present in just three of them, comprising 50 percent of participants in one assembly, a handful in two, and none in the others. Chavistas sabotaged only two zonal assemblies in 2010 (Giusti and De Viveiros 2012, 55) and none in 2011. Data I collected on the first six zonal assemblies in 2011 show a major change. Chavistas were present in all six and were a majority in two. Table 3.1 tracks the changes from 2009 to 2011 in these six zonal assemblies.[12]

Why did Chavistas oppose Sucre's PB in 2009 and 2010 (to a lesser extent) and largely come to accept it by 2011? My fieldwork points to three reasons for their initial (and for some, continuing) opposition. First, there was pervasive distrust of the opposition due to the 2002 coup. Rafael Blanco, a Chavista leader from Guaicoco, told me he would never work with the Ocariz administration, as 'these are the people who carried out the coup d'état in 2002.' Second, Chavistas who participated in Ocariz administration activities, like PB, faced the threat of sanctions from national and local institutions of, or supportive of, the government. Elvira, one of the only Chavistas who openly participated in PB in Guaicoco in 2010, told me,

'The "radical Chavistas" have it in their heads that if they participate here they won't be eligible to receive funding from Fundacomunal,' which registered and helped fund communal councils. An oppositionist in Guaicoco told me a Chavista who participated in PB was 'accused of having joined the opposition' by other Chavistas. Violeta, a Fundacomunal official I spoke to, bragged of punishing Chavistas who worked with Ocariz. 'If you want to receive resources from Ocariz, we'll stop giving them to you. And there are a lot more resources available from the ministry than from him. Their projects might be fifteen thousand *bolívares*, but we have a lot of resources. We have all the resources of the national government. If you accept resources from Ocariz, we'll be closed to you.'[13] Violeta's coworker, Astrid, said they refused to register communal councils led by non-Chavistas. 'We exclude them. We put hurdles in their way.' Violeta added, 'We have a list . . . the *Lista de Tascón* . . . It includes all who signed the revocation referendum against Chavez.[14] And we compare the names and ID numbers of everyone on this list, and if anyone is on the list, we won't approve them.' I asked, 'Isn't that a bit antidemocratic?' Violeta replied, 'Yes, it's antidemocratic, but it's strategic. Sometimes so they won't think we're so antidemocratic, we'll take their folders, and not register them, but tell them there have been delays in the process.'

The third reason (many) Chavistas initially opposed participating in Sucre's PB is that a number of zonal coordinators opposed their participation, which shows Chavistas did not have a monopoly on exclusion. Angel Alvarado, Sucre's director of community affairs, ran the zonal coordinator program, and he described it using participatory rhetoric often associated with Chavismo: 'It's a counterweight to the power of directors and bureaucrats. . . . It [power] shouldn't go from the top to the bottom, but from the bottom to the top. . . . This is a way to nourish communities, to have communities govern City Hall instead of having City Hall govern communities. It's a space of encounter between City Hall and the communities. . . . The coordinators are mini-mayors . . . they ask what the [zone's] needs are, and are the link between projects and the communities.'

Zonal coordinators typically came to their positions through campaigning for Ocariz in 2008 for Primero Justicia or one of the other parties that supported Ocariz, such as COPEI and Un Nuevo Tiempo. This may explain why around a third of Sucre's zonal coordinators appeared to support excluding Chavistas from PB and other events they ran. One of the many zonal coordinators I spoke to about this issue, from Barrio Union, told me, 'Among my colleagues there are many who want to exclude the Chavistas. They say, "If they didn't give anything to us, why should we give anything to them."' I came across a case of exclusion in August 2010 when a group of Chavistas complained that the zonal coordinator in La Bombilla, a zone in Petare, had not invited them to a workshop. Maribel Piñango overhead someone telling me about this and, with a half laugh and smile that seemed to indicate amusement and some support, said, 'Sometimes they only invite our allies.' Fundasucre's top brass disapproved of these practices. When I shared this example with him in an interview, Alexander said, 'We never agree with coordinators not telling people about meetings.' Alexander acknowledged that Primero Justicia officials occasionally pressured him to not work with Chavistas. 'They say, "Why are you giving any resources to Chavistas?" . . . They [the party] had to wait eight years [to take city hall] and now they want to take their revenge.' Chispiao said he confronted the handful of coordinators who excluded Chavistas whenever he found out it was happening and sometimes directly invited Chavistas to events if he thought they might face exclusion from lower-level officials.

To illustrate how inclusion and exclusion played out locally I discuss a conflict between Chavistas and oppositionists over the Casa Kamoca community center in the barrio of Guaicoco. The zonal coordinator, Chepa, a Primero Justicia militant I came to know well, told me COPEI's Enrique Mendoza built the center in the 1990s when he was Sucre's mayor. Chepa said that when José Vicente was mayor Chavistas had proposed holding a referendum on turning Casa Kamoca into a Barrio Adentro clinic. Chepa and other oppositionists fiercely opposed this but the referendum was held and won, according to local Chavistas, leading to the clinic being established. After Ocariz became mayor, oppositionists moved to retake the center. Chepa said, 'They [Chavistas] had it for ten years. . . . It was a garbage dump. It was our goal to recover the space. . . . We worked like ants.' Chavistas resisted. On April 19, 2010, a holiday marking the

Venezuelan independence movement's birth, things came to a head. Chepa said, 'We broke the lock [and] took it by force.' Chavistas were furious as 'we were marching in a parade with the president,' one told me. In May 2010 the Ocariz administration brokered an agreement giving both sides keys to the space and specific times to access it.

But tensions remained high. I learned this directly while attending the August 16, 2010, PB technical assistance session in Casa Kamoca's upper level, which was held from 6–8 p.m. During the session loud sounds came from the lower level, where a government-run Info Centro-internet café and Barrio Adentro clinic were housed. Chepa went down to investigate and I followed a bit later. I found a small group of senior citizens. The group's leader, José, who I learned was a Chavista, said they had come to use the Casa Kamoca's upper level for a physical therapy class. He took out a copy of the agreement the Ocariz administration had brokered in May. Chepa (who had gone back upstairs) had signed, along with other oppositionists. The agreement clearly said Casa Kamoca's upper level was reserved for physical therapy classes Monday, Wednesday, and Friday nights from 6–7 P.M., precisely the time it now was. It seemed clear Chepa was violating the agreement by holding the technical assistance session. I asked José if Chepa had invited him to attend the session. He said, 'Yes, I was invited. But I don't trust them. How can you trust someone who signs an agreement and then violates it?' When I got back upstairs I told Chepa what José had said and asked about the agreement, which I had just learned of. Chepa said it was 'invalid' because the Chavistas had agreed but failed to give 30,000 bolívares (alongside 150,000 provided by the Ocariz administration) to fix the space. Chepa also matter-of-factly said it was impossible for anyone else to use the space just now because the technical assistance session was using it.

This conflict illustrates the intense polarization found in Sucre and throughout the country at this time. This was partly because we were just weeks away from the September 2010 parliamentary elections. Polarization was particularly intense in Sucre since this was the first big election since the PSUV had "lost Petare" to Ocariz and Primero Justicia in 2008. I stayed abreast of the Casa Kamoca situation until October 2010 when I went to

El Alto. The conflict remained intense throughout this time. I was thus surprised to find that the conflict appeared to have been resolved when I returned to Sucre in April 2011. When I met up with Chepa again she gave a positive report of a meeting she had recently attended in Guaicoco's *sala de batalla* (battle room), the coordinating body for local Chavista work. This would have been unthinkable six months earlier.

The data presented above showing the dramatic increase in Chavista participation in Sucre's PB in 2011 suggests the improvement in Chavista-oppositionist relations was not limited to Guaicoco but found throughout Sucre. My fieldwork points to three reasons for this change. First, 2011 was a nonelectoral year. Second, top Fundasucre officials made significant efforts to welcome Chavistas to events like the PB. And third, various other factors seem to have made Chavistas more open to working with Ocariz by 2011.

During my fieldwork I regularly chatted with Chispiao, who spoke often of the importance of including Chavistas in Fundasucre programming, including PB. This was presented as a noble effort guided by principle. But statements from other officials, like Alexander, show that electoral considerations were also important. He acknowledged as much when recounting a controversial Fundasucre decision to transfer an approved PB project from a group of Primero Justicia activists to a group of Chavistas. Alexander said the reason for this was that the Primero Justicia group had failed to implement the project. Those activists were, unsurprisingly, opposed to the project's transfer. In explaining why Fundasucre did so anyway, Alexander said, 'We probably won't win the votes of the [Chavista] group but we might get some votes of those watching from outside who see what is happening.'

Electoral data, presented below, suggest this strategy worked as Alexander hoped it would. These and other data also show that by mid-2011 Chavistas were increasingly open to participating in Ocariz administration programs, including PB. Conversations with Chavistas point to several reasons for this. Many spoke of increased difficulty getting projects through national channels versus the relative ease of doing so via Sucre's PB. An organizer told me, 'In the last year there haven't been any projects' from the national government available to the group of thirty-five communal councils she worked with in Petare Norte. A Chavista from Barrio Union said her communal council participated in Sucre's PB in 2011 because 'we weren't able to get funding anywhere else.' A Chavista in a zonal assembly in Caucagüita said, 'We'll go wherever there are benefits.' Another detailed why his and other Chavistas' views had changed: 'At first people didn't believe that there would be resources given through this [Sucre's PB] . . . [b]ut they've seen that resources have come. They replaced an elevator in the building that hadn't been fixed in twenty years.' Yet another Chavista from Caucagüita said, 'There are resources here to get. [In the future] the president [and] the mayor won't be around, but we'll still be here.'

The ruling party's stance toward Chavista participation in Ocariz administration programming also appears to have softened. Many Chavistas I spoke with in 2011 said Fundacomunal still opposed this, but others said this was no longer true. To my initial surprise, several Chavistas told me, 'The party told us to participate' in Sucre's PB in 2011. Chavistas justified doing so by saying things such as 'this is our money,' and 'the president wants us to participate.' There also seems to have been a decline in symbolic violence against Chavistas who participated in Sucre's PB. In mid-2011, Edison, a Chavista in Caucagüita, said, 'Last year lots of people commented that [Chavista] communal councils that were participating with the mayor were *escualidos* . . . but that's not happening this year.' Other Chavistas made similar comments about this shift.

Chavistas who wanted to avail themselves of the benefits of working with Ocariz but still felt pressure from Fundacomunal to not do this sometimes defied the institution or found creative workarounds. One form this took was for "mixed" communal councils to submit "sly paperwork." By this I mean a practice wherein communal councils with both Chavistas and oppositionists in elected positions submitted inaccurate forms to Fundacomunal indicating a purely Chavista leadership to avoid sanctions for having oppositionists in leadership. I learned of various cases of this in Sucre, with Chavistas involved in such mixed councils saying they had grown frustrated with nominally Chavista leaders who were corrupt or lazy and preferred working with trustworthy, hardworking oppositionists.

The Libertador communal council shows that open challenges to Fundacomunal's efforts to enforce Chavista-only leadership sometimes succeeded. At the April 30, 2011, Caucagüita zonal PB assembly, a Black Chavista from the Libertador communal council told me, 'We had just four [Chavista] people who ran things for years, and we didn't get anything.' Residents had recently come together to elect a new slate of leaders that had both Chavistas and oppositionists. This man pointed to a white woman nearby and said, 'She's an *escualida* but she's a leader in the community. . . . We had to struggle against Fundacomunal. . . . They came to our assemblies and told us we couldn't have someone [in the leadership] who was from the opposition. . . . We forced them to accept what the community had decided. When they told us we couldn't have opposition people, we took the law to them.'

FIGURE 3.4 Chavista paricipants at Ocariz administration community event, May 2011.

Source: Photo by author.

The increase in Chavista participation from 2009 to 2011 improved the quality of popular control in Sucre's PB in two ways. First, Chavista participation occurred through communal councils that, as a matter of course, vetted proposals in collective assemblies before submitting them to the PB. During an April 2011 technical assistance session in Caucagüita, Edinson, a Chavista from the Don Bosco communal council, told me, 'All the communal councils discuss projects in assemblies before they are presented here.' Oppositionists who participated in Sucre's PB usually did so without any affiliation or as members of civic associations, which did not vet proposals in collective assemblies. My conversations with such participants suggested their proposals had been discussed by a few people at most, and often not at all, before being submitted to Sucre's PB. Fundasucre officials recognized the challenge this posed. During a conversation in mid-2010 (notably a time when few Chavistas participated in Sucre's PB), Maribel commented,

> Communities should do diagnoses prior to the community encounters, but almost none of them do. If we're having a meeting on a Saturday, the community should get together beforehand and decide about the needs they have, and their priorities. The need that I might put forward is not the same as the need that you'll put forward. . . . I might, for instance, say that I want to have handrails on the sidewalk stairs in my neighborhood, owing to my physical disability, but this might not be what the whole community wants, which might be a road. If you don't talk to anyone else, then you'll just think that they agree with you.

The increase in Chavista, and thus communal council, participation reduced this problem, and it also improved the quality of popular control in Sucre's PB in a second way. As the example involving Tacho shows, Chavistas complained about aspects of Sucre's PB they found wanting, like the command-and-control decision-making some officials used. These complaints served the important function of alerting higher-level officials about the PB's shortcomings. Alexander, for instance, told me he was aware of Tacho's complaint from the April 30, 2011, Caucagüita PB assembly. At a technical assistance sessions a few days later, Alexander recounted how a group of Chavistas had complained to him about the incident. 'They told me they didn't agree with how the infrastructure projects were chosen Saturday.' Alexander and Chispiao both said they were working to address Chavistas' and others' concerns about the PB's limitations.

INSTITUTIONAL EFFECTIVENESS

Sucre's administered democracy scores highest on institutional effectiveness, equaling Torres and surpassing Santa Cruz and El Alto. Evidence shows a robust link between participatory inputs and policy outputs. Official data on Sucre's budgetary execution rate are unavailable (like all the cases). Unofficial data, which appear credible, suggest Sucre's project implementation rate between 2009 and 2012 was high. Chispiao reported that this rate was 85 percent in 2012 (Giusti and De Viveiros 2012, 56). He acknowledged that project implementation was not perfect but said, "When there have been problems the causes have more to do with disorder than misappropriation of funds" (56). He also reported that communities themselves executed 70 percent of PB projects (57). This is similar to Torres, which had a 76 percent rate of community execution from 2009 to 2012 and a reported 90 percent rate in 2016. (As noted, Torres's PB covered all municipal investment while Sucre's covered 20–40 percent of this.)

Self-reported figures must, of course, be treated with caution. But subjective data are consistent with the view that the Ocariz administration was institutionally effective. The key evidence of this is the fact that many Chavistas held relatively positive views of Ocariz. For instance, a woman in Petare Norte told me, 'I'm Chavista but I recognize that this mayor's doing a good job.' When I asked about her view of Ocariz's Chavista predecessor, she scoffed and scornfully said, 'What did José Vicente do?' Her answer was not unique, as many Chavistas seemed to view Ocariz more favorably than his predecessor.

POLITICAL EFFECTIVENESS

Sucre's administered democracy was politically effective, albeit to a lesser degree than Torres's participatory democracy. During Ocariz's first two years in office his party's political fortunes improved. Primero Justicia won Sucre's seat in the 2010 National Assembly election, which Primero Justicia and the PSUV both portrayed as a referendum on Ocariz's rule.[15] Primero Justicia's vote share increased 4 percent compared to Ocariz's 2008 election. Most notably, the party's vote rose 15 percent in Sucre's poorest (and most Chavista) parish and 10 percent in its second- and third-poorest (and also highly Chavista) parishes. These results, shown in table 3.2, suggest Ocariz's participatory policies, like PB, led to increased popular sector support, just as top administration officials hoped.

In 2013 Ocariz was reelected, another indicator of the political effectiveness of the regime he led. Ocariz notably defeated a strong challenger: Elías Jaua, a prominent, well-respected Chavista, who had previously served as Chávez's vice president for a time. I score Sucre as less politically effective than Torres for two reasons. First, the incumbent party won reelection with a new candidate in Torres, while in Sucre the sitting mayor was reelected.

TABLE 3.2 Primero Justicia vote (%) and turnout, Sucre, 2008–2013

		2008	2010	2013
		MAYORAL	NATL. ASSEMBLY	MAYORAL
PARISH	Caucagüita	34.8	44.31	35.56
	Filas de Mariches	22.32	37.07	26.05
	La Dolorita	27.51	38.57	26.1
	Leonicio Martínez	81.65	81.83	79.96
	Petare	55.8	59.73	52.69
	Total PJ (%)	55.6	59.89	52.79
	Turnout, all voters (%)	61	67	60

Source: CNE.

Second, Primero Justicia's vote share declined 3 percent from 2008 and 7 percent from its high mark in 2010. Ocariz sat out the 2017 election since the opposition coalition Primero Justicia boycotted it. As discussed in the next section, this is indicative of the opposition's return to intransigence against a ruling party that was no longer hegemonic.

THE DEMISE OF ADMINISTERED DEMOCRACY
(2013–2017)

This chapter has argued that the presence of left-populist hegemony in Venezuela from 2005 to 2013 is a key reason Sucre's center-right mayor, Carlos Ocariz, embraced participatory governance in an unexpectedly robust way during his first term. If this argument holds, the dissolution of left-populist hegemony from 2013 on should have negatively affected Sucre's administered democratic urban regime. Evidence I collected during later visits to Sucre in 2015 and 2016 show this is precisely what happened. From 2014 on Ocariz increasingly governed in a "typically right-wing" manner, doing little to facilitate popular participation in decision-making.

Sucre's PB remained in place in 2013, but there was a marked decline in Chavista participation. In 2014, the PB was suspended. Officials in Sucre said their focus that year was completing unfinished projects, what Maribel called 'paying our debt.' In 2015 a greatly diminished participatory initiative, the Rapid Attention Program (PAR), was rolled out. PAR differed from PB in four ways. First, it covered just 15 percent of the investment budget versus 40 percent going to PB in its final full years (2011 and 2012). Second, PAR focused on very small projects. Maribel spoke of PAR as 'the fast track of participatory budgeting. . . . It's small projects that are very important' to the people they help. Examples include fixing a staircase and putting up lights in a neighborhood. Third, PAR involved far fewer people compared to PB. Juan Vicente Mijares, who became Fundasucre's president in 2015, said, 'Instead of an assembly with 120 people [as was common in Sucre's PB] we might have 15 people, [representing] 15 families that live on a particular street.' And fourth, in large part due to the drop-off in Chavista participation, PAR tended to involve unorganized or weakly organized individuals rather than organized communities. Notwithstanding Maribel's argument that PAR was a 'fast track of PB,' the differences between PAR and PB are very significant, indicating a major turn away from the Ocariz administration's previous commitment to participatory rule.

Several pieces of evidence support my argument that the dissolution of left-populist hegemony contributed to Ocariz's abandonment of participation. First, left-populist hegemony's material base disappeared as Venezuela entered into a severe crisis marked by plunging oil prices, increasingly stringent U.S. sanctions (first in a relatively indirect from and later brutally direct), falling state spending, and rapidly rising inflation. Fundasucre officials said rampant inflation undermined budgeting of any kind, including participatory budgeting, since annual price rises of 700 percent and much more made it impossible to budget for projects that would be completed a year later. Maribel said, 'Budget problems made it hard to complete many projects.' She and other officials said PAR could overcome this issue since it involved small projects that could be completed "immediately." But PAR was a far cry from what Sucre's PB had been.

A second facet of the crisis of left-populist hegemony was increased polarization between Chavista and opposition forces. The trigger for this was the unexpectedly close April 2013 special election to replace Hugo Chávez. Primero Justicia's Henrique Capriles lost by just 1.5 percent. This likely pushed him to adopt a confrontational stance, in which he refused to recognize the results as valid and called for opposition protests in the streets, some of which turned violent and led to a number of civilian deaths. Polarization was further exacerbated during the February–April 2014 protest wave.

The effects of this were acutely felt in Sucre since Ocariz was Capriles's longtime confidante and campaign manager in 2013. Fundasucre officials said Chavistas stopped participating in Ocariz administration activities, including PB, in July 2013. It seems likely Primero Justicia's shift to a more confrontational stance toward the government contributed to this. Fundasucre officials said Chavistas told them they had 'received instructions from above to stop working with Ocariz' around this time. Local processes also contributed to Chavistas' diminished willingness to work with Ocariz. A group of Chavistas in the barrio of Turumo, in Caucagüita, had worked with Ocariz in a cooperative way for several years but abruptly stopped in July 2013. Andrés Tovar, one of the group's leaders, said there was 'a grassroots decision' to stop working with Ocariz because his administration failed to complete a large staircase approved through the PB.

The end of Chavista participation contributed to what Fundasucre's new president, Juan Vicente Mijares, called 'the transformation of community organization.' By this, Juan Vicente meant an increase in what might be called thin associationalism, in which new associations were formed, just to obtain public resources. 'We found that many [newly-formed civic associations] were created with the purpose of obtaining resources, and that's okay, but forming a community organization just for the purpose of obtaining resources is not the same as forming a community organization to develop your community. Having an interest in receiving resources is different than solving problems in your community.' He commented that the switch from PB to PAR allowed Fundasucre to work around this issue: 'We don't need community organizations. We approve funding and it goes directly to suppliers, for example, the hardware store.' This workaround, of course, did not resolve and arguably contributed to the problem.

The result of these various changes was that Ocariz governed in a much less participatory manner during his second term. This stands in contrast with Torres, where Julio Chávez's successor, Edgar Carrasco, continued to govern in a highly participatory way. This suggests left-populist hegemony was more central to Sucre's administered democracy than Torres's participatory democracy since the end of left-populist hegemony saw a major shift in Sucre's urban regime, which was not the case in Torres.

Sucre does not fit the mold of a city built for participatory success. From 2009 to 2017 Primero Justicia, a center-right anti-Chavista opposition party with a middle- and upper-class core base, governed Sucre. In the beginning of this period, Venezuelan president Hugo Chávez was at the height of his power and well into a radicalization process that started around 2001. According to literature on democracy, urban participation, and conservative parties, one would have expected a right-of-center party in such a context to govern in an antidemocratic or safely democratic manner in which the protection of elite interests was paramount.

This is not what occurred. During the first of his two terms as mayor, Primero Justicia's Carlos Ocariz embraced participatory governance to a degree that some of his own advisers found surprising and distasteful. Ocariz implemented a participatory budget that within a few years covered 40 percent of Sucre's investment funds and totaled 35 million USD a year. He and his staff devoted many hundreds of hours to the PB, which at its height (around 2011–2012) involved around a thousand meetings a year with a few thousand total participants. The process was socially and politically inclusive, with popular and middle classes both well represented and Chavistas coming out in force after two years of boycotting the process. The shortcomings of Sucre's PB are apparent when compared to Torres, with Sucre's administrated democracy being more paternalistic and limited, following a logic of "give the people some but not too much power." But when compared to right-governed Santa Cruz and (more surprisingly) left-governed El Alto, in Bolivia, Sucre's participatory success stands out as a notable, indeed impressive, achievement.

In this chapter I have sought to show that explaining this achievement requires paying close attention to how Venezuela's national context of left-populist hegemony shaped the way Ocariz governed. My argument in brief is that this hegemony compelled Ocariz to embrace participation in an unexpectedly robust way.[16] This argument finds support in the fact that Ocariz embraced participation only during his first term, 2009–2013, when left-populist hegemony was present, and not his second, when this hegemony eroded and then collapsed. The broader import of this case is that leftist hegemony can push forces on the right side of the political spectrum to react to the real and apparent threats posed by radical left parties in office in an unexpected way, by embracing participatory democracy, rather than seeking to end democracy or make it safe again.

PART II

BOLIVIA

Refracting Passive Revolution,
Perpetuating Clientelism

4

BOLIVIA

From Active to Passive Revolution

O n December 18, 2005, Evo Morales was elected Bolivia's first Indigenous president. This followed a five-year protest cycle dubbed a "classic revolution" (Gilly 2007, xiv), "revolutionary moment" (Hylton and Thomson 2007, 20), and "revolutionary epoch" (Webber 2011a, 2). Alongside Morales's longtime leadership of the coca growers' union, this raised expectations for sweeping, even revolutionary, change. Morales stoked such beliefs by promising to "rule by obeying" in a "democratic and cultural revolution" that would decolonize Bolivia and empower its long-suffering Indigenous majority.

Morales's election led to major changes, but many have objected to calling them revolutionary. This chapter views Bolivia's trajectory under Morales as a movement from active to passive revolution. Following Modonesi (2011), this label highlights Morales's increasing demobilization of previously activated popular classes. The Morales years had three phases: insurgent reform from 2006 to 2009, passive revolution from 2010 to 2016, and crisis from 2016 to 2019. The argument I make to explain Bolivia's post-2009 consolidation of passive revolution parallels that made for Venezuela, starting with the similar effects of neoliberal reform, which led to low growth, rising poverty and inequality, widespread protest, and party system collapse in both cases. Bolivia differs from Venezuela in how its party system collapsed, which occurred through a revolutionary (versus involutionary) crisis of hegemony. This led Bolivia to enter the left turn with a movement-left ruling party, which emerged from and was initially tightly linked to a strong and autonomous civil society. Morales's identity and early actions—partially nationalizing gas, writing a new constitution, and pursuing major land reform—infuriated the Right, which from 2006 to 2009 fought the ruling party, the Movement Toward Socialism (MAS), with legislative stonewalling and violent protest, with a dozen MASistas killed in 2008 in what some call a "civic coup." I contend that since Morales did not need to build an already-existing popular bulwark, and feared civil war, he worked to contain right-wing backlash via limited mobilization and demobilization of popular forces. From 2010 on Morales moved rightward, backtracking on land reform, reconciling with the agrarian elite, and openly clashing with the popular movements that previously backed him. This led to a passive revolutionary regime. The chapter begins by discussing the centrality of Indigeneity to Bolivia's past and present and closes by examining MAS's crisis, fall, and resurgence between 2016 and 2020.

THE CENTRALITY OF INDIGENEITY
TO BOLIVIA'S PAST AND PRESENT

Bolivia is an Indian country, a place where two-thirds of the population
recognizes and declares itself to be Aymara, Quechua, Guaraní, or of other
Indigenous groups governed since Spanish conquest by a white and mestizo
minority. Since the sixteenth century, the relationship between rulers and ruled,
and between dominant and subaltern groups, has had a specific feature, indelible
as skin color. As in the rest of the colonial universe born in that century, the
relationship took the form of racial subordination.

—ADOLFO GILLY (2007, XIV)

No discussion of Bolivia can ignore the centrality of Indigeneity to its past and present. Its Indigenous majority has faced and resisted centuries of racist oppression and exploitation. "The basis of the colonial order [established in the sixteenth century] was a state-community pact in which diverse native peoples, now lumped together under the rubric of 'Indians,' provided labor and tribute to the Spanish crown in exchange for protection of their land base and a relative degree of local autonomy" (Hylton and Thomson 2007, 36). From 1780 to 1781 this order was nearly destroyed in "the greatest anti-colonial revolution yet seen in the Americas" (39). Under the leadership of Túpaj Katari (né Julián Apaza Nina, sometimes spelled Túpac), Aymara forces fought for Indigenous autonomy and self-rule, laying siege to La Paz for months before Spanish forces brutally crushed the uprising. Indigenous struggles have invoked Katari's memory ever since, drawing on the horizontal-democratic organizational forms, centered on the popular assembly, established in the tumultuous decades preceding the uprising (Thomson 2002; Hylton and Thomson 2007).

Post-Independence governments repeatedly sought to abolish Indian tribute and communal landholdings. These attempts foundered until the 1870s when silver and tin mining increased the state's revenues, giving it leeway to aggressively pursue Indigenous landholdings, which were significantly reduced from the 1880s to 1930s. Indigenous communities resisted with legal and direct action, with major uprisings in 1899, 1927, and 1947. These "revolts coincided with petition drives, rural labor strikes, political assemblies, and congressional lobbying" (Gotkowitz 2007, 3). Rural mobilization in 1947 was the largest in Bolivian history and helped foment the 1952 Revolution.

The Revolution highlights the "disarticulation, dissonance [and] *desencuentro*" (Hylton and Thomson 2007, 10) between "Indian" and "national-popular" struggles. The latter refers primarily to the tin miners, who fought for socialism and labor and political rights in the 1930s and 1940s and were key to the Revolution (Young 2017). From 1952 to 1964, the mining-led Bolivian Workers' Central (COB) cogoverned with the Nationalist Revolutionary Movement (MNR). Miners and the COB played a central role in struggles against military rule and for the restoration of democracy in the 1960s, 1970s, and early 1980s. The 1952 Revolution established universal suffrage, nationalized tin, enacted sweeping land and educational reforms, and created a model of state-led development (the "State of '52") that endured until 1985. Indigenous peoples were incorporated into the nation but at a high cost. In the name of modernity and equality, the MNR sought to transform Indians into workers, peasants, and citizens. This never fully succeeded, as Indigenous traditions survived in state-promoted institutions such as peasant unions (Rivera Cusicanqui 1984; see also Soliz 2021).

Indigenous organizing surged from the 1970s on. It took multiple forms. Cultural work revalorized Indigenous culture, language, and traditions. *Katarista* peasant unions waged a combined struggle against capitalism and Indigenous oppression (Hylton and Thomson 2007, 86–87). Multiple Indigenous parties were formed between the 1970s and 1990s. From 1986 to 1992 the Ejército Guerrillero Túpac Katari (a guerilla movement) fought the Bolivian state, until its leading members, including future vice president Álvaro García Linera, were imprisoned. Indigeneity was central to the 1990s' "neoliberal multiculturalism," which combined marketization, decentralization, and cultural and educational reform. It was also central to new forms of organizing like the *cocalero* movement led by Evo Morales.

NEOLIBERAL REFORM AND THE CRISIS AND COLLAPSE OF THE OLD ORDER

Morales's election, and the revolutionary crisis that led to it, were a response to neoliberal reform from 1985 to 2000. Market reform, in turn, responded to the failure of the 1982–1985 center-left Democratic Popular Unity (UDP) government that took office after democracy was restored. Hobbled by debt incurred by 1970s military rulers, and facing mobilization from the Left and Right, the UDP failed to deliver stable governance and called early elections in 1985 amid hyperinflation, which reached 20,000 percent annually.

MARKETIZATION

The election brought the MNR back to office to dismantle its own legacy through the "New Economic Policy" (NEP), which devalued the currency, established a uniform, free-floating exchange rate, liberalized interest rates, trade, and prices (leading to rising fuel, utilities, and services prices), eliminated wage and price controls, froze public-sector wages, severely downsized public-sector employment, reduced state spending, initiated privatization of state-owned enterprises, and established new value-added taxes as well as externally funded compensatory social spending (Silva 2009, 107). This was done in a technocratic and repressive manner. Power was centralized in the hands of the president and a small team of technocratic advisers linked to international financial institutions. Executive power was expanded through frequent presidential decrees that bypassed legislative debates. Debate was further limited by pacts between Bolivia's leading parties. The national state used coercion to quash dissent, most notably from labor (107–8).

The NEP's effects were dramatic. Currency devaluation ended hyperinflation but brought a recession. Modest growth resumed in the late 1980s, and there was 4.4 percent annual growth from 1991 to 1998 (111). But poverty and inequality remained high due to the increase in informal work, rising prices, and the reduction and elimination of state subsidies (110). The Bolivian Mining Corporation fired twenty thousand miners in the 1980s and by 1991 forty-five thousand had been fired. This decimated the miners' union and the COB, which unsuccessfully fought the NEP through a 1985 general strike involving twenty-five thousand workers in the mining, manufacturing, transport, education, oil, telecommunications, and banking industries. The Bolivian Peasant Trade Union Confederation (CSUTCB), erected rural blockades in support (112). In response, President Paz Estenssoro declared a ninety-day state of siege, arrested thousands of union officials and strikers, and sent 150 labor leaders into internal exile. "The COB framed resistance in Polanyi-like defense of traditional urban union-centered concerns: the protection of formal sector employment, pay, and working conditions along with nationalist defense of public enterprises and industrial policy to counterbalance international capital and its domestic allies, perennial enemies of the popular sector" (112). This resistance continued through the Jaime Paz Zamora administration (1989–1993), but "although the COB still called general strikes, by the early 1990s its capacity to mobilize large numbers of workers and peasants and to ensure adherence to the strike call was significantly diminished" (113). The COB would never recover its earlier glory.

In 1993, Paz Estenssoro's planning minister, Gonzalo Sánchez de Lozada, was elected president. This led to a second round of market reforms through Sánchez de Lozada's Plan de Todos (Plan for All). The plan entailed significant privatization of state-owned enterprises, including the oil and natural gas, telecommunications, airline, electricity, and railway industries (Hylton and Thomson 2007, 99). There was also reform to education, pensions, and agriculture, along with political decentralization. These "multicultural neoliberal" reforms were contradictory (Hale 2005; Postero 2007). The Education Reform Law promoted bilingual education and multicultural teacher training, which some Indigenous leaders supported. But it was also an attack on teachers' unions, who bitterly resisted it. The 1996 Agrarian Reform Law recognized communal property, meeting a longtime demand of lowland Indigenous movements, but sidelined concerns of the highlands-based CSUTCB (Silva 2009, 116). The 1994 Law of Popular Participation (LPP) increased the number of municipalities from fifty to over three hundred and established direct mayoral elections and mechanisms for popular participation in local governance. This facilitated the rise of new left parties like Evo Morales's MAS (Grisaffi 2019). But the LPP was also an attempt to weaken labor unions (Kohl and Farthing 2006).

Popular forces resisted the Plan de Todos. The COB and CSUTCB unsuccessfully fought the LPP and Law of Capitalization, which enacted privatizations (Silva 2009, 120). Teacher unions supported this resistance and led opposition to the education reform law, forcing the government to rewrite it (122). The Chapare-based cocaleros emerged as a leading antineoliberal force. Through the 1990s the cocaleros fought the U.S.-backed War on Drugs, framing their struggle as nationalist, anti-imperialist, and pro-Indigenous. But for popular forces as a whole the 1990s appeared largely as a time of defeat and triumphant market reform.

A REVOLUTIONARY CRISIS OF HEGEMONY

The 2000–2005 protest cycle shattered this image and led to the collapse of Bolivia's party system in a revolutionary crisis of hegemony characterized by a sudden and sharp uptick in popular mobilization, which was sustained and involved significant links between socially and spatially disparate forces, with Indian and national-popular struggles converging around a cohesive set of demands (Hylton and Thomson 2007, 20). The crisis culminated in the fall of successive presidents due to bottom-up pressure.

Economic and political exclusion caused and exacerbated by marketization fueled the protest wave, with state repression of protest leading to more mobilization. Protesters' core aim was democratic control over natural resources. Webber (2011a, 143) links the start of the protest cycle to heightened exclusion caused by the 1999–2003 economic crisis. During this time, annual growth averaged 1.9 percent and per capita growth was flat. This crisis showed the hollowness of Sánchez de Lozada's "claim that the privatization of state-owned enterprises, and the foreign investment this would attract, would create 500,000 new jobs and a GDP growth-rate of between 4 and 10 per cent annually" (136–37). Poverty, which had remained high throughout the neoliberal era, increased from 62 to 65 percent in this period, and extreme poverty and inequality also grew (143). Privatization and reforms related to it (e.g., reclassifying contracts with foreign firms) cost the state hundreds of millions of dollars in lost revenue (Hylton and Thomson 2007, 101).

The protest cycle commenced with the 2000 Water War against the privatization of Cochabamba's water supply. Mobilization was led by the Coalition to Defend Water and Life ("La Coordinadora"), comprised of peasants, factory workers, students, middle-class professionals and environmentalists, and others. The Coordinadora spearheaded a series of massive marches and public assemblies of fifty to one hundred thousand people from January to April 2000. Lethal state repression brought more to the streets. In April protesters declared victory, with water becoming municipalized instead of privatized (Bjork-James 2020).

While this was occurring, the CSUTCB mobilized peasants in the highlands, who erected highway blockades against water privatization and neoliberal land reform. State forces killed two protesters, and two army officers were killed in retaliation. Large protests were also held in September and October 2000 and June and July 2001. Cocaleros in the Yungas mobilized in April 2000 against the state's forced coca eradication policy.

A second, more intense, protest wave occurred in 2003. In February there were protests in La Paz and El Alto against an IMF-mandated salary tax increase. Police went on strike at the same time and engaged in deadly clashes with military forces. State repression left twenty-nine dead and more than two hundred injured (Hylton and Thomson 2007, 109). These events were a prelude to the gas war in September and October, which brought three mobilization streams together. CSUTCB led the first stream, which sought the release of Edwin Huampu, a peasant leader held for an act of collective violence against cattle rustlers in Cota Cota. El Alto's Federation of Neighborhood Associations (FEJUVE) and Regional Workers' Central (COR) led the second mobilization stream against a new tax, Maya y Paya ("One and two," in Aymara), proposed by El Alto's mayor. The third stream involved mobilization against Sánchez de Lozada's plan to export Bolivian gas to the United States through Chile.

By mid-September protest engulfed the entire department of La Paz and parts of other departments. The CSUTCB blocked La Paz's major highways. FEJUVE and COR shut down El Alto. And the Coalition for the Defense and Recuperation of Gas, led by Oscar Olivera (a famed leader of the 2000 Water War) and Evo Morales, held rallies with fifty thousand people in La Paz and twenty thousand in Cochabamba. The military killed three protesters when it cleared blockades to "rescue" foreign tourists stranded in Sorata. This repression sparked new mobilizations, with the city of La Paz soon under siege.

In October, El Alto became the epicenter of protest, which now centered on two demands: halting the export of gas and nationalizing and industrializing it instead; and the resignation of Sánchez de Lozada for the rising death toll from state repression. Protesters effectively controlled

El Alto for the first half of October. FEJUVE and COR played a role, but it was ordinary Alteños who led daily road blockades and popular assemblies throughout the city. "The lack of centralized authority stymied government efforts to suppress the uprising, even by the application, in the Bolivian context, of extraordinary levels of lethal violence" (Hylton and Thomson 2007, 115). By the end of the conflict at least sixty-three civilians were dead (Gutiérrez Aguilar 2014, 120). This brought the middle class to the streets, which helped lead to Sánchez de Lozada's resignation on October 17.

Carlos Mesa replaced Sánchez de Lozada as president. Mesa had served as vice president but denounced Sánchez de Lozada and resigned days before the president. Mesa's interim presidency lasted through June 2005. During this time Mesa functioned as an arbiter between two blocs: a revolutionary left-Indigenous bloc based in the highlands and a reactionary "eastern-bourgeois" bloc centered in Santa Cruz and the lowlands (Webber 2011a). The left-Indigenous bloc sought the nationalization and industrialization of gas and calling a constituent assembly (CA). The eastern-bourgeois bloc pushed for regional autonomy that would give departmental elites extraordinary control over decisions about natural resources and more (Eaton 2007).

Mesa was unable to reconcile these competing demands and was ousted in a final protest wave, the second gas war of May and June 2005. For three weeks large protest marches were held in El Alto and La Paz demanding Mesa's resignation and the full and immediate nationalization of gas. The Right maneuvered to replace Mesa with the Senate president, Hormando Vaca Díez, who was firmly aligned with the eastern-bourgeois bloc. Protesters successfully mobilized to prevent this and bring about a caretaker government that called for elections in December 2005. MAS strongly favored this resolution. To radicals it was a betrayal of their hopes for a revolutionary solution to the crisis. Writing amid the crisis, Hylton (2005) argued, "Not for the first time, Morales functions as a dam against a popular flood onto the nation's highways, into its streets and perhaps even the presidential palace. . . . Morales has a vested interest in maintaining a dynamic of limited mobilisation." Webber (2011a) and Gutiérrez Aguilar (2014) concur that MAS actions foreclosed possibilities for more radical

TABLE 4.1 Support for traditional parties in Bolivia,
1985–2005 presidential elections

	VOTE % (MNR + MIR + ADN)
1985	73
1989	73
1993	57
1997	57
2002	42
2005	7

Sources: Nohlen 2005, 152–54; Silva 2009, 118.

and revolutionary change, in particular an open CA process and a more far-reaching nationalization of gas.

Morales's election in December 2005 put an end to the protest cycle and marked the collapse of Bolivia's party system. Table 4.1 shows this collapse, with the vote share for the three parties that dominated politics in the 1980s and 1990s—the MNR, MIR (Revolutionary Left Movement), and ADN (Nationalist Democratic Action)—declining sharply in 2002 and disappearing in 2005. Morales won the presidency with 54 percent. MAS became the fulcrum of a new party system, winning a slight majority with 72 of 130 seats in the Chamber of Deputies and securing 12 of 27 Senate seats.

THE RISE OF A NEW MOVEMENT-LEFT REGIME: INSURGENT REFORM AND RIGHT-WING BACKLASH, 2006–2009

If Morales's election provisionally ended Bolivia's "third revolutionary moment" (Hylton and Thomson 2007, 21), it nonetheless constituted a momentous political shift and was an unabashed triumph for Indigenous peoples, social movements, and the Left. In two inaugural ceremonies held in January 2006, Morales signaled his intention to reshape Bolivia. The first ceremony was on January 21, 2006, in the pre-Inca site of Tiwanaku. Morales walked barefoot over coca leaves, was blessed by Indigenous religious leaders as Apu Mallku, the highest Indigenous authority, and declared, "A new millennium has arrived for the original peoples of the world" (Postero 2010, 18). The next day in a ceremony in La Paz Morales honored Indigenous anticolonial resisters, miners who fought the dictatorship, cocaleros killed in the drug war, those killed in 2003, and Túpac Katari and Che Guevara as "martyrs of liberation" (18).

MORALES'S FIRST TERM: INSURGENT REFORM

Morales's first term, 2006–2009, was a period of insurgent reform that led to four major gains. The first was the profound effect electing an Indigenous president had on the country's Indigenous majority. Mamani Ramírez (2011, 43) discusses this as follows:

> The driving force of this process is the populations' increasing identification with references to the *popular* and to indigeneity. . . . An Aymara, Evo Morales, is now the direct representative of this. The conditions for the production of an indigenous self-government on a national scale have spread across the whole space of the territory of the state, in spite of the fact that those in positions of leadership have yet to make sense of these emergent territorial articulations. There is a feeling of owning those territories, and in those spaces, the privileges once held by the white-mestizo are now questioned, especially those gained by the exploitation of indigenous labor and natural resources in those territories.

Silvia Rivera Cusicanqui offers a similar take: "Just having Evo elected president allowed indigenous people to see themselves mirrored proudly every day. This has had an immeasurable impact on self-esteem, as it allows many people who previously were ashamed to be Indians to lift their heads up for the first time" (Farthing and Kohl 2014, 37). Indigenous political representation went beyond Evo: "There was now ethnic-class political representation, unlike anything witnessed before, in the executive, top ministries, congress, and the constituent assembly" (Hylton and Thomson 2007, 142). The new constitution also committed Bolivia to decolonization and plurinationalism.

The second gain was the partial nationalization of gas, announced in a decree on May 1, 2006. Farthing and Kohl (2014, 38) note the limits of this: "Despite the posturing . . . the May Day decree was far from nationalization in the classic sense. No assets were expropriated and no companies expelled. Instead, Morales forced private firms to either renegotiate new contracts or abandon the country." In late 2006 gas companies signed new agreements giving the government 50 percent of royalties (versus 18 percent pre-Morales) and 70 percent of total gas revenues. While falling short of past nationalizations and present demands for full nationalization, this was still a major change that significantly increased government revenues.

The third gain was Morales's March 2006 convocation of a constituent assembly.[1] With this and the partial nationalization of gas, Morales could boast of fulfilling the 2003 "October Agenda." The demand for a CA was first made by lowland Indigenous movements in the early 1990s and then taken up by Indigenous and other movements in Bolivia's valleys and highlands, such as the Water War protesters. The CA was inaugurated on August 6, 2006, and contained many Indigenous and women delegates, a far cry from the country's twelve previous constituent assemblies (the last in the 1960s), which had no women or Indigenous participants (Hylton and Thomson 2007, 142). The CA became a central axis of conflict with the Right.

The fourth gain was the attempt to implement major land reform. Like the CA, this became a major axis of left-right conflict, which is detailed in the next section.

CONFLICT WITH THE RIGHT AND INCREASING TENSIONS BETWEEN MAS AND POPULAR MOVEMENTS

From 2006 to 2008 the CA was the main arena of left-right and intra-left conflict. This conflict initially centered on how to choose delegates. Social movements favored rules that would allow them to be directly represented in the CA. The Right favored rules whereby delegates could come only from parties and citizens' groups. MAS sided with the Right on this and a related rule allowing candidates who finished in third place in the seventy district elections for the CA to be seated if they won at least 5 percent of the vote. MAS also agreed to the Right's demand for a regional bloc of delegates. These rules gave the Right considerably greater representation than it would have achieved through majoritarian rules. MAS's willingness to compromise shows its desire to placate the Right, as well as its willingness and interest to subordinate movements to itself. Hylton and Thomson (2007, 141) argue that MAS's "refusal [to accept movements' demands on the CA format] began the effective closure of the revolutionary process."

In the election for the CA, MAS won 54 percent of the seats, giving it an absolute but not two-thirds majority. This led to another round of conflict, lasting seven months, over the rules for voting on measures within the CA. MAS favored majority rule, while the Right demanded that measures pass only with two-thirds support. The question of whether the CA would be "originary" and produce an entirely new constitution also led to sharp conflict, with MAS and social movements in favor of this and the Right strongly opposed.

The Right confronted MAS within and beyond the CA. Right-wing delegates boycotted the CA for months to protest Morales's "dictatorial" push for majoritarian voting. Right-wing forces also staged marches against Morales and for the increasingly radical regional autonomy agenda in Sucre, where the CA was held, and other Media Luna departments. Indigenous peasants responded by marching in support of the government in Sucre (Webber 2011b, 95). MAS received critical support from the Unity Pact (Pacto de Unidad), comprised of the Confederation of Indigenous Peoples of Bolivia (known by its original acronym, CIDOB), the National Council of Ayllus and Markas of Qullasuyu (CONAMAQ), CSUTCB, the "Bartolina Sisa" National Federation of Women Peasant Workers of Bolivia (FNMCB-BS), the Syndicalist Confederation of Intercultural Communities of Bolivia (CSCIB), various small organizations, and leftist intellectuals. Unity Pact delegates pressured MAS from the left to support its transformative agenda of plurinationalism, decolonization, Indigenous autonomy, and sweeping land reform (Garcés 2011).

During this period MAS served as an arbiter between left-popular and right-wing forces, reprising the role the party played during Carlos Mesa's presidency. Vice president Álvaro García Linera offered an aggressive initial response to the Right's CA boycott, calling on social movements to defend the government with arms if necessary, but he quickly retreated to a less incendiary position (Webber 2011b, 95). An external report rated the chance of "imminent civil war" within Bolivia at the time at 56 percent (96), showing the immense pressure MAS faced. Conflict intensified in December 2006 and January 2007 when the Right's largest party, Podemos ("We Can"), rejected MAS's compromise proposal for "mixed" voting wherein CA measures deemed noncontroversial would need a simple majority and items deemed controversial two-thirds support to pass. Morales called on the armed forces to defend Bolivian unity but quickly backtracked. In February 2007 a complicated compromise was struck whereby two-thirds support was needed for measures to pass within CA commissions and in the full assembly; measures with less support would go directly to voters for a yes or no vote in a later referendum, with voters also voting yes or no on the overall constitutional text (97–98; Postero 2017, 50).

The peace bought by the February 2007 compromise was short-lived. In March 2007 the Right launched a new effort to sabotage the CA, demanding that Sucre become Bolivia's capital and resume the status it had until the late nineteenth century. Conflict over this took the form of right-wing street violence in Sucre and pro-MAS marches in El Alto and La Paz. "Violent protests ground the Assembly to a halt for over a month. 'Sucre turned into a battleground,' remembers Raúl Prada [a prominent leftist intellectual and Unity Pact delegate], who was assaulted by a mob. By late November 2007, three people were dead and two hundred had been wounded" (Farthing and Kohl 2014, 41). This led the CA to relocate first to a military building outside Sucre and then to Oruro. The Right responded by resuming its boycott. In December 2007 two-thirds of delegates present in the CA (with the Right vocally absent) approved a final draft of the constitution. The Right refused to recognize this text as legitimate and engaged in further street violence that claimed three more lives.

The Right also redoubled its fight for regional autonomy. In December 2007 a massive *autonomista* rally, which organizers claim attracted a million people, was held in Santa Cruz (Farthing and Kohl 2014, 47). Referenda on regional autonomy were held in the Media Luna departments of Santa Cruz, Beni, Pando, and Chuquisaca in May and June 2008. Over 80 percent voted in favor in each department. The government declared the polls illegal, and abstention was high. Street violence continued with right-wing forces violently attacking a dozen Indigenous leaders in central Sucre during Morales's May 2008 visit.

Under pressure from the Right, the government agreed to an August 2008 recall referendum for the president, vice president, and eight (of nine) departmental prefects. Morales, García Linera, and six prefects, including the four Media Luna prefects, easily won their votes, with right-wing prefects recalled in La Paz and Cochabamba. In the coming weeks right-wing Media Luna prefects fomented violence and unrest aimed at ousting Morales. This culminated in what the government and some analysts called a civic coup in early September (Webber 2017). Right-wing vigilantes attacked government facilities in the Media Luna departments, occupying seventy-five buildings and national airports. Morales responded by expelling the U.S. ambassador, who had met with those prefects in the preceding days. On September 11, vigilantes apparently allied with the prefect of Pando killed at least a dozen peasants marching to support MAS (Farthing and Kohl 2014, 49).

The Pando massacre turned the tide toward MAS. The Union of South American Nations condemned the Right's actions, and in late September twenty thousand peasants marched to Santa Cruz in support of the government. This forced the Right to resume negotiations with the government over the stalled constitution, which led Congress to approve a revised constitutional text in October. The public approved the constitution in a January 2009 vote. MAS could claim victory: it had put down the right-wing unrest and succeeded in getting a vote on the new constitution. But popular movements were deeply upset about the behind-door negotiations that led to major changes, including a significantly reduced land reform.

Morales had announced an "agrarian revolution" in May 2006. In November 2006 MAS introduced the Law of Communitarian Renewal of Agrarian Reform (Webber 2017, 214). It sought to change Bolivia's grossly unequal land distribution, wherein 90 percent of farmers were smallholders owning 10 percent of arable land, with the 10 percent of farmers who were medium and large owners holding 90 percent of this land. Hylton and Thomson (2007, 137) argue, "More than [gas] nationalization—which stands to benefit all, albeit unequally—it is the threat of agrarian reform in the lowlands that has stoked the fires of reaction and increased pressure for regional autonomy."

During the 2006–2009 insurgent reform period MAS aggressively pursued land reform (Webber 2017). Alejandro Almaraz, a longtime militant and cofounder of MAS who favored radical land reform, spearheaded this in his role as vice minister of land.[2] Until he was dismissed from this post in 2010, Almaraz pushed for sweeping land reform, including radical redistribution. The state titled 11.7 million hectares between 2007 and 2009, almost equaling the amount titled between 1996 and 2006, with priority given to titles for small producers (219). A novel feature of land reform under Morales was the creation of Communitarian Lands of Origin (TCOs), in which land was collectively given to Indigenous communities. Webber (2017) highlights the limits of what was the high point of land reform under Morales: the state expropriated few large private properties, and nearly 75 percent of land given to TCOs was state-owned and less productive marginal land, with wealthy, well-connected large landowners maintaining control over productive land.

The Unity Pact made land reform central in the CA. "The original constitutional text approved in Oruro in December of 2007 reflected, in large part, the proposal of the Unity Pact" (Garcés 2011, 58), including provisions on land reform that limited holdings to a maximum of five thousand hectares. The "negotiated text" Congress approved in October 2008 eliminated the retroactive nature of this limit and allowed an unlimited number of "associates" to hold up to five thousand hectares, letting large landholders circumvent the limit (62). Unity Pact delegates sharply criticized MAS for altering the text approved in Oruro in December 2007. Their critique was that MAS had fundamentally changed the character of the CA from a process based on the assembly's constituent power to a process derived from constituted power (47).

In a January 25, 2009 referendum, 61 percent of voters approved the new constitution (specifically the revised text negotiated in Congress in October 2008). The document declared Bolivia to be a plurinational state with direct, communitarian, and representative democracy, enshrined state control over the economy, and established guaranteed access to health care, social services, and education. On the night of January 25, with the results in, Morales declared, "The colonial state ends here. Internal colonialism and external colonialism ends here. Sisters and brothers, neoliberalism ends here too" (Dangl 2009).

CONSOLIDATING PASSIVE REVOLUTION, 2010–2016

By the end of 2009 MAS was firmly in control of the Bolivian state. Morales won reelection in December with 64 percent of the vote and MAS gained a two-thirds supermajority in both houses of Congress, giving it power to enact laws that would concretize the new constitution. MAS's sweeping victory dealt the Right a crushing electoral blow and ended the intense confrontation of preceding years. Some hoped this would lead to the full enactment of the revolutionary changes Morales promised when first elected. Instead it set the stage for the consolidation of a passive revolutionary regime, with Morales's second and third terms in office marked by an alliance with the agrarian elite (ending hopes for major land reform) and increasingly strained relations with popular movements.

I trace the emergence of this regime to Morales's response to right-wing backlash from 2006 to 2008. This response had two key features. The first was the mix of mobilization and demobilization of popular sectors.

MAS regularly mobilized its base during this period but worked to keep it within relatively clear bounds. MAS also demobilized popular classes in this period, with demobilization increasing from 2010 on. The second feature, which was found in a limited way from 2006 to 2008 and became more prominent after 2010, was Morales's efforts to conciliate the Right. This can be seen in the compromises MAS made over the rules for electing CA delegates and in the final "negotiated" constitutional text. MAS's embrace of passive revolution can, paradoxically, be explained by the strength of popular movements, and the party's close links to these movements shown, for instance, in Morales's continued leadership of the cocaleros and the Unity Pact's firm, if critical, support for Morales. Therefore, Morales did not need to create a popular bulwark to withstand the intense right-wing backlash he faced in his first term. Morales was also concerned with civil war. All this likely contributed to MAS's continuation of its strategy of prioritizing electoral politics over street protest, which Webber (2017) traces to the party's near-win in the 2002 presidential election.

After Morales's second term commenced in 2010 he established an alliance with the lowland agrarian elite. As Webber (2017, 223) notes, this marked a 180-degree shift:

> After the political defeat of the autonomist movement of the lowlands, the agro-industrial elite changed tactics and opted for a close working relationship with the Morales government. They were in turn embraced by officialdom. Recall that in 2008 Rubén Costas was plotting Morales's ouster from office. By 2013, he was regularly lunching with Morales and joining García Linera for formal government ceremonial acts in Santa Cruz. The president is also now entirely at home in his regular consultations with CAO [Eastern Agricultural Chamber of Commerce], ANAPO [Association of Wheat and Oilseed Producers], CAINCO [Chamber of Industry, Commerce, Services and Tourism of Santa Cruz], and the Confederación de Empresarios Privados de Bolivia (Confederation of Private Employers of Bolivia, CEPB)—that is, precisely those business organizations that backed the civic-coup attempt of 2008.

MAS's alliance with the agrarian elite unsurprisingly led to diminished support for land reform. Morales dismissed Alejandro Almaraz as vice minister of land in February 2010, mere weeks into Morales's second term. In 2012 Almaraz wrote, "The [agrarian] reform process has slowed since 2011, and we are faced with the challenge of avoiding the reversion of community titling" (Farthing and Kohl 2014, 122). The government continued to title collective lands, but TCOs (Communitarian Lands of Origin) were given marginal land of limited or no agricultural value, while the state provided large and medium holders productive land. This meant "that the most valuable land in the country will continue to be held by a small group of agro-industrial capitalists at the expense of the landless and the land-poor majority" (Webber 2017, 230).

Land was also at the center of the deterioration of the ruling party's relationship to social movements. To be sure, the relationship was never conflict free, but the balance between cooperation and confrontation shifted dramatically after CIDOB launched a June 2010 march from Trinidad, capital of the lowland department of Beni, to protest the new Organic Plurinational Electoral Law and the Framework Law for Autonomies. CIDOB and other Indigenous organizations "saw [the laws] as falling short of historic demands for designated seats in congress for Indigenous self-representation; they also argued that the new legislation did not sufficiently encompass respect for consultation with Indigenous communities before any developmental projects are initiated in their territories, and minimized the integrity of Indigenous territorial autonomy and therefore self-determination in the lowlands" (Webber 2017, 224–25). Seven lowland Indigenous MAS senators went on hunger strike in support of protesters, but the Morales administration dismissed the protests as divisive and beneficial to imperialism and the domestic Right (225).

Relations between MAS and movements took a sharp turn for the worse in 2011 when conflict emerged around the government's plan to build a road through the Isiboro Sécure National Park and Indigenous Territory (TIPNIS). Morales argued the road would bring "development" to poverty-stricken lowland communities. Brazilian companies and the cocaleros strongly supported the road, which would benefit both groups by opening up access to foreign markets. Indigenous communities living in TIPNIS were split with some supporting and some opposing the road. Over a thousand predominantly Indigenous protesters marched against the road in August 2011. Morales told them, "I want to tell you, like it or not, we are going to construct this road and this administration is going to deliver the Villa Tunari-San Ignacio de Moxos highway" (Postero 2017, 123). According to Postero (123), "Mónica Tapera, a Guaraní journalist who worked as part of the communications committee of the march, told me that the marchers were mostly concerned that they had not been consulted about the placement of the road or the potential damage to the environment. This was the crux of the crisis: the government had begun the highway project without carrying out any consultation with the local Indigenous organizations, and then, when challenged, took an intransigent stance."

TIPNIS became a domestic and international lighting rod. Critics saw MAS's stance as a betrayal of its pro-Indigenous, promovement rhetoric. CONAMAQ and CIDOB, two of Bolivia's most important Indigenous associations, supported the TIPNIS marchers. In June 2011 a group of prominent leftist intellectuals who had served as ministers under Morales or had close ties to MAS, including Lino Villca, Román Loayza, Félix Patzi, Alejandro Almaraz, Alex Contreras, Raúl Prada, Gustavo Guzmán, and Pablo Solón issued the "Manifesto of the Plurinational Coordinator for Renewal: For the Recovery of the Process of Change for the People and with the People" (Webber 2017, 226). García Linera responded by dubbing the group the "infantile left" (226). On September 25, 2011, a video emerged showing national police assaulting and tear-gassing marchers, with seventy wounded (Achtenberg 2017; Postero 2017, 124–25). Public opinion shifted toward the marchers, Morales's defense minister, María Chacón, resigned in protest, and Bolivia's national ombudsman sharply condemned the actions (127).

CIDOB and CONAMAQ left the Unity Pact shortly after this, marking the most significant rupture between MAS and popular movements of Morales's presidency up to this time. The government dismissed the organizations as "stooges of imperialism" and the Right. The charge is false, but it points to the fact that Morales's domestic and foreign opponents did seek to take advantage of the TIPNIS conflict. In 2012 MAS used dubious means to install progovernment leaders at CIDOB and CONAMAQ, with MASistas physically occupying the organizations' headquarters in La Paz and Santa Cruz (Postero 2017, 126).

All this caused irreparable harm to MAS's relationship to social movements and leftist activists and intellectuals who had previously supported the party. Morales retained significant popular support despite this due to his economic policies, which significantly reduced poverty and led to sustained growth. From 2006 to 2018 Bolivia achieved 3.2 percent real (inflation-adjusted) per capita annual GDP growth, double the Latin American average (Arauz et al. 2019, 6). Poverty was cut from 60 to 35 percent and extreme poverty declined from 38 to 15 percent (15). As Arauz et al. (2019, 1) note, Morales's (partial) nationalization of hydrocarbons was crucial to securing these gains: "In the first eight years of the Morales administration, national government revenue from hydrocarbons increased nearly sevenfold from $731 million to $4.95 billion. Although some of this was from price increases, most was a result of the nationalization and associated policy changes." This economic success led Morales to a landslide third reelection, with 61 percent of the vote, in 2014. Morales won in eight of Bolivia's nine departments, only losing in Beni by a small margin. MAS also retained its two-thirds majority in both houses of Congress.

CRISIS, COUP, AND MAS'S RETURN, 2016–2020

Morales's third term commenced in an atmosphere of triumphalism, but within two years the horizon dimmed. There were concerns that Bolivia's robust economic growth would not be sustained. The main source of conflict, however, was Morales's attempt to end the limit of two consecutive presidential terms established in the 2009 constitution. Morales initially pledged to respect this, but he changed his mind and held a controversial referendum on the issue in February 2016. Many thought Morales would score a narrow victory but he narrowly lost. His supporters blamed a "dirty campaign" centered on allegations that Morales had fathered a child out of wedlock with a much younger woman who allegedly "enjoyed a high-level post in a Chinese company which has received multi-million dollar no-bid contracts from the MAS government" (Achtenberg 2016). It is also likely that Morales lost some support due to a protest that turned deadly in opposition-governed El Alto just days before the referendum, with MAS supporters implicated in a fire that killed six people and burned down city hall.

Morales initially accepted the 2016 referendum result, but in 2017 MAS asked Bolivia's Plurinational Constitutional Court to end the two-consecutive-term limit. The court ruled for MAS in December 2017, holding that "term limits were an infringement of human rights" (Gustafson 2020, 234). This set the stage for Morales to stand for his third reelection since the 2009 constitution took hold, and fourth overall, in October 2019. The months leading up to the election were marked by largely middle-class protests opposing Morales running. Protesters also claimed, without evidence, that he was planning to commit fraud to win the elections and that this was the only way he could win.

The election took place Sunday, October 20, 2019. "Quick count" results released that night showed Morales winning but with a margin under 10 percent. If this held, the election would go to a second round with Morales facing second-place finisher Carlos Mesa. The quick count transmission was then abruptly suspended, and the next results released, on October 21, showed Morales with a 10.56 percent margin, enough to avoid a runoff. Morales's opponents immediately called fraud and took to the streets. This was not spontaneous but "clearly reflect[ed] a predetermined plan with coordination and financing" (Gustafson 2020, 249).

Protesters received a boon when the Organization of American States (OAS) issued an unusual press release on October 21 expressing concern about "a drastic and hard-to-explain change in the trend" of the vote between the release of the quick count vote on Sunday night and the nearly complete vote results provided on Monday afternoon. This clearly supported protesters' allegations that Morales had committed fraud. Concurrent and subsequent analyses by the Center for Economic and Policy Research (Weisbrot 2019), and researchers based at MIT (Curiel and Williams 2020) and elsewhere (Idrobo, Kronick, and Rodríguez 2022) found no clear evidence of fraud, with the change in trend explicable based on later results coming from rural areas with a higher pro-Morales vote.

Irrespective of this, the OAS statement had an explosive effect, adding fuel to the opposition protests that roiled Bolivia for the next three weeks. The Santa Cruz Civic Committee's far-right president, Luis Fernando Camacho, held a leading role in the sometimes violent protests, which took up Fernando Camacho's demand for Morales to resign. Morales's troubles intensified when police seeking higher pay mutinied on November 8 and his presidential guard declined to protect him. The OAS released a report on November 10 stating that the October 20 election was marred by serious irregularities and calling for a new election. Morales had agreed to respect the report's results and called for a new election. But the die was cast for the coup that would oust Morales, with the head of the army "suggesting" he resign for the good of the nation. Morales did so hours later. Fearing for his life, he fled to the Chapare and then to Mexico two days later.

Like Latin America's many previous right-wing coups, the one against Morales enjoyed a not-insignificant degree of popular support, particularly from Bolivia's middle classes. Popular movements were split, with some supporting and others opposing the call for him to resign. Morales's ouster did not spark immediate widespread popular mobilization. Part of the reason for this is the increasingly strained relations between MAS and social movements from 2010 on. The lack of more widespread protest against the coup can be seen as one of the factors that allowed it to succeed.

The coup led to a brutal right-wing dictatorship led by Jeanine Áñez, a far-right senator from Beni who stepped into the void created by the resignations of Morales, García Linera, and the heads of Bolivia's two houses of Congress, all of whom feared for their own safety and that of their families. These resignations cleared the way for Áñez to declare herself interim president. She was sworn in holding an enormous Bible and declared, "The Bible has returned to the palace." This was one of many acts of real and symbolic violence against MAS and Indigenous peoples throughout

Bolivia. Just after Morales's resignation, Áñez's close ally Luis Fernando Camacho entered the presidential palace and kissed a Bible atop a Bolivian flag. A pastor accompanying Camacho said, "Pachamama will never return to the palace." Over the next weeks Bolivia was engulfed by racist violence. Multiple groups were captured on video burning the Indigenous Wiphala flag and attacking Indigenous people. Police in Santa Cruz were filmed cutting the Wiphala flag from their uniforms. The initial cabinet Áñez assembled included no Indigenous ministers.

The Áñez regime's actions fostered Indigenous-led mobilizations across Bolivia. Protesters called for Áñez's resignation, new elections, the military's return to the barracks, and the freeing of detainees. Áñez responded with violence, which she set the stage for by secretly issuing a November 14 decree exempting state security forces from prosecution for the use of force. The very next day police and military forces opened fire on a protest in Sacaba, Cochabamba, leaving nine dead. A few days later, on November 19, state security forces killed eight protesters at El Alto's Senkata gas plant. Human rights reports indicate that state repression led to at least twenty-three civilian deaths, all of them Indigenous, and over 230 injured, in the weeks after Áñez took over (International Human Rights Clinic 2020). The Áñez regime also systematically persecuted MAS leaders, with many going into hiding. Arturo Murillo, Áñez's minister of government, promised to "hunt down" Morales, calling him "an animal." Murillo also boasted of having a list of MAS leaders he would detain for "sedition and subversion."

After taking over, Áñez promised to hold elections within weeks. She repeatedly reneged on this promise, scheduling and postponing the election multiple times. One of the excuses Áñez gave for this was the COVID-19 pandemic. This held little water since her bungled and corrupt response to the pandemic led to an estimated twenty thousand deaths above normal between June and August 2020 alone, "indicating Bolivia has suffered one of the world's worst epidemics" (Trigo, Kurmanaev, and McCann 2020; Hetland 2020).

Áñez's response to the pandemic and repeated postponement of elections sparked massive mobilizations in July and August 2020, which succeeded in forcing her to finally hold an election in October 2020. MAS's candidate was Luis Arce, who served as finance minister under Morales and is widely credited with the sustained growth Bolivia achieved during Morales's presidency. Arce defied polls predicting a close race to win comfortably with 55 percent of the vote, nearly twice the percentage of his closest rival, Carlos Mesa. Arce's victory indicated Bolivians' firm rejection of the repression, racism, and ineptitude that characterized Áñez's brutal rule. The magnitude of Arce's win – with a margin well beyond what Morales had achieved in 2019 – also suggests that voters wanted a return to the stability and prosperity found during the Morales years but were more comfortable doing this without Morales himself in office.

5

SANTA CRUZ

Technocratic Clientelism, or Fear of the Masses

f Torres approximates the ideal-typical "democratic city," Santa Cruz is the opposite, approximating the ideal-typical antidemocratic city. My research shows that from 2005 to 2016 city residents had virtually no control over political decisions, which were made by avowedly apolitical experts, who justified their power by pointing to the "dirtiness," "parallelism," and "non representativeness" of neighborhood associations. This critique is accurate as far as it goes. Clientelism permeated barrio-based politics in Santa Cruz. Yet city officials neglected the fact that the administration they worked for was key to this system, with Santa Cruz's center-right mayor using clientelism and repression to control popular classes. I label Santa Cruz a case of "technocratic clientelism," with clientelism serving as the disavowed foundation of technocratic decision-making. This regime provided extremely limited, very low-quality popular control over decisions. There was a veneer of institutional effectiveness, but projects implemented bore almost no relation to citizens' professed needs. Officials were aware of this, but they were indifferent or even proud of it. Corruption appeared to be extensive. The mayor, Percy Fernandez, was relatively politically successful. He won reelection twice but his antidemocratic actions sparked repeated "protests for inclusion" by the marginalized. Popular forces' weakness and MAS's prioritization of intra-elite pacts over popular mobilization post-2010 doomed these protests and generated demoralization among those who had risen up.

At first glance Santa Cruz's technocratic clientelistic regime seems to have a simple explanation: an antiparticipatory right-of-center mayor closely linked to powerful dominant classes and popular sectors with limited capacity for autonomous mobilization. This explanation, however, appears wanting in light of three ways Santa Cruz is similar to Sucre: both had center-right mayors during periods of national left rule; both mayors had experimented with participatory reform in the 1990s; and each city had a large informal poor sector that tended to support the left ruling party. This makes Santa Cruz's outcome seem less inevitable. I argue that explaining this outcome requires paying attention to Bolivia's national regime. During the period of insurgent reform (which lasted through 2010 locally), MAS Santa Cruz supported popular struggles against the mayor's technocratic clientelistic rule. As MAS consolidated a passive revolutionary, and thus demobilizing, regime, from 2010 on, Santa Cruz's local elected officials faced little to no pressure to adapt their rule to MAS's participatory rhetoric, which was disconnected from concrete governance institutions and practices. By 2011 MAS Santa Cruz had aligned itself with the national party's passive revolutionary-demobilizing shift, which facilitated the mayor's ability to govern in a "typically right-wing" antidemocratic way.

FROM FRONTIER TOWN TO CAPITAL OF THE MEDIA LUNA: A BRIEF HISTORY OF SANTA CRUZ

Until the 1940s Santa Cruz de la Sierra, capital of the department of Santa Cruz in Bolivia's eastern lowlands, was an isolated frontier town of little economic or political importance. The Cruceño elite's wealth derived from "agricultural plantations that used forms of debt peonage to produce goods for regional markets, and in a much more limited fashion, for the national market to the west" (Eaton 2007, 73). In 1952 a highway linking Santa Cruz to Cochabamba was built through Plan Bohan, created by a 1942 U.S. mission to Bolivia. With this, Santa Cruz's integration with the rest of Bolivia commenced. The city's (and region's) population exploded in coming decades. Between 1950 and 2010 Santa Cruz's annual growth averaged 6 percent. As of 2006 Santa Cruz was the world's fourteenth fastest growing city (with population of over a million people) and it was Bolivia's largest city after 2000 (Kirshner 2013, 549).

Significant state investment from the 1960s on, and foreign investment beginning in the 1980s, transformed Santa Cruz's economy, which was the most dynamic in Bolivia by the 2000s. "By 2004 the city and its immediate environs produced 42 percent of the nation's marketed agricultural output and 34 percent of its industrial gross national product" (Kirshner 2013, 549). Agriculture retained its centrality, with large plantations reliant on a mix of free and unfree labor "produc[ing] sugar, wheat, cotton, soy, and beef for both national and export markets" (Eaton 2007, 73). Land ownership was highly unequal, in large part because Bolivia's 1953 land reform was not implemented in the eastern lowlands.

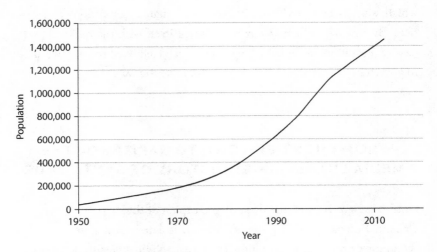

FIGURE 5.1 Population of Santa Cruz de la Sierra, 1950–2012.

Source: Kirshner (2013).

The Cruceño elite's economic profile diversified in the 1970s and 1980s to include not only export agriculture, cattle ranching, and forestry, but also financial and banking services, and agro-industrial processing of soy, sugarcane, cotton, and coca leaf (Prado 2005, 162–69). The city and region's elites benefitted from 1970s military rule, through loans that were rarely repaid, and national investment, and from neoliberal policies in the 1980s and 1990s, which opened opportunities for foreign investment and trade.

The regional elite portrayed its success as endogenous, ignoring the privileged access to national power they enjoyed from the 1960s through 1980s. This changed with decentralization reforms implemented by President Sánchez de Lozada in the 1990s, which prioritized municipalities over regions. Eaton (2007) views this change as critical to the emergence of the regional autonomy movement, which Santa Cruz led, and which was a response to the Cruceño elite's declining national political fortunes beginning in the 1990s. The regional autonomy movement comprised political and material demands, for regional control over resources and decision-making, and racist ethnoregional cultural identity politics. The latter centered on the divide between "cambas," portrayed as genuine lowlanders who are modern, civilized, and white(r), versus "collas," portrayed as darker-skinned, "backward" Indigenous migrants from the highlands and valleys.

This split is central to the racial political geography of Santa Cruz, which is comprised of a series of concentric rings (*anillos*). Wealthier, predominantly white and mestizo residents live in the central zone, districts 1–4, and 11, within the city's fourth ring, where less than 10 percent of residents live in poverty (Kirshner 2013, 550). During my research, residents in these districts tended to identify as cambas and support regional autonomy and right-wing politics. Predominantly poor, darker-skinned Indigenous residents, many of whom migrated from Bolivia's highlands and valleys, are concentrated in districts 6–10 and 12, which lie beyond the city's fourth ring and have poverty rates of 30–50 percent (350). These districts house the bulk of the city's workforce, which is two-thirds informal, with many working in micro enterprises, street vending, and domestic work.

Residents of the outer rings were more likely to support MAS and oppose or hold ambiguous views on regional autonomy (for instance, opposing the autonomy movement's right-wing politics but supporting demands for decentralization).

CLIENTELISM AND INTERRUPTED REFORM
(1990–2004)

The 1982 restoration of democracy paved the way for the reemergence of formal politics in departmental capitals, including Santa Cruz. The city held direct elections for municipal council in 1987 and for mayor in 1989. Percy Fernandez (known to all by his first name), an engineer, won this election and the next two in 1991 and 1993 on the MNR (Nationalist Revolutionary Movement) line. Percy had an extensive public service background. He directed each of Santa Cruz's three utility cooperatives and was president of the Santa Cruz Civic Committee, the Regional Development Corporation, and the city's Committee of Public Works. From 1982 to 1985 Percy served as a minister in the national Democratic Popular Unity (UDP) government.

In 1989 Percy presented himself "as an alternative candidate to those promoted by regional groups of power and pressure" (Mayorga 1997, 29). He performed best in this election and the next two in the city's poor and working-class zones (34–40, 52). The first of Percy's two periods as mayor was marked by confrontation with dominant classes and an innovative attempt to foster popular participation through the program "La Alcaldía a los Barrios" (the mayor's office in the barrios) program, established in 1993. Percy visited popular zones to talk to residents and inspect works in progress. Neighborhood participation committees were established "to gather [residents'] aspirations for neighborhood improvement and transmit them to the municipal government through the respective district coordinator" (59). The program was a form of consultative participation, where citizens influence but do not control decisions. In a 2008 interview,

Fernando Prado, an urban planner who oversaw this program, said, 'It went further than the Law of Popular Participation' in terms of resident control over decisions. Fernando said the program ended after just six months. 'It didn't go anywhere because the MNR used it instrumentally, and ended up by just giving resources to their people. . . . The problem was the MNR's neighborhood councils thought they owned the Mayor's Office. They didn't want to share with anyone else.' He believes the failure of this program led to Percy's subsequent disdain for participatory planning. 'I think that was how the mayor began to distance himself more and more from participation, saying, "That's just for the dogs, I don't want to know anything about it."'

During his first period as mayor, Percy confronted the city's "groups of power." This nebulous term is widely used locally to refer to the city and region's dominant classes, and the real and perceived control they hold over local and regional institutions, including through secretive local social clubs known as lodges. Ferreira (2010a, 174–75) contends that in the 1990s and after, the city's two main lodges controlled the Santa Cruz Civic Committee, Federation of Private Entrepreneurs, Chamber of Commerce and Industry (CAINCO), CORDECRUZ (a precursor to the regional government), Federation of Fraternities, Federation of Professionals, College of Architects, Society of Engineers, College of Lawyers, 24 de Septiembre Social Club, and the city's utility cooperatives. This list notably includes the organizations that led the regional autonomy movement.

In common lore, the lodges do the bidding of the "groups of power," i.e., the dominant classes. Per Fernando Prado, however, the truth is different. 'All the important members of the lodges are middle-class professionals . . . [and] the upper class is content to leave the institutions in the hands of the lodges.' Fernando traces the formation of the lodges to local middle-class professionals' fears in the early 1980s that they would lose their jobs to the growing number of professionals from La Paz. 'The middle classes organized the lodges because they were afraid *Paceños* would take all the professional jobs.' Fernando said the lodges 'built up the idea of Cruceño identity and the fear of a Colla invasion' to justify their control over professional jobs. The lodges also criticized 'the communists of the UDP.'

Percy confronted the lodges in 1992 and 1993. He called "directly on the people to unite and struggle 'against these antidemocratic groups that have supplanted popular power'" and "denounced that the majority of Santa Cruz's cooperative, business and even cultural institutions were run by these secret groups" (Mayorga 1997, 47–48). CAINCO's head publicly said neither he nor his organization had anything to do with the lodges. The Santa Cruz Civic Committee president denounced Percy's efforts: "It's ridiculous that he wants to fight the lodges; there are other problems that are more serious and need to be resolved" (quoted in Mayorga 1997, 47–48.). These comments indicate local elites' displeasure with Percy at this time.

Elite opposition likely doomed Percy's 1995 bid for a third reelection. Jhonny Fernandez, the son of Max Fernandez, who owned one of Bolivia's largest breweries and in 1989 founded the neopopulist party Unidad Cívica Solidaridad (UCS), won the election. Jhonny (as he was known) "waged an intense campaign amongst the popular sectors, with help from the groups of power, who saw in the UCS's populism a way to stop the mayor's reelection" (Ferreira 2010b, 18). Accounts indicate that Jhonny governed in a clientelistic way during his one and a half terms as mayor. Prior to the 1995 election—in which "the lodges openly supported Jhonny Fernandez against Percy Fernandez" (Ferreira (2010b, 70)—Jhonny used his family fortune to make large contributions of equipment and tools to schools and health clinics, "leaving the impression of a generous candidate, with a social sensibility and populist style" (Kreidler 2010, 197). He held large rallies in popular zones in which he bestowed "gifts of chicken, hats, headbands [and] plastic bags of groceries" (197). In his 1999 campaign, he "hired a foreign marketing firm and immediately launched his campaign with acts in the barrios in the style of UCS, giving away sweaters, headbands, hats, flags, groceries, with paid operatives in all the different districts of the city" (245–46).

Jhonny resigned halfway through his second term, amid charges of corruption, inefficiency, and ineptitude. Fernando called Jhonny's mayoralty "a disaster," a view shared by other analysts (Ferreira 2010b, 74; Kreidler 2010, 273). After his resignation, his brother, Roberto Fernandez, became mayor. Roberto's administration was viewed much more favorably. After taking office, Roberto (who was also known by his first name) announced, "We're going to realize a change in direction, [and] City Hall will be run with transparency and residents' participation" (quoted in Kreidler 2010, 301). He held participatory planning workshops and created an Urban Planning Board (Kreidler 2010, 303). He also supported a municipal ordinance establishing election of district submayors by neighborhood council (NC) presidents. Roberto placed first in the 2004 election but with a margin too low to win outright. City council was accordingly charged with determining the final result. This allowed Percy, who had come second, to assume the mayoralty by making a deal with the third-place finisher, Oscar Vargas, in which Percy would be mayor for the first half, and Oscar the second half, of the term.

TECHNOCRATIC CLIENTELISM (2005–2016)

Percy's return to office raised hopes for a resumption of the interrupted reform of his first mayoral period. But his first year back was hard, according to Omar Andrade, an urban planner from Fundación PAP (Foundation for Citizen Participation and Poverty Alleviation). In a 2010 interview with him and his colleague, Martha Elcuez (also an urban planner), Omar said, 'The mayor's office had lost a lot of credibility' since a large inherited debt inhibited its ability to complete projects. '2006 was a conjunctural year' as well as a time when 'planning was in fashion.' This led Percy to contract Fundación PAP to implement a new participatory planning program, Neighbor Demand.

Omar and Martha ran Neighbor Demand. In my interview with the two of them, in their office, Omar said, 'The mayor's office's idea of participation is to go and have a two-hour meeting with communities, ask them what their demands are, and then leave. Our idea is very different. We spent three to four months in neighborhood units.' Fundación PAP worked with seventeen partners, including local universities and NGOs, to reach the city's 680 neighborhood units. Each partner traveled to a set of neighborhood units to gather residents' input about their priorities. Omar said they set up the process so clientelistic neighborhood councils could not take over. 'To evade cooptation by the neighborhood councils we included all the neighborhood functional organizations, the sports' clubs, Mothers' clubs, churches, etc.' Neighborhood councils 'were just one amongst many.' Omar and Martha told me the process generated high expectations within communities. Working-class residents of Plan 3000 (district 8) also said this was the case, pointing to 2006 as the last time real participatory planning took place in the city. Omar said city officials 'committed themselves to these projects . . . but haven't followed through.' In addition to showing Percy's disregard for his own program, this hurt Fundación PAP 'since communities thought we were going to execute projects that had been planned.'

In retrospect it seems 2006 was a conjunctural year, marking the Percy Fernandez administration's decisive turn away from any semblance of commitment to participatory planning and toward technocratic clientelistic rule. In interviews with dozens of city residents, officials, and urban planners I was repeatedly told no participatory planning had taken place in Santa Cruz since sometime around 2006 or 2007. Echoing a line I heard repeatedly, in July 2010 Omar said, 'There's been no participatory planning in the last two years.' According to a report by Desafío (2013, 9), a community-based organization committed to empowering Santa Cruz's marginalized communities, "Until 2008 we saw that a small percentage of the funds included within the rubric of Municipal Deconcentration was destined to this end [participatory planning], but now no amount is specified."

After I first arrived in Santa Cruz for fieldwork in July 2010 I obsessively sought to find someone with knowledge of Neighbor Demand. As days turned to weeks I began to wonder why my search was coming up empty. After several dead ends I was elated when I secured an interview with a senior official from the Department of Parks and Gardens, Richard Iturralde, whom I was told had helped run the program and could answer my questions. I made my way to Richard's office, which as one might expect was housed in a city park, and we sat down to talk. My hopes that he could grant me access to attend a Neighbor Demand session were dashed within minutes when he told me he had no knowledge of the program operating after 2006. Richard seemed proud of this. 'Neighbor Demand was a disaster,' he said. 'Participation works best when it's imposed by the executive. . . . We [officials] try to learn from experiences in other countries. . . . [Take] traffic . . . a traffic solution doesn't come from a resident . . . he's just in his car and knows he doesn't want traffic, but he doesn't know how to make that happen.'

My interviews with other top officials suggest that Richard's "participation is a disaster" and "experts know best" attitude was near universal among the Fernandez administration's upper echelons. These officials viewed participation with scorn and endorsed technocratic decision-making where experts make rational decisions benefitting "the city as a whole." They made clear that this required that experts like themselves be insulated from residents' narrow-minded, self-interested, and "capricious" ways.

In a March 2011 interview in his office, Juan Carlos González, the head of monitoring and control in the Department of Public Works, criticized the 'extreme [of] too much participation' of Neighbor Demand in 2006. Juan Carlos also explained why experts like him should have control over decisions for the city. 'We analyze the city as a whole. . . . It doesn't work to leave all the planning in the hands of residents because they don't look at how the city is growing.' Like other top officials, he felt *experts know what citizens need better than citizens themselves do.* Consider his discussion of the last participatory planning session he had attended, some four years earlier. 'Residents' priorities were health, education, paving, and drainage, in that order.' The Fernandez administration's spending was the reverse of this, with the most spent on paving and drainage and the least on health and education. To Juan Carlos this showed that 'there's a difference between what residents say they want and what they actually need.' To illustrate this, he discussed the difference between how residents and experts decide which streets need to be paved. 'We [experts] view things from the technical angle, and we want to finish important streets [and] finish off the rings [the major concentric roads circling the city] or complete a certain corner' of particular importance to traffic. Pointing randomly on a map of the city he hastily drew, Juan Carlos said residents 'want a street here and here and here . . . [because] your grandma lives on this street.' The takeaway was clear: residents are narrow minded, while experts know what is best for all.

Juan Pablo Rollano, the director of institutional planning, held a similar view on the superiority of expert-led over participatory decision-making. In an interview he repeatedly referred to residents' "whims" (*caprichos*) and 'lack [of] long and medium-term vision.' To illustrate this Juan Pablo offered a seemingly hypothetical example of residents arguing against having a new school built on the site of an existing soccer field. To him it showed that 'they don't realize that the school would benefit everyone in the neighborhood.' (He did not consider that residents might not be against the school but merely want it built elsewhere.) He was also highly critical of neighborhood leaders, viewing them as corrupt and solely guided by personal or political interests. In his words, these 'leaders use projects to destabilize [things] . . . to do politics.' Juan Pablo saw neighborhood leaders as a key reason why participatory planning was impossible. 'The problem is the neighborhood leaders. Since there is parallelism, there might be one recognized leader, a second leader who is recognized by others, and a third waiting to rise. . . . This leads to the outsourcing of demands, which are based on personal and political interests. . . . [The leaders] don't even respond to representativeness, much less to technical criteria.' Residents' "whims" and neighborhood leaders' 'personal and political interests' meant participatory planning should be avoided. 'Residents don't see the technical needs . . . so why even enter that arena [of participatory planning] . . . It doesn't even respond to representative criteria. . . . They [the leaders] have other interests.'

These comments point to a second key feature of Santa Cruz's urban political regime in the post-2005 Percy period: its clientelistic nature. Interview and observational data suggest Juan Pablo's charges about neighborhood leaders were accurate. Across Santa Cruz many, if not most, of the neighborhood and district leaders I came across, particularly leaders officially recognized by the municipality (in exchange for supporting the mayor), appeared to regularly act in ways that benefitted their personal and political interests over and above residents' collective interests. Popular politics was riddled with parallelism that prevented duly elected leaders from fulfilling their duties and empowered illegitimate leaders, who entered their posts through corruption and fraud. It also created confusion as to which neighborhood or district leaders and associations were legitimate and generated widespread disgust and rejection of popular politics as irredeemably tainted.

To Juan Pablo and other city officials, technocratic decision-making was the only way to deal with the clientelism and corruption of popular politics. When I shared this point of view with poor residents from barrios in the outer rings, they regularly offered three critiques. First, they questioned if experts were truly the disinterested parties they claimed to be. Second, they pointed out that experts regularly failed to note or respond to what residents said they needed. Third, they argued that the clientelism Juan Pablo and others bemoaned was not natural or inevitable but something produced and reproduced by Percy's administration. My research suggests the clientelistic and technocratic aspects of governance in Santa Cruz are not separate. Nor can technocratic decision-making be seen as a necessary response to the unfortunate-but-inevitable existence of clientelistic politics. Santa Cruz's clientelism was the foundation of its technocratic decision-making: it kept popular sectors in check and excluded from decisions, which experts could thus make without undue popular and political (i.e., democratic) "interference."

I encountered one official who worked for Percy but did not hold the views noted. Fernando Prado was the director of the Office of Planning from 2005 to 2007. He then resigned and became a vocal critic of the mayor. In the first of a number of lengthy interviews I conducted with him between 2010 and 2016, Fernando said, 'This administration is not at all interested in popular participation.' He also said Percy made this crystal clear to his staff. 'He would tell us, "These little projects [chosen through Neighbor Demand] only hurt the municipality. I want to do big projects."' To achieve this Percy worked to insulate his administration from any real popular input, a key means being clientelism. Fernando said Percy controlled Santa Cruz's Oversight Committee (OC), established by the 1994 Law of Popular Participation to allow civic associations to influence municipal decisions. Fernando told me, 'If MAS [the city's key opposition party] got two-thirds control of [the OC] it could make things much harder for the mayor.' Fernando said Percy financed OC candidates loyal to him in NC elections to prevent this. 'These candidates have more money and can make more promises.' This helped them win most of the time, 'and when they don't win there are problems. There are charges of fraud and sometimes even physical force is used to take over the neighborhood council.' Like Juan Pablo, Fernando also pointed to the problem of parallelism in neighborhood councils. 'There are also parallel Neighborhood Councils, which are formed in the same neighborhood unit.' Fernando felt all of these practices were a means to 'keep a lid on participation.'

EXPLAINING SANTA CRUZ'S TECHNOCRATIC CLIENTELISTIC REGIME

If Santa Cruz's technocratic clientelistic regime is neither "natural" nor inevitable, what explains it? Conjunctural local politics is part of the story. As noted, Percy placed second in the 2004 mayoral election but because none of the candidates had enough votes to win outright Percy was able to become mayor (starting in 2005) through a deal he struck with the election's third-place finisher, Oscar Vargas, whereby each would serve half the term. But when the time came for Percy to step aside in mid-2007, he refused. One consequence of this was that Percy needed new local allies. He found them by moving to the Right and embracing the regional autonomy movement, which Fernando said Percy had kept his distance from before breaking with Oscar. 'Percy went to [autonomy events] but was in the last row. At the last Town Hall [in 2007] he was one of the key speakers. At this point, Percy accepted becoming part of the *Verdes* group,' i.e., allying with Santa Cruz's right-wing prefect Rubén Costas. Percy's embrace of the Cruceño Right's language is evident in a statement he made in August 2008, in the tense days just before the recall referendum (mentioned in chapter 4) on Evo Morales and department prefects. "This government has not learned how to govern, and for that reason I ask the armed forces to overthrow the president of the republic" (Romero 2008).

Part of the reason Percy moved to (and stayed on) the Right, rather than moving left like Sucre's Carlos Ocariz, is the increasingly passive revolutionary character of Evo Morales's administration, which was reflected in MAS Santa Cruz's politics. After 2010 MAS Santa Cruz prioritized backroom deals over organizing and mobilizing its base. This meant Percy faced very little pressure to organize or mobilize popular sectors, which allowed him to govern in the "typically right-wing" antidemocratic manner he did.

Santa Cruz's balance of class forces also shaped Percy's governance strategy. As noted, in the 1990s Percy was more aligned with popular classes and clashed with elites (e.g., over the lodges). After 2005 things were different. Percy was now firmly allied with dominant classes and clashed with organized popular classes. In a June 2011 interview, Fernando said, 'To return to City Hall Percy had to promise to not go after the lodges.' He also noted that 'Percy is allied with big construction companies and the traditional families' based in agro-industry and real estate. This elite-professional class-force balance explains (and underlies) the state-controlled nature of Santa Cruz's technocratic clientelistic regime. This can be seen in the types of officials found in Percy's administration: Percy himself came to the office with extensive government and private sector experience. Other administration officials held degrees from prestigious national and international universities, including Argentina's Universidad de Córdoba and Santa Cruz's most prestigious one, the Universidad Autónoma Gabriel René Moreno.

ASSESSING SANTA CRUZ'S TECHNOCRATIC CLIENTELISTIC REGIME

Of the four cases, Santa Cruz has the least extensive and lowest quality of popular control. Residents had virtually no control over local political decision-making, although there were forms of pseudo participation. I found that there was a veneer of institutional effectiveness, but a closer look showed a yawning gap between citizens' expressed needs and the policies and projects Percy's administration implemented. There appeared to be political effectiveness, but evidence beneath the surface showed significant dissent.

EXTENT OF POPULAR CONTROL

My research indicates that during Santa Cruz's period of technocratic clientelistic rule, there was a near-total lack of popular control over political decision-making. Two pieces of evidence support this claim. The first are the many statements, already provided in great detail, from top city officials expressing disdain for participation and affirming the fact that the Fernandez administration did virtually no participatory planning after (around) 2006. Second, there are statements and reports from residents, former city officials (e.g., Fernando Prado), urban planners (e.g., Omar Andrade and Martha Elcuez), and NGOs (such as Desafío) also indicating a lack of participation.

I also found extremely little popular control over nonbudgetary decisions. One piece of evidence showing this is that after returning to the mayor's office in 2005 Percy refused to implement an ordinance passed by his immediate predecessor, Roberto Fernandez, that gave NC presidents the power to elect submayors, as opposed to the mayor appointing these posts. Fernando Prado told me, 'Percy just ignored this and said, "They're just like any other functionary and so I'll name them myself."'

QUALITY OF POPULAR CONTROL

Evidence I collected indicates that Santa Cruz lacked meaningful participatory planning but had instances of pseudo participation. I use this term to refer to apparently participatory spaces that were highly flawed in multiple ways, including being racially and politically exclusionary, and marked by officials imposing their own preferences over and above citizens' choices. This section discusses an instance of pseudo participation in district 9, one of the four outer-ring districts where I conducted significant fieldwork.

(I repeatedly sought out opportunities to observe instances of participation in this district and others but was unable to do so. This difficulty is, I argue, indicative of the lack of participatory spaces within Santa Cruz, since my efforts to observe participation in the three other study cities were similar but much more successful.) District 9 is one of the city's poorest districts, with a reported 25 to 40 percent of residents living in poverty. My discussion focuses on a (purportedly) participatory budget planning session I attended in the district the night of March 23, 2011, in a meeting space in the submayor's office. My discussion focuses on three issues: Did decision-making approximate deliberation, who had control over decisions, and how inclusive was the process in terms of residents' access to decisions and resources?

The meeting included three district officials: the submayor, the OC representative, and president of the District Federation of Neighborhood Councils; four municipal department officials; and around forty NC presidents. The meeting's official purpose was to reformulate the district's 2012 annual operating plan or POA. An engineer from the Department of Parks and Gardens kicked off the proceedings by writing the amount of money the district had for plazas and an urban park on a blackboard at the front of the room. 'This is the money they've assigned us. We're here to tell you about your plazas.' After this there was a brief discussion and vote on which neighborhood would receive a plaza. Next there was a longer discussion about walkways. The NC presidents and municipal technicians engaged in back-and-forth questions and answers. This led to a decision, which all seemed to agree with, to build walkways in four neighborhoods. Next an engineer spoke about school buildings, explaining, 'The decision about where to do this is yours. . . . We'll just tell you how much [money] you have.'

The most interesting part of the assembly came toward the end and centered on a conflictual and deliberative discussion about sports fields. The NC presidents repeatedly interrupted the municipal architect who was facilitating the discussion to pose questions, mostly about incomplete projects from previous years. The presidents vigorously debated where and how to spend the funds the district had been allocated. A woman said she did not have a field in her barrio, since the one there had been turned into a market. This meant local kids had nowhere to play. Another woman asked for money to install a net on one side of the field in her barrio. She said the field was next to a busy road where a child playing had recently been hit by a car. A few other women also made pleas for fields to be built in their barrios. (Several men spoke at various points as well.)

Ever Romero, the OC representative, then told everyone that a particular company had been contracted to build fields in the past in several districts, including district 9, but had failed as a business, leaving half the contracted projects unfinished. Ever said the district should not contract this company again. Throughout the discussion NC presidents voiced complaints against the municipal government. (This was likely due to the municipal technicians' presence.) The discussion eventually moved to a vote on whether to fund two new sports fields or provide lighting for several already-built fields. After several somewhat chaotic rounds of voting, it seemed relatively clear that a majority of the NC presidents favored funding two new fields. But the president of the district Federation of Neighborhood Councils, who was facilitating the vote, was not happy with this result. In a manner that was not transparent (at least to me), she kept the vote going until the group agreed to fund three fields, the outcome she seemed to want.

At first glance this example seems to show a reasonably deliberative participatory budget meeting. But closer inspection reveals that this is more appearance than reality due to several major limitations. The first limitation became apparent before the meeting ended. Officials (in this case the district Federation of Neighborhood Councils president) could and did override residents' choices. Discussions with other NC presidents showed that this was a common practice in district 9. One group of presidents told me of an example involving Ever, the district OC representative (and romantic partner of the district Federation of Neighborhood Councils president, which illustrates another layer of the nepotism and personalism of the city's barrio politics). According to the group, Ever altered a paving project on an avenue connecting the fifth and sixth rings. One of the presidents drew a line and said, 'It was supposed to be a straight road.'

He then drew a crooked line and explained that the road had not been paved in a straight line. It was paved up to a certain point but then went off course for several blocks before continuing to be paved from a subsequent point. The unplanned section of paved road passed by two condominium buildings. The presidents said Ever had accepted a bribe to alter the project and follow the unplanned route. I asked if they had proof this happened. Omar, one of the presidents in the group, traced a crooked line in the air with his finger and said, 'The proof is that the road is paved like this.' (It is worth noting that this example illustrates a problem Juan Pablo Rollano pointed to: neighborhood leaders do things in a way that benefits their personal and political interests rather than residents' general interests. What Juan Pablo, and other officials, did not note was that the person most responsible for this was the mayor, whom they all professed great respect for.)

A second limitation of the process was the NC presidents' decision-making power, which concerned only where predetermined small-scale projects could go. Officials decided what projects were discussed and how much money went to specific project domains (e.g., sports fields versus plazas). The third, and most critical, limitation of the process was its clientelistic nature. This limitation was not immediately apparent but became abundantly clear through months of participant observation in this district and others.

My research shows that clientelism manifested itself in two ways. First, NC presidents were pressured to support the mayor. In a conversation with a group of NC presidents in district 9 aligned with Ever, one of the presidents commented on the 2010 mayoral campaign: 'Ever tried to force us to change our politics, and work for Percy's campaign. . . . [After the campaign] Ever came to our barrio and told people, "I didn't see your president in the campaign so you won't be getting machinery."' Second, there was exclusion of people called MASistas. This term had overlapping racial, political, and geographic meanings. It was used not only or primarily for MAS supporters but also and especially for city residents with darker skin, Indigenous "looks," highlands origins, or who lived in an outer-ring district (particularly district 8) identified as pro-MAS.

The flipside of the exclusion of MASistas (which in the following paragraphs is used in the broad sense just noted) was the inclusion of autonomistas. This term officially referenced supporters of the regional autonomy movement. But during the main period of my fieldwork in Santa Cruz (2010–2011) it was used to refer to supporters of Percy and the local and regional Right more broadly. Almost all the presidents attending the budget-planning meeting just discussed were self-proclaimed autonomistas. This was not coincidence but by design. I asked an NC president at the meeting if any MASistas were present. He said, 'We're all autonomistas here.' 'Why?' I asked. He replied, 'There were some troublemakers affiliated with the government [i.e., MAS] who used to come and criticize everything . . . but we got rid of them.' I asked how. He responded, 'We didn't stop them from coming, but we ignored them whenever they tried to speak. Then they stopped coming.' Ever, an autonomista like all the current OC members, confirmed that MASistas no longer came to district 9 meetings. MASista NC presidents from the district whom I spoke to told me they were not invited to participatory planning sessions or other district meetings. They also said many of the NC presidents who attended these meetings were not legitimate leaders since they had been elected in illegal "parallel" gatherings open only to autonomistas.

My fieldwork in three other districts—6, 8, and 12—that resemble district 9 in having high poverty and lying beyond the fourth ring, and are thus considered "outer ring," indicates that the pattern of clientelism, racism, and exclusion just noted was prevalent throughout the city's outer-ring districts. In July 2010 I sat down for the first of several interviews (over the next year) with Gualberto Flores, a longtime pro-MAS neighborhood leader from district 6. Gualberto was elected president of his neighborhood council in 2006 and then reelected in 2008. He said he could attend district-wide meetings from 2006 to 2008 but not after 2008 because he supported MAS. 'I've been marginalized because of my political views.' He said the district OC representative, Carlos Diaz, who was allied with the mayor, stopped inviting him to the meetings. 'I'm not alone in this. There are twenty-five neighborhood councils that no longer go to these assemblies.' Gualberto also said Diaz should not be the representative since he had only invited his "friends" to the meeting where he was elected to the position. Gualberto said that he and other dissident NC presidents from district 6 'managed to obtain a list' of one hundred NC presidents loyal to Diaz who were invited to district meetings and able to participate in discussions and obtain benefits; those not on the list, i.e., MASistas, were excluded.

Other (genuinely) MASista neighborhood leaders I spoke with in Santa Cruz provided similar accounts. Lorenzo Justiniano told me about local politics in district 12 and serving as an OC representative from 2005 to 2007. After he joined, Lorenzo said he was told to align himself with Percy's political group and offered a "phantom" job in the mayor's office. Lorenzo's wife, Martha, who took part in the interview and was also a neighborhood leader, said phantom jobs were common. The term referred to a practice of officially holding a municipal job, and getting a salary for it, without doing any work. Lorenzo said he turned down the offer, which was repeated several times during the year and a half he served on the oversight committee.

Lorenzo 'got quite an education' from his time on the OC. According to the 1994 Law of Popular Participation that established it, the OC offered a way for civil society to exercise control over local political decision-making. Lorenzo said Santa Cruz's OC did not do this, since the fourteen other representatives were bought off by the mayor. He said, 'They all had family members working in City Hall.' To illustrate their illicit gains, Lorenzo told me of one rep who 'used to own a beat-up car and now has a whole fleet of TRUFIs' (informal taxis). He said when he began his time on the OC he was approached by one of Percy's "operators" and told, "'Choose ten of the most conflictive neighborhoods'" to get projects. 'We'll give something for you too,' the operator added.

Lorenzo said he refused this offer and all others and adopted a conflictual stance toward the mayor, in accord with his understanding of what the OC was for. In October 2006 Lorenzo led a protest at city hall demanding that the mayor complete unfinished projects. He said three thousand people from his district turned out. Their demands included paving and lighting projects and finishing drainage works in district 12. Lorenzo said the protest was met with repression. 'I myself was beaten by the municipal police.' But the protest had an effect: the district got most of the unfinished projects completed. He then told me of a meeting he had attended the previous night. The meeting reaffirmed the president of the district 12 Union of Neighborhood Councils in his position—despite the fact that Percy had just named this man as the district's new submayor. 'This is like having the rat guard the cheese,' Lorenzo said.

I asked Lorenzo and Martha when Neighbor Demand had last occurred in district 12. Martha said it was in 2007, and she recounted the extreme disrespect the municipal officials in attendance showed residents who came to the session. 'They told us, "You're a bunch of useless idiots"' in response to a request to pave a specific road. ' "That won't be paved any time in the next forty years,"' Martha recounted the technicians then saying.

I found the same pattern captured in this anecdote—of largely white municipal officials treating darker-skinned Indigenous and mestizo residents of outer-ring districts in a paternalistic, disrespectful, and racist way—in district 8, the city's most pro-MAS district, often called "the bastion of MAS." The district is called Plan 3000, in reference to three thousand families resettled there in 1983 after being displaced by major flooding elsewhere in the city. Plan 3000 saw intense struggles between pro-MAS residents and leaders and the mayor's office. These struggles occurred in neighborhood councils and centered on alleged corruption and actual or alleged MASistas' exclusion from resources and decisions.

MASistas (used here to mean party militants and residents who opposed the mayor and by default supported or sympathized with MAS) and some oppositionists in Plan 3000 were highly critical of their OC rep, Victor Hugo Selis. Jorge "Don Chichi" Castedo, an oppositionist and lifelong activist in his sixties who worked closely with MASistas, said Don Selis (as he was called) was 'servile to the municipality' and 'has done lots of damage' by facilitating and not condemning the widespread practice of leaving projects half-finished for years. Don Chichi said Don Selis 'manipulated people into voting for him' in his first election to the OC (in 2007 or 2008) by promising things he did not deliver. Don Chichi also said Don Selis's 2010 reelection was fraudulent. 'He tricked everyone. All the [NC] presidents were told that they were signing up for a vaccination program, but in actuality they were signing a document for the certification of the OC representative.' 'You mean they reelected him without knowing they were?' I asked with surprise. 'Yes, they reelected him without knowing it,' Don Chichi told me.

For several years Don Chichi partnered with a respected MASista, Carmen Alvarez, to try to change things. When I spoke to Carmen a few days after talking with Don Chichi, she gave me more dirt on Don Selis. 'He takes advantage of everything, and he just did the [2011] POA [annual operating plan] with Jesus Alvarez and Fanny Nuñez within four walls [i.e., behind closed doors] in the name of everyone.' Jesus and Fanny were powerful district 8 officials allied with the mayor. MASistas like Carmen reviled both of them, and Don Selis, due to their history of racist and exclusionary actions.

In several months of participant observation I met many MASistas in Plan 3000 who repeated Carmen and Don Chichi's criticisms of Jesus, Fanny, and Don Selis. In an April 2011 meeting of Plan 3000's MASista Union of Neighborhood Councils (with the district also having a parallel autonomista Union), Raul Magne, president of the district's Federation of Neighborhood Councils, commented, 'We know we weren't consulted for the 2011 POA. I was a leader then [he showed his NC badge indicating this as he spoke] and I wasn't asked. We know it was just Fanny Nuñez, Jesus, and Victor Hugo Selis and a little group of people.' Earlier in the meeting a woman, on the verge of tears, said, 'I've been elected and reelected [president of my NC], but there's a parallel [NC] and [the president of this parallel NC] has lights for her plaza and I haven't gotten any projects.' Still fighting back tears, she added, 'They don't want us.'

The evidence presented (a fraction of what I collected in my fieldwork) paints a damning picture of neighborhood and district politics in Santa Cruz: civic leaders under the thumb of a powerful mayor; systematic exclusion of those not aligned with the mayor; systematic corruption and malfeasance, with civic leaders aligned with the mayor repeatedly using fraud to gain and maintain power; and widespread parallelism, with pro-MAS residents regularly winning elections they (and many outside observers) viewed as legitimate only to have autonomistas form parallel associations (neighborhood councils, unions, and federations) that gained the mayoral recognition denied to MASistas. All this makes it hard to dispute that there was no real participation in Santa Cruz.

The apparent lack of genuine participation in Santa Cruz also makes it challenging to assess other indicators about the quality of popular control in the city, though a few remarks can be made. In terms of gender, district-level meetings I attended in districts 8, 9, and 12 were inclusive, with high numbers of men and women. Compared to El Alto, I found much greater gender inclusivity in Santa Cruz, visible in the fact that many women were NC presidents and more than a few were in higher positions, e.g., serving as president of a district federation or union of neighborhood councils, as submayor (which happened in several cases in Santa Cruz), or on the OC. I did not observe overt exclusion based on class. There was widespread exclusion based on racial and ethnic categories and (perceived) political ideology, which also translated to class exclusion since residents labeled MASistas tended to be among the poorest in the city. Data on turnout should also be taken with a grain of salt. In the handful of budget-planning sessions I attended there appeared to be significant turnout of forty to fifty NC presidents per district. I was told that there was generally good attendance at NC meetings. But, as noted, such meetings were highly exclusionary.

INSTITUTIONAL EFFECTIVENESS

Percy's central claim to fame was being a mayor who "gets things done," as his official municipal biography put it during his time as mayor. During his 2010 campaign for reelection, he plastered the city with placards that read "Vote for Percy: So the projects continue . . ." Evidence suggests this strategy worked politically, at least to an extent. Lorenzo (Justiniano) told

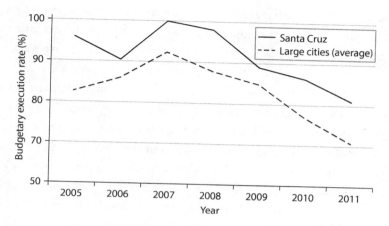

FIGURE 5.2 Budgetary execution in Santa Cruz versus Bolivia's large-city average, 2005–2011. (The average is of Bolivia's six largest cities: Cochabamba, El Alto, La Paz, Oruro, Potosi, Sucre, and Santa Cruz.)

Source: Ejecución Presupuestaria, http://vmpc.economiayfinanzas.gob.bo/Ejecucion PresupuestariaVarios.asp?t=GM, April 1, 2012, last accessed June 12, 2015.

me that people in his district voted for the mayor in 2010 and said, 'Percy is getting work done.'

Official data appear to back up Percy's claim of being institutionally effective. As figure 5.2 shows, from 2005 to 2011 Santa Cruz's budgetary execution rate was consistently above the average of Bolivia's six largest cities. From 2005 to 2009 the city's budgetary execution rate was close to or above 90 percent, and it declined less than the large Bolivian cities' average in 2010 and 2011. Santa Cruz's rate decreased to 64 percent in 2012 (*La Razón* 2013) before rebounding to 70 percent in 2013 (*El Deber* 2014). Notably, in both years, its budgetary execution rate was the highest among all large Bolivian cities.

But a closer look suggests that Santa Cruz's institutional effectiveness was more apparent than real. The rosy picture portrayed in Figure 5.2 is complicated by evidence suggesting widespread corruption, taking the form of "phantom projects" that are complete on paper only, and the private use of public resources. Carmen Alvarez estimated that over 50 percent of all projects listed as complete in Plan 3000 were phantoms. She provided numerous specific examples. 'In [Neighborhood Unit] 156 there was a project for a small school, which cost 10,000 [US] dollars and there's nothing there.' She continued, 'There was a community center and it's not even a community center, it's a police module . . . and in Barrio Paititi [a neighborhood in the district] 460,000 bolivianos was spent for a sports field fitted with nets and links and stairs, but there's nothing there . . . not even a single stone. And the Oversight Committee [representative] Victor Selis has been overseeing all of this. . . . There's no projects in the barrios, only a few very small projects for lighting a plaza and a few multi-use sports fields.'

Carmen also gave numerous examples of corruption relating to her OC rep. 'Don Selis has held barbecues and we have the receipts of all this. . . . We have proof of false signatures, and of meetings, of false projects. . . . We have 550 pages of denunciations that are with the public prosecutor right now.' 'Can you give some examples?' I asked. Carmen pointed and said, 'There's a receipt for 38,000 [bolivianos] for a meeting.' 'Just a single meeting?' I asked. 'Yes,' she replied, 'for a single meeting . . . there were 66 people present . . . for a barbecue . . . and there was a barbecue for 1,600 bolivianos. . . . There was a receipt for a gas inspection, that was supposed to cost 150 bolivianos, but then on the last page they added 1,000 more to make it 1,150 bolivianos.' I asked Carmen to estimate the extent of phantom projects in Plan 3000. She replied, 'This is at least 50 percent. . . . In the [district's] 106 neighborhood councils there are around 60 phantom projects.'

My research in other districts suggests that widespread phantom projects and corruption were not unique to Plan 3000. During a weekly meeting of NC presidents and district leaders in district 9 in June 2011, the OC rep, Ever, took out a book of photos and started to list finished projects. As he showed the photographs, he commented, 'The pictures don't lie,' and read off a number of projects. Monica, an NC president taking notes during the meeting, came over when he mentioned a project in her barrio. She glanced at the photo and shook her head to indicate that while the book might say the project was done, it was not. A number of other NC presidents then commented that projects supposedly finished in their barrios were not. The president of the district Federation of Neighborhood Councils promised to submit a formal denunciation. In reaction to pictures Ever showed, several women commented, 'Those could've been taken in another neighborhood.' The negative reactions prompted Ever to do an about-face. Moments after having said 'the pictures don't lie,' he noted that several photographs were taken from too far away to tell if the projects shown had been completed or not.

Another very widespread problem in Santa Cruz was the lack of correspondence between projects that were implemented and residents' expressed needs. As noted, top officials in Percy's administration spoke proudly of ignoring what residents said they wanted by, e.g., choosing projects in the reverse order given by residents. This "officials know best" attitude helps explain the prevalence of costly, large-scale projects that residents said were not priorities for them. Don Chichi, of Plan 3000, told me, 'The POA [annual operating plan] isn't decided upon by us, by the neighborhood councils. We ask that the POA be decided in the district, *so that we define what we want for the barrio. We don't want another cemetery, as the municipality is proposing. We already have a cemetery . . . [and] that isn't what we want*' (emphasis added). Eduardo Correa, a Plan 3000 NC president and then district submayor, commented, 'They [the Fernandez administration] haven't taken into account what the neighbors want. . . .For instance, they've paved roads which don't have sewers yet! That's not planning a city.' In one of my interviews with Fernando Prado, he said the mayor had 'built five Level II hospitals [but] budgeted no money for doctors!' I learned from chatting with residents in outer-ring districts that shiny new school modules had been built but then stood empty since the mayor did not allocate funds to hire teachers. Each year Percy's administration prioritized a large-scale cookie-cutter project to implement citywide: hospital modules one year, school modules the next, urban parks the following. But residents repeatedly told me (and others) that these projects were not what they needed. Fernando said, 'Neighbors' demands aren't listened to; they aren't priorities.'

POLITICAL EFFECTIVENESS

As with institutional effectiveness, Santa Cruz's technocratic clientelistic regime initially appears politically effective, but a closer look reveals a more complicated reality. Electoral data show Percy was relatively politically effective. He won reelection in 2010 with 52 percent of the vote, 32 points above his 2004 total of 20 percent. Turnout increased from 58 percent to 85 percent.[1] In 2015 Percy won again but with just 42 percent. His ability to secure reelection twice indicates political effectiveness, though Santa Cruz does not match Torres, where the local incumbent party won reelection with a new mayoral candidate.

Evidence from districts 6, 8, 9, and 12 (8, 9, and 12 being the city's three poorest) shows Percy faced significant dissent among outer-ring residents excluded from benefits and decisions. In each case a similar pattern occurred at some point between 2006 and 2011 with residents collectively protesting to remove the submayor or OC representative who excluded them, often in racist ways; and in many of the cases to support a submayor who was inclusive and whom Percy sought to remove from office because of this. In some cases these struggles achieved initial success, but it never lasted. An analysis of two struggles points to two reasons for this. The first was popular classes' limited capacity for autonomous mobilization. The second was MAS's shifting willingness to support popular struggle; when the party supported protesters their prospects of success were much greater than when the party declined to provide support.

During my fieldwork a pronounced struggle took place in Plan 3000, the district with the highest percentage of highland migrants that, as noted, was known as the "bastion of MAS." As already discussed, district and municipal leaders, particularly the submayor and OC representative, had excluded MASistas for years. In June 2010 a breaking point was reached. For a week between one and three hundred protesters, mostly MAS supporters, blockaded the submayor's office and a nearby municipal dump. They wanted Percy to let the district's NC presidents choose their own submayor.

The protest worked. Percy designated Eduardo Correa as the district's submayor after an assembly of mostly MASista NC presidents chose him for the position. Correa was unlike any previous submayor in Plan 3000: a dark-skinned migrant from Potosí who spoke Spanish as a second language, a MASista, and as Correa himself told me, 'I am the only submayor designated by pressure.' His designation led to a sea change in how the submayor's office was run. I interviewed Correa three times. The first was in April 2011, nine months into his tenure as submayor. We spoke in his office, which was mostly empty. Correa told me, 'The submayor before me [Fanny Nuñez, whom Percy appointed] only received people from her group. . . . Residents who came from more distant [and poorer] barrios had no chance to meet with her. . . . Things happened in a totally arbitrary way. . . . The submayor only served people of her political line . . . [and] she would never meet with a MASista. . . . In order to meet with her I had to come with three hundred neighbors, Alteño style, bringing placards and marching. . . . That was the only way she'd meet with us. . . . She wouldn't meet with a *morenito* [short brown man] like me.'

Correa said he was opening the submayor's office to all. 'For the 2012 POA [annual operating plan discussions] I'm going to convoke everyone regardless of whether they are with the Right. . . . I'll consider everyone, and we'll prioritize everything. . . . I'm not just the submayor for the MASistas, but for everyone.' Correa noted that in his nine months as submayor he had attended all residents who came to see him, regardless of their political affiliation. Correa specifically mentioned that he attended those he knew to be opponents of MAS, as well as MASista NC presidents and residents, who referred to him as "one of ours." Correa contrasted his approach to his predecessor's when 'there was never, never any convocation for the elaboration of the POA. . . . There [was] very little participation . . . [and] the leaders weren't taken into account for the 2011 POA.'

Correa's time as submayor was immensely challenging and short-lived. When we first spoke in April 2011, he said he regularly thought of quitting because of the obstacles the mayor's office put in his way. 'I don't have the personnel to attend residents' demands. . . . I can't contract anyone. That all happens in the central office . . . and they deprive me of things,' such as machinery and material needed to attend to residents' requests for projects. Correa also said, 'They [the mayor's office] have meetings [in downtown Santa Cruz, an hour or more drive from Plan 3000] and they only let me know thirty minutes in advance, so I get there late and look bad. They're trying to crush me.' Correa's inability to effectively fulfill his duties generated frequent complaints from NC presidents, including the MASista presidents who had supported him from the beginning and whose protest had put Correa in office. In meetings of Plan 3000 MASista civic associations in April 2011 I regularly heard people say, 'The submayor isn't doing anything.' I also heard this exact complaint from autonomista NC presidents. Correa was aware of all this but said the mayor's office had tied his hands.

In May 2011, a month after this conversation, the mayor replaced Correa with Jesus Alvarez, who, as noted, was reviled by many (particularly MASistas) for his racist and exclusionary ways. Despite their criticism of Correa, MASistas in Plan 3000 were outraged by his removal. As they had a year earlier, they protested. But this protest was much smaller than the one that led to Correa becoming submayor, and it quickly fizzled out without success.

Both protests had to confront the historical weakness of popular sectors in Santa Cruz, including in Plan 3000, which many considered the city's most combative and organized district. While this might have been true, Plan 3000's own activists pointed to its mobilizational weakness. When I told Correa I was doing research in El Alto, he said, 'We're not at the level of social organization that they have in El Alto. If El Alto is 100, we're a 10 in terms of organization. . . . Sometimes people say "*Plan 3000 de pie, nunca de rodillas*" [Plan 3000 on its feet, never on its knees], taking off from the [well-known] saying "*El Alto de pie, nunca de rodillas,*" but we're not there yet.' He pointed to the greater racial-ethnic heterogeneity of Plan 3000 (and Santa Cruz generally) versus the greater homogeneity in El Alto as a key reason for this difference. 'El Alto has all Alteños, and everyone there is from La Paz; they are all Aymara. . . . The problem in Plan 3000 is that it's the compendium of all Bolivia; it's Chuquisaca and Potosí and Oruro and Cochabamba and Beni and La Paz and Pando and Tarija and Santa Cruz. It's all nine departments of Bolivia. But that means that the neighbor in front of you or across the street might speak Quechua or Aymara or

Spanish . . . so we're a long way from El Alto.' He further noted, 'I can't say that in Plan 3000 we can convoke 20,000, 10,000, or 5,000' for a march. By contrast even poorly attended marches in El Alto attracted five thousand or more, with the biggest bringing out tens or hundreds of thousands.

The reason the June 2010 protest managed to overcome these obstacles, while the May 2011 protest did not, is because of the distinct role of MAS in the two protests. The party played a leading role in the June 2010 protest. The Regional Council for Change (CRC), an umbrella organization that brought together seven pro-MAS social organizations in Plan 3000, directed the protest. (CRC is the Plan 3000 equivalent of pro-MAS umbrella organizations found at the national and urban levels, e.g., CONALCAM and El Alto's CORELCAM.) CRC leaders and others said that CRC initiated the protest, facilitated the selection of Correa as the submayoral candidate, maintained and increased pressure on higher officials, and coordinated with local and regional MAS elected officials, who served as brokers. José Luís Guachalla, the head of the CRC, told me a critical turning point in the week-and-a-half struggle came when the CRC gave the mayor an ultimatum after a week of blockading the submayor's office, telling Percy he had to recognize their choice for submayor or face a blockade of the municipal dump. Forty-eight hours later the blockade began. José Luís said Percy settled 'in three hours,' agreeing to appoint Correa as submayor. Protesters say Santa Cruz's four MASista city councillors helped make this happen, with the district 8 councillor, Arminda Velasquez, acting as a go-between and convincing Percy to appoint Correa as submayor.

MAS's role in the May 2011 protest was very different. Protesters say MAS city councillors offered no support. A likely reason was that at this time MAS was negotiating a power-sharing agreement with Percy and the right-wing city council president, Desiree Bravo. This shocked and angered many grassroots MASistas, who reviled Bravo. MAS's willingness to seek an alliance with the Right, and related refusal to support grassroots MASistas' popular mobilization, is indicative of the broader shift happening within the party at the time, namely the move toward consolidating a passive revolutionary regime.

This shift and its apparent consequences for district-level struggles in Santa Cruz can also be seen in a second struggle I observed in May 2011, in district 12. I learned of this protest when I happened upon a blockade of city hall by about a hundred people. The struggle resembled that of district 8: a group of dissident NC leaders protested Percy's dismissal of a submayor who these leaders said was highly inclusive.[2] The district 12 struggle had two features not found in district 8's struggle: it was led by NC presidents previously affiliated with Percy, and it centered on a submayor who had also been close to Percy in the past but had recently opposed the mayor.

The key issue was Percy's refusal to support a submayor who worked with all residents regardless of party. One protester I met told me the submayor, known as "Pocho," 'was working with the majority, and attending to all the neighborhood councils. . . . We all elaborated the POA together. The submayor called us for a meeting, but they [the mayor's office] wouldn't recognize the results.' Fidel Honor, president of the district Federation of Neighborhood Councils, and Iver Ijanes, another district neighborhood leader, led the protest. Both said they supported Percy. Fidel said he was trying to avoid antagonizing Percy so he could continue working with him in the future. Fidel and Iver presented their struggle as one of inclusion. Iver said, 'The submayor [Pocho] doesn't look at people's political colors. . . . He works with everyone.'

MASistas in district 12 confirmed that Fidel and Iver were longtime Percy supporters. Lorenzo, a MASista who served a few years earlier as the district 12 OC representative, said Fidel and Iver had themselves been very exclusionary in the past. 'We [MASistas] couldn't even enter the submayor's office for meetings before. They would physically remove me from the meetings. [As he says this he mimics holding onto a bench.] Women would come and pick me up, as I held on. And Fidel and Iver threatened me on the phone, telling me not to come to the meetings. . . . Until last year we [MASistas] were in permanent opposition and they [those loyal to the mayor] controlled the [district] Union of Neighborhood Councils . . . but then they came over to our side, and we form the majority now . . . The other side now only has fifteen Neighborhood Councils at most, out of eighty, and we now have more than fifty.'

The district 12 struggle started just after Pocho's May 9 dismissal and petered out by mid-June 2011. As with the district 8 struggle, the historical weakness of popular classes and limited support from MAS appear as key factors explaining the protest's failure. The highpoint of the protest, the aforementioned blockade of city hall, lasted just two days. On the second day, municipal police and security forces arrived, telling those present to disband or face arrest. Lorenzo said, 'People are somewhat fearful and say, "They're going to injure us."' In the face of municipal repression, the protest was disbanded, with a smaller protest continuing for the next several weeks outside the district 12 submayor's office. During one of the final meetings before the protest ended, an NC president commented that he thought they should give up, saying, 'We need a new patron.' This statement indicates protesters' decidedly limited sense of possibility. Their hope was not for major change but simply a "new patron" who could link them to benefits. Like the failed district 8 protest in May 2011, MAS provided very little support in district 12. Fidel and Iver were labeled MASistas; although it was a false accusation, it led them to approach MAS for help, but they and others say their entreaties fell on deaf ears. Like the second Plan 3000 protest, the result was failure leading to protesters' demoralization.

CODA: THE CONSOLIDATION OF TECHNOCRATIC CLIENTELISM AMID MAS'S SHIFT FROM INSURGENT MOBILIZATION TO *TRANSFORMISMO*

The analysis I've presented is largely based on research conducted in 2010 and 2011. In August 2016 I revisited Santa Cruz, interviewing a dozen people, including three key contacts from my earlier fieldwork, to see what had and had not changed in the intervening years. The interviews pointed to two interrelated findings. The first was the consolidation of technocratic clientelism in Santa Cruz. The second was MAS's incorporation into the city's political power structure. This second finding showcases MAS's transformation within Santa Cruz from an insurgent force for change to the junior partner in a process of "transformism," in which the old and new political elite merge and serve to perpetuate the status quo. While MAS's incorporation into Santa Cruz's political power structure reinforced the technocratic and clientelistic character of local governance, I found that it also marked an important transition away from highly overt and violent racism to more subtle "everyday" racism in the city and region's politics.

The first person I spoke to in 2016 was Gualberto Flores, a MASista activist from district 6. I asked him what I had missed since 2011. He said, 'Nothing has changed.' He quickly made a slight amendment. 'It's worse than it was five years ago. . . . There's been no advance in participation, in planning, in social control.' Gualberto said the patterns he told me of in 2010 and 2011—the often-violent exclusion of darker-skinned (real or imagined) MASistas such as himself from decision-making and resources—were further entrenched. He placed the blame for this on MAS's shoulders, saying, 'They've gone with the old logic.' This was a reference to the party's decision to openly ally with Percy from 2013 on. This alliance further diminished the popular classes' already feeble mobilizational capacity. It also exacerbated fragmentation of popular-sector associations. Speaking of the city's multiple Federations of Neighborhood Councils, Gualberto said, 'When you were here five years ago there were two, [and] now there are seven.' This was largely due to leaders' cooptation by different political parties, citizens' groups, and political factions. (Figure 5.3 offers visual evidence of the shift in MAS's relations with Percy and the Cruceño Right. The photo shows Evo Morales, Percy Fernandez, and Santa Cruz governor Rubén Costas meeting in May 2014. The evident warmth the leaders show for each other is markedly different from the enmity that characterized their relations before 2010.)

I next spoke to Fernando Prado. When I asked, 'How have things changed since 2011?' his answer was similar to Gualberto's. 'The situation of the municipal government has gotten much worse in the last five years. There are no mechanisms of participation. There's no transparency. Spaces [of supposed participation] have been totally coopted. Powerful economic interests totally control the municipal government, and there's no political

FIGURE 5.3 Rubén Costas, Evo Morales, and Percy Fernandez.

Source: "El 2020 marca el ocaso de tres caudillos que dominaron la política," *El Deber*, December 20, 2020, https://eldeber.com.bo/pais/el-2020-marca-el-ocaso-de-tres -caudillos-que-dominaron-la-politica_212878.

alternative.' Like Gualberto, Fernando felt that MAS had been fully incor-porated into the city's political power structure. Fernando noted a reduction in overt racism, specifically a decline in 'the instrumentralization of racism' by the political Right in the service of the regional autonomy agenda. But he said the city's persistent clientelism had not diminished. 'Contacts in the peripheral zones told us it's worse than ever. If you aren't friends with the mayor, if you don't go to meetings of Percy's Santa Cruz Para Todos political party, you get nothing. . . . They just leave you in the freezer.' Juan Pablo Sejas, the director of the Centro Cultural San Isidro, a small com-munity cultural organization, corroborated Fernando's view. 'If you're not with Santa Cruz Para Todos you're out,' he told me at the center, which is located on the periphery of Plan 3000 and accessible only by traveling on an extremely poorly maintained dirt road. Juan Pablo added, 'There's no mobilization now,' due to 'the numbing of the neighborhood movement.'

Other people I spoke with made similar comments, saying the city was as technocratic and clientelistic as ever, there was less participation than ever, and MAS was not a political alternative, just the mayor's junior partner. Several interviewees noted the change referenced by Fernando regarding less overt racism. A concrete indicator of this was the presence of dark-skinned Indigenous MASistas working in city hall, something that would have been nearly unthinkable in 2010 and 2011. Dr. Carlos Herbert Camacho was an example of this. Camacho called himself a "Colla," the term for an Indigenous person from the highlands. He told me he started working on participatory initiatives (which he had a rosier view of than nearly everyone else I spoke with) in Percy's administration in late 2015. Before this he had spent eight years working directly under Evo Morales and Álvaro García Linera in the national government. Camacho's presence in the Fernandez administration indicated a shift from overt to subtler forms of racism. Despite being a fairly high-ranking city official, Camacho said he suffered regular if somewhat subtle racism. 'Many people won't listen to me because I'm a Colla.'

Gualberto also referred to the continuing presence of racism in the city. He said, 'Racism is again taking form' and gave an example of a school director in his district being replaced. 'They [school leaders] refused to seat the new director because he's short [and] has Indigenous features.' He pointed out, "The previous director was tall like you [referring to me]' and white. Racism was clearly still present in Santa Cruz in 2016, though the form it took seemed distinct from what had occurred in previous years. In April 2011 I spoke with a group of MASista leaders from Plan 3000. They referenced the violence that occurred in September 2008, during the right-wing civic coup referred to in chapter 4, in which right-wing political and civic leaders shut down Santa Cruz and other Media Luna departments and took over public institutions. This led to major violence in Plan 3000, with the quasi-fascist Cruceño Youth Union (Union Juvenil Cruceño) attempting to enter the district's central roundabout and shut down a government radio station. In an April 2011 interview, one of the leaders I spoke with said, 'They shouted "you damn Collas, you damn MASistas" at us.' Another leader made a play on words when he spoke of being beaten during the opposition civic strike at the time: 'El paro cívico se convirtió en palo cívico (the civic strike was turned into a civic beating)'.

My 2016 visit to Santa Cruz thus suggested a decidedly mixed picture. People I spoke with pointed to the lessening of overt racism, and specifically racialized violence toward dark-skinned highland migrants deemed to be MASistas, as a very welcome change. But nearly everyone I spoke with felt that elite control, clientelism, and corruption were more entrenched than ever. A key reason for this, in my informants' view, was the transformation of MAS from a political alternative to another cog in the machine that perpetuated ordinary residents' marginalization from decision-making.

Like Sucre, Santa Cruz does not fit the mold of a city where one would expect participatory success. But unlike Sucre, Santa Cruz fulfills this expectation of participatory failure. From 2005 to 2020, Percy Fernandez, a center-right mayor with close links to dominant classes, governed Santa Cruz. As this chapter has shown, Percy did so in a markedly antidemocratic manner, with the city's residents having virtually no ability to shape local political decisions. Such decisions were instead the province of well-credentialed experts who disdained the idea and practice of participation. But, as the chapter has shown, this technocratic rule rested on a clientelistic basis, with Percy using repression and particularistic resource distribution to dominate popular classes.

This domination, and the racist and classist exclusion it rested on—with darker-skinned Indigenous residents and MASistas conflated and locked out of decisions and resources—brought forth repeated cycles of popular resistance, in which the marginalized sought to be included. These struggles sometimes aimed to build a more real form of democracy and at other times involved the excluded just trying to gain access to a new patron. As the chapter has shown, these struggles for inclusion nearly always failed. A major reason for this was the limited support such struggles received from MAS, Santa Cruz's main opposition party, which after 2010 shifted from a stance of insurgent mobilization to transformismo and demobilization. Among other things, this left popular classes largely at the mercy of Percy's technocratic clientelistic regime.

Santa Cruz's participatory failure seems to have a clear explanation: a markedly antiparticipatory center-right mayor linked to dominant classes in a city where popular classes possess limited capacity for autonomous mobilization. This explanation, however, seems limited when Santa Cruz is compared to Sucre. As noted, the cities have several notable similarities: center-right opposition mayors with a history of supporting participation (in however mild a way) governing cities with a large class of informal workers who tended to support the left national ruling party. I have argued that explaining the cities' strikingly different forms of governance requires paying attention to national context. In the case of Santa Cruz, having a left ruling party in the midst of a passive revolutionary turn is a key factor that shaped Percy's governance strategy. This occurred in an indirect way, with Percy able to govern in a "typically right-wing" antidemocratic manner due to the lack of pressure from MAS and (organizationally weak and unsupported grassroots) MASistas to govern in a fairer, more democratic manner.

The following chapter shows that the negative effect MAS's passive revolutionary turn had on urban participation can also be seen in cities the party governed.

6

EL ALTO

Inverted Clientelism in the Rebel City

O f the four cases studied in this book, El Alto would seem the best positioned to develop into a robust participatory democracy. The city is globally renowned due to the organizational and mobilizational capacity of its inhabitants. This capacity is expressed both directly and through the city's powerful social organizations, in particular the Federation of Neighborhood Councils (FEJUVE-El Alto) and Regional Workers' Central (COR). El Alto's contentiousness was famously demonstrated in the 2003 gas war that overthrew neoliberal president Gonzalo Sánchez de Lozada and led scholars to dub El Alto the "rebel city" (Lazar 2008). According to Jeffery Webber (2011a, 184), "El Alto earned its position as the vanguard of left-Indigenous struggle in Bolivia, and as one of the most rebellious urban locales in contemporary Latin America." This position was reaffirmed in the second gas war of May–June 2005, which was also centered in El Alto. This uprising prompted the resignation of Sánchez de Lozada's successor, Carlos Mesa, and directly led to Evo Morales's election as Bolivia's first Indigenous president six months later.

In April 2010 Morales's MAS won El Alto's municipal elections, gaining the mayoralty and a city council majority. Edgar Patana, the

FIGURE 6.1 "Ruling by obeying" billboard next to El Alto City Hall.

Source: Photo by author.

COR's leader, became mayor, and Zacarías Maquera, a peasant trade-union leader who led the Federation of Agrarian Communities of the El Alto Urban and Suburban Radius (FESUCARUSU), became city council president. With social movement leaders from a movement-left party holding the city's top elected positions; with this party officially committed to "ruling by obeying," as a billboard adjacent to city hall stated during Patana's first years in office (see figure 6.1); and given the continued strength of the city's social organizations, El Also seemed ideally situated to implement bold participatory reform that would allow MAS to live up to its rhetoric.

This did not come to pass. As this chapter documents, Patana's term as mayor did not result in anything approaching participatory success. It instead perpetuated an inverted clientelistic urban regime. This awkward label seeks to capture the unusual mix of popular power and clientelistic relations found in El Alto at this time. I argue that the city was character-ized by a local state that was controlled by civil society, but it was done in a corrupt and clientelistic way rather than being participatory and genu-inely democratic. El Alto's inverted clientelistic regime featured extensive popular input into local political decision-making but a lack of real popu-lar control over decisions, extremely weak policy outputs, and significant conflict within and between social organizations, the local incumbent party, and the local state. A striking, and unexpected, characteristic of the regime was the movement-left local incumbent party's *antiparticipatory* governance strategy.

What explains this outcome, which appears surprising in light of exist-ing research on participatory urban governance and MAS's history of highly participatory governance in Chapare municipalities it ran in the 1990s?[1] Like the other cases I contend that the combination of national regime type and local balance of class forces helps to explain El Alto's urban political regime. Patana's demobilizing governance strategy closely resembles the passive revolutionary national strategy that MAS increas-ingly adopted from 2010 on. There are reasons for thinking this resem-blance is not entirely coincidental, since Morales chose Patana to be MAS's candidate for El Alto's 2010 mayoral race (over the objections of more than a few grassroots MASistas). Patana's demobilizing governance strategy, in combination with El Alto's popular power balance of class forces, helped perpetuate and deepen inverted clientelistic rule, which had taken hold in El Alto between 2004 and 2010.

The chapter begins with a brief overview of El Alto's socioeconomic structure and historical development. I then discuss the clientelism found in the 1990s and early 2000s. This was interrupted by the 2003 gas war, in which anarchic self-rule briefly took hold. The bulk of the chapter assesses El Alto's inverted clientelistic regime. I end by examining the regime's dynamics and 2015 implosion. Patana was jailed for corruption after his term. His successor was a center-right mayor strongly opposed to participation.

THE MAKING OF THE REBEL CITY

Three facts define El Alto as a city: its poverty, Indigeneity, and contentiousness.

At the time of my research, circa 2010, approximately 70 percent of Alteños lived in poverty. According to Jeffery Webber (2011a, 189–91), 93 percent of the city's economically active population (EAP) can be considered working class, understood "in an expansive sense to refer to those whose labour has been commodified in some way and who do not live off the labour of others" (18). This 93 percent has subcategories: 41 percent of the EAP work as manual laborers, 21 percent as non-manual laborers, and 9 percent as domestic workers and nonremunerated family laborers. Dominant classes, comprising independent professionals, bosses, and owners, account for 7 percent of the EAP. It is critical to note that around 70 percent of El Alto's employment is informal, and this increased in the neoliberal era (191).

El Alto is an important commercial and industrial center. On a daily basis high quantities of commodities pass through the city, which serves as a conduit to the Chilean Pacific coast, the Peruvian Altiplano (high plain), and destinations across Bolivia. El Alto is a market town with an immense open-air market held on Thursdays and Sundays in the 16 de Julio neighborhood. A smaller, but still impressive, daily market is held in the bustling zone of La Ceja (the eyebrow), the main point connecting La Paz and El Alto. According to residents, you can buy any and everything in these markets: produce, clothing, electronic goods, auto parts, cars, and more. El Alto is also one of Bolivia's primary manufacturing centers, with over five thousand production units (Webber 2011a, 189). Ninety-eight percent of these units are small or micro enterprises, with 59 percent of the city's industrial employment occurring in these units. El Alto's few large industries include a Coca-Cola bottling plant, a tannery, and factories producing wooden doors, plastics, and woven goods (191).

Commerce and industry are the two largest sources of employment; other sources are construction, transport and communications, and social and

FIGURE 6.2 La Ceja.

Source: Photo by author.

community services (190). Women predominate in the commercial sector and men in other sectors. Thousands of Alteños work in La Paz as day laborers, domestic workers, street vendors, and in inter-city transport (Arbona and Kohl 2004, 261). Most live, as well as work, in precarity. As of 2001, 93 percent of the city's population lived in substandard housing that lacked one or more basic necessities such as gas, water, and electricity. Seventy-seven percent lived in simple adobe houses. And 37 percent lived in houses lacking toilets (Webber 2011a, 188–89). The near-universality of poverty in El Alto has made the city relatively egalitarian, though scholars argue that economic processes, such as the burgeoning trade in used clothing from the United States, have generated an incipient process of bourgeois class formation that is making the city less equal (Gill 2000, 43; cited in Webber 2011a, 191).

El Alto is also fiscally poor. As of 2003, its tax revenue was one-third that of neighboring La Paz, despite the cities having roughly equal populations at the time (Arbona and Kohl 2004, 263). El Alto collected just one-sixth as much as La Paz from taxes generated from local revenue and one-fourth as much from investment taxes (263). One reason for these differences is that "Bolivian law requires businesses to pay taxes where they are incorporated and have their administrative offices, regardless of where they do business. Remarkably, most factories located in El Alto pay their share of corporate municipal and value added taxes only in La Paz" (263). El Alto's tax base is also limited due to the preponderance of informal employment and its population's contentiousness. Attempts to generate more revenue by increasing residents' taxes have regularly been met with fierce and sometimes violent resistance, with examples of this occurring in 1997 and both February and September 2003 (Hylton and Thomson 2007).

El Alto is not only Bolivia's poorest large city but also its most Indigenous. As of 2001, 81 percent of Alteños self-identified as Indigenous, with 74 percent identifying as Aymara, 6 percent as Quechua, and 1 percent as another Indigenous group or Afro-Bolivian (Webber 2011a, 188). The salience of Indigenous identity is visible in everyday life and the city's politics. The neopopulist party CONDEPA (Conciencia de Patria; Conscience of Fatherland) electorally mobilized Indigenous, and specifically Aymara, identity with great success in El Alto in the 1990s, which helped the party govern the city for a decade. Webber (2011a, 260) argues that during the 2003 gas war Alteños developed a "combined oppositional consciousness" that drew on elements of Indigenous and class struggle. Alteños also express Indigenous identity through architecture, clothing, food and language, with Aymara and (to a lesser extent) Quechua spoken in many neighborhoods. There are at least two reasons for the salience of Indigeneity in El Alto: the racism that has plagued Bolivia since the colonial era and the resistance it has sparked, as well as the fact that most Alteños are from the highlands and retain close ties to surrounding rural communities where Indigenous practices and traditions are integral to everyday life.

As much as by its poverty and Indigeneity, El Alto is defined by its residents' contentiousness. Protest is constitutive of El Alto in many ways, including the most literal: contentious collective action led to El Alto's designation as a city in 1985 and its designation as an autonomous municipality in 1988. (Before this El Alto was a neighborhood and then a district within La Paz.) FEJUVE was the leading force behind the series of increasingly combative mobilizations during the 1980s that resulted in El Alto becoming a city of its own. In his authoritative study of FEJUVE, Máximo Quisbert Quispe (2003, 62) notes that "El Alto's autonomy was the most important political demand of the 1980s." In addition to social mobilization by residents, this victory was also made possible because of the political calculations of La Paz-based political elites, who worried about the strain El Alto's growing population would present for La Paz's fiscal resources and the electoral threat El Alto's residents could pose (Arbona and Kohl 2004, 262).

Protest is also constitutive of El Alto in a material sense, as the city's history shows. In 1950 El Alto was a marginal neighborhood of eleven thousand on La Paz's outskirts. Its population exploded over the next half century, driven by rural-to-urban migration in the 1970s and 1980s and an influx of thousands of ex-miners after the industry was decimated in 1985. El Alto experienced dizzying 8.2 percent annual growth from 1950 to 2002, making it Bolivia's fastest-growing city and one of the fastest-growing cities in the world.

This torrid growth generated a torrent of social needs, which were met—however partially and inadequately—through clientelism and protest. Alteños were present in the urban mobilization that was key to the success of the 1952 Revolution. The Revolution, in turn, enhanced El Alto's importance. During the twelve-year national revolutionary period, the ruling Nationalist Revolutionary Movement (MNR) practiced "single party clientelism" in El Alto, forming clientelistic links to neighborhood councils (NC) that were formed in the 1940s and 1950s (Quisbert Quispe 2003). Through the MNR's intermediation the councils helped link El Alto residents to the national state. The councils also helped lead protests, which forced the state to install public lighting, construct new schools, and implement small-scale social works in the neighborhood of El Alto (42).

The installation of military rule in 1964, and the intense repression of miners and urban workers that accompanied this, led to an initial decline in protest in El Alto (and across Bolivia). Protest reemerged with vigor in El Alto in the late 1970s, particularly with the 1979 formation of FEJUVE-El Alto, which Quisbert Quispe (2003, 45) links to "the growth of the population and basic needs associated with this growth." FEJUVE played an important role in the struggle to end military rule in the late 1970s and early 1980s. The federation also assumed the leading role in local struggles for basic needs and municipal autonomy. According to Quisbert Quispe (2003), El Alto's neighborhood movement engaged in more than eighty episodes of collective action, against rising prices and goods shortages, in the tumultuous period of Democratic Popular Unity (UDP) rule from 1982 to 1985. FEJUVE led the way. In 1984, its president was named mayor of El Alto district, an important step on the path to municipalization four years later (46). FEJUVE spearheaded marches, mass rallies, hunger strikes, road blockades, and more during this period.

I turn now to the clientelism that characterized El Alto's politics in the 1990s and early 2000s.

CLIENTELISM (1990S–EARLY 2000S)

From 1989 to 1999 CONDEPA governed El Alto. Scholars categorize the party as neopopulist due to its personalistic leadership, use of populist rhetoric, and lack of ability or interest in organizing and mobilizing its base through the creation of new civic or partisan institutions. The party differs from other neopopulist forces, such as Argentina's Carlos Menem and Brazil's Fernando Collor de Mello, in two ways: its (vague and inconsistent) opposition to neoliberalism[2] and its emphasis on Indigeneity.

CONDEPA's political articulation of Indigeneity was key to the party's success in El Alto (and La Paz). The central figure behind this approach was the party's founder, Carlos Palenque, who rose to fame in the 1970s and 1980s as the immensely popular host of several radio and television programs catering to working-class Aymara migrants in La Paz and El Alto (Mayorga 2002, 98). Palenque spoke of this work as follows: "We've brought a communitarian conversation of Quechuas and Aymaras to electronic media communication" (Mayorga 2002, 114). The party's 1989 foundational document opposes "any form of colonialism or neocolonialism, including cultural and ideological [forms]" (225). A 1993 programmatic statement of the party's principles critiques "neoliberal policies . . . [which] are characterized by scorn for the value of human life, of health, nutrition, education and employment" (226).

In his media and political work, Palenque assumed the role of the Godfather (or compadre) who came to the rescue of the poor and needy. According to him, the Godfather is "a person identified with the popular sectors, who knows their anxieties and concerns, who knows their problems" (quoted in Mayorga 2002, 114). This quote shows that the party appealed simultaneously to Indigenous and popular-class identity (which in Bolivia have been linked, at times in complex ways). Palenque explained, "There has almost always been a lack of appreciation of the poor classes. So that these sectors have been seen as marginal not only by the governments but also by the press itself." (113).

CONDEPA was electorally dominant during its decade ruling El Alto. The party won 58 percent of the vote in the city's first mayoral election in 1989 and was then reelected three times, winning with a 33 percent plurality in 1991, a 58 percent blowout in 1993, and a solid 49 percent plurality in 1995. It also controlled El Alto's municipal council with a majority throughout this time; one exception was 1991–1993 when the party held a plurality with five of the council's eleven seats (Quisbert Quispe 2003, 64–67). Palenque's 1997 death led to a terminal crisis for the party. It lost El Alto's 1999 mayoral election and disappeared entirely from politics shortly thereafter (Mayorga 2002, 341).

In its decade of rule, CONDEPA exerted significant control over El Alto's key civic institutions, including FEJUVE, COR, and the Asamblea de la Alteñidad (Assembly of Alteño-ness), an umbrella organization active from 1992 to 2000 that played a leading role in the formation of the Public University of El Alto in 2000 (Quisbert Quispe 2003). Other parties also gained influence within these institutions but in a more limited way. This led to a steep decline in these associations' autonomy and mobilizational capacity. According to Quisbert Quispe (2003, 69): "For a considerable length of time FEJUVE lost its capacity to maintain its function as an organic civic structure, and the effects of this were felt in a context of the splitting of the political space." This "splitting" was expressed in two ways: civic organizations' and leaders' loyalty was divided among multiple parties, and organizations literally split into multiple bodies supporting different parties. Examples of this include FEJUVE and the Federation of Small Merchants, which split in 1994, with one branch supporting CONDEPA and another the rival neopopulist UCS party (69).

Scholars judge CONDEPA's rule harshly. Per Aliendre (2002, 14), the party was able to stay in office "despite its administrative management being characterized by a high level of improvisation, completely disordered administration, misuse of resources and scant attention given to the needs of the population." He also holds that "mayors and councillors were switched [on Palenque's orders] even as CONDEPA remained in control of the municipal government. The comptroller initiated charges but the Condepista municipal councillors did not implement the corresponding penalties. To this date, all of the ex-Condepista mayors have active judicial cases against them. The administrative machinery operated according to partisan, and in many cases familial, criteria" (14–15).

From 1999 to 2005, José Luis Paredes of the Revolutionary Left Movement (MIR) was El Alto's mayor (like the MNR, it was a formerly leftist party that embraced neoliberalism in the 1980s and 1990s). Like Palenque, Paredes came to politics through media: he owned a television station and hosted a popular TV program. He spoke of modeling himself after Palenque and Max Fernandez of Unidad Cívica Solidaridad (UCS) (Mayorga 2002). Like these leaders, Paredes adopted a personalistic and populistic political style. He valorized ordinary people on his TV show and mimicked UCS by using a series of well-publicized strategic donations of public works to lay the groundwork for his later political career (Lazar 2007, 103). Paredes also resembled Palenque and Fernandez in running against neoliberalism and then supporting neoliberal policies while in office, specifically promoting free trade and supporting regressive taxation on the poor.

While he copied Palenque's political style, Paredes sought to draw a sharp contrast between his own administration practice, which he claimed was efficient and modern, and CONDEPA's corruption and inefficiency (Lazar 2008). But studies suggest his administration was much like CONDEPA's in practice. Aliendre (2002, 15) found that Paredes "initiated his administration with technical and innovative criteria" but proceeded to run it in a personalistic and politicized fashion. Aliendre points to the fact that only two of the twenty-five employees Paredes hired at the beginning of his term for administrative and financial work had professional or administrative experience. He had an autocratic reputation. Aliendre notes that he had four heads of personnel between 1999 and 2002, since Paredes was unable to get along with any of them for long. He was known for "getting things done" and implemented a number of highly visible works across the city (Revilla 2009). But as of 2002, over halfway into his first term, Paredes's administration had "meager levels of budgetary execution" and poor coordination between administrative levels. Aliendre contends that this inhibited the administration's ability to attend to the population's needs. Paredes's MIR also resembled CONDEPA in the regular accusations of corruption in office directed at the party's leaders (Lazar 2008).

The clientelism of the CONDEPA period also appears to have continued in the Paredes years. Lazar (2008) reports that a pattern of "corporate clientelism," in which communities offered collective support to the party they felt was most likely to win office, remained intact under Paredes. When Paredes won in 1999, communities switched their support from CONDEPA to MIR, and in 2004 they switched again from MIR to Paredes's newly formed Plan Progreso para Bolivia party, as I discuss in the next section. According to Lazar, this clientelism often took the form of MIR and Plan Progreso distributing T-shirts, hats, and food items during campaign rallies. She found that communities offered their support to a given party or candidate in the hopes of receiving preferential treatment if that party won office.

"A TRUE REVOLUTION": ANARCHIC SELF-RULE IN RED OCTOBER (2003)

The 2003 gas war momentously interrupted the workings of politics and everyday life in El Alto, as well as Bolivia as a whole. Hylton and Thomson (2007, 20) view the "October insurrection" as Bolivia's "third revolutionary moment" (the first was the 1780–1781 anticolonial revolution led by Túpac Katari and the second was the 1952 Revolution). They justify this claim by drawing on Trotsky's (1980, 17) famous understanding of revolution:

> The most indubitable feature of a revolution is the direct interference of the masses in historic events. In ordinary times the state, be it monarchical or democratic, elevates itself above the nation, and history is made by specialists in that line of business—kings, ministers, bureaucrats, parliamentarians, journalists. But at those crucial moments when the old order becomes no longer endurable to the masses, they break over the barriers excluding them from the political arena, sweep aside their traditional representatives, and create by their own interference the initial groundwork for a new regime.

Firsthand and scholarly accounts suggest there is truth to the view that "Red October" constituted a revolution in this sense. I view the period as a time of anarchic self-rule, in which communities throughout the city governed themselves in a process of decentralized direct democracy, via what Mamani Ramírez (2005) calls "neighborhood micro-governments." Firsthand accounts emphasize that it was not social or political leaders but ordinary Alteños who made key decisions about what happened in the city during this time. At an October 2010 event commemorating the seventh anniversary of October 2003, Carlos Arce, an Alteño and economist with the leftist think tank CEDLA (Center for Studies of Labor and Agricultural Development), offered this direct account:

> The neighbors were the police, the mayors, they were the power, and they decided who could go where. . . . This was the [people] governing

themselves, surpassing the vision of the leaders . . . In El Alto a true revolution was taking place, in which the workers, who toil daily [. . .] didn't feel capable of governing, but they were doing it. . . . They organized themselves, and they didn't need doctors or lawyers [. . .] to govern.

Wilma Plata, a representative of the La Paz teachers' union, gave this first-hand account:

> The districts were converted into liberated territories in which the neighbors made decisions and carried these decisions out. . . . The neighborhood councils were the leaders, and this was a true popular democracy, a true workers' democracy, in which they made decisions and carried these decisions out. . . . And the method of this, of the October Days, was direct action. . . . We trusted our organization and our strength.

The event where these remarks were made was held in FEJUVE's auditorium, which was filled to capacity. The existence and popularity of fora like this one highlight the long-term significance of the gas war within El Alto. Among other things it continued to serve as a symbolic resource for the city's residents and social and political leaders, who pointed to it as proof of El Alto's importance and rebellious essence.

The city's defining features—its poverty, Indigeneity, and contentiousness—were all key to the October 2003 uprising. In addition to drawing strength from the national cycle of protest that engulfed Bolivia from 2000 to 2005, the gas war built on El Alto's history of collective mobilization. A number of major protests occurred in the city in the three years leading up to October 2003. These include May 2000 protests to create the Public University of El Alto, April 2001 protests against plans to privatize the city's water supply, and February 2003 protests in El Alto and La Paz against an IMF-imposed national government plan to raise local taxes (Mamani Ramírez 2004, 36, 37, 41). The February 2003 protests left thirty-three dead in the two cities and showed the increasing disconnect between civic associations and parties and the local state in El Alto, with protesters burning city hall and the local offices of Bolivia's three traditional parties—MNR, MIR (the local incumbent party), and ADN—as well as that of UCS (41–42).

This severing of the link between civil and political society, which underpinned El Alto's clientelism, was a key precondition for the social explosion that started in September 2003. The proximate cause of this explosion was the mayor's imposition of new tax measures on home ownership and construction, known as the Maya y Paya forms, in August. FEJUVE and COR responded by organizing two civic strikes against the measures, the first on September 8 and the second on September 15–16. The second strike pushed Paredes to abrogate the new taxes.

At the same time, two separate protest streams also engulfed El Alto. One stream demanded the release of Edwin Huampu, a peasant trade-union leader from Cota Cota held in La Paz's San Pedro prison for the murder of two cattle rustlers. As Hylton and Thomson (2007, 110) note, this amounted to an individual punishment for an act of collective justice, since, in accord with Indigenous communal norms, Huampu had carried out a decision that had been made by the community as a whole and sanctioned by the district subprefect. The second protest stream demanded that the government abrogate its plan to export Bolivian gas to Chile; this demand soon morphed into a call for the industrialization of Bolivian gas (113).

The government responded to the protests with heavy repression that left a total of more than sixty dead in El Alto. This brutal and heavy-handed response spurred further protest, with El Alto experiencing a full-scale insurrection during the first two and a half weeks of October. The neighborhood microgovernments that formed during this period of anarchic self-rule served two basic functions: a military one of territorial defense and a political one of coordinating decision-making around the provision of basic goods, particularly food and first aid (Mamani Ramírez 2005). Military-type activities included the construction of road blockades and the control of movement within neighborhoods. Mamani Ramírez reports that residents detained anyone unknown within a neighborhood to protect against police infiltration. During the uprising the military and police regularly sought out neighborhood leaders. Neighborhood microgovernments also exercised control over hours in which stores and pharmacies could be open. Mamani Ramírez (2005, 102) quotes an NC president on how this worked:

> In these days we were converted into a small government (like) we we're saying: what we did to close all the stores, how we put out orders that they should only attend people during certain hours. That alcoholic beverages not be sold; that the people were really united, that the stores, and the pharmacies too, attend to the people. Because of all this, I think that in this moment yes we were a government in the zone. We had to care for children and the elderly. And I think that we were a government, unexpectedly revolutionary, in this moment, right? And the leadership of the neighborhood councils didn't decide everything. The leadership didn't do everything, but rather it was the people ourselves who demanded that we hold meetings and it was us who carried out what was planned; because there [in meetings] we came to conclusions, we made determinations and finally we evaluated what we had done.

This quote highlights a point discussed earlier and emphasized in innumerable accounts of October 2003: the extraordinary decision-making power ordinary Alteños possessed.

This power was exercised in a highly decentralized manner throughout the city. FEJUVE and COR played an important role in setting what came to be known as the "October agenda." It comprised three demands: halting the export of gas to Chile, holding a constituent assembly, and demanding Sánchez de Lozada's resignation for his role in the deaths of dozens of civilians. FEJUVE and COR led three strikes to support these, and earlier, demands. But during the uprising "FEJUVE, COR and the leadership of the street vendors' union were not authorized to meet with the government. As a result the leaders had to follow and comply with the mechanisms of action and collective decisions of the neighborhoods and residents" (Mamani Ramírez 2005, 100). To further illustrate this, Mamani Ramírez gives the example of Jesús Juárez, a local priest the national government asked to intervene with protest leaders. Juárez could not comply and told the government, "There's not even anyone to speak with in

El Alto, every head of a neighborhood is a little king [reyezuelo], everyone is demanding Goni's head" (105).[3]

Accounts of October highlight the entire population's involvement. Young people, particularly young men, played a critical role in the uprising, especially in military-type territorial defense. This central role for youth contrasts with the marginality they faced in El Alto's civic and political life during "normal" times, although youth mobilization was very important in the struggle to create the Public University of El Alto. Neighborhood leaders, such as NC presidents and zone and block leaders, also played a key role, though due to the heavy military presence (which limited leaders' movement) many residents without previous leadership experience were heavily involved in decision-making. Ex-miners, rural and urban Indigenous activists (especially those connected to the Katarista movement), students, the unemployed and street vendors also played important roles (110). The assembly-style participatory democracy through which decision-making occurred drew on two traditions: Indigenous *Ayllus*, a form of collective decision-making practiced in the Altiplano since the eighteenth century (Thomson 2002) and the assemblyism of the miners' union (Mamani Ramírez 2005).

TOWARD INVERTED CLIENTELISM (2004–2010)

The October 2003 uprising produced major immediate and long-term effects on national politics in Bolivia. It forced President Sánchez de Lozada to resign and set the stage for Evo Morales's 2005 election. The uprising's effects within El Alto were more ambiguous. The anarchic self-rule that took hold during that month did not persist. The years following the uprising saw clientelism reconstituted within El Alto, with citizens' access to public resources contingent on supporting particular people. But this clientelism differed from the past because leaders of civic associations, rather than of the local state or political parties, were increasingly positioned as patrons, with citizens and (in a more uneven and messy way) elected and administrative officials positioned as clients. This system can be considered an inverted form of clientelism since the local state and parties are relatively subordinate to civil society, thus reversing the pattern of classical clientelism in which civil society is subordinate to the state or parties.

My fieldwork indicates that this inverted form of clientelism began to take hold in El Alto between 2004 and 2010 (though I cannot establish with precision exactly when it occurred). Local elections were held in December 2004, marking the end of a politically important year. Those hoping for revolutionary change were disappointed when the mayor, José Luis Paredes, was reelected with a 53 percent absolute majority, a rare feat in Bolivian politics.

This outcome would have been hard to imagine during October 2003 since Paredes's attempt to impose new taxes had helped set the uprising in motion. What then explains it? One factor was the failure of those involved in the uprising to channel their insurgent energy into formal politics, which was at least in part due to the youthful character of the uprising. As noted, while young people played a key role in it, this was not true of social and political life in El Alto before. Nor was it true after, according to young activists, such as Abraham Delgado, a participant in the uprising and leader of a radical Katarista group called Jóvenes de Octubre (Youth of October). In an interview, Abraham said that after the uprising corrupt older leaders, who saw their positions 'as a means of social advancement,' reasserted their control over social organizations. These leaders 'closed the door' on youth like Abraham. Since civic associations—specifically FEJUVE, COR, the street vendors' union, the Public University of El Alto, and the urban peasants' union (FESUCARUSU)—controlled candidate selection, Abraham said it was impossible for anyone not a leader of these associations to win an election or even mount a serious candidate. Thus (often more radical) youth were locked out of city politics.

Paredes's skill as a politician also explains his rehabilitation. When the uprising reached its height and it seemed Sánchez de Lozada was unlikely to stay in office, Paredes supported the mobilization, directing members of his party, MIR, to participate in pickets across the city. After it was over, Paredes left MIR (which had allied with Sánchez de Lozada) and formed a new party, Movimiento Plan Progreso. With an eye to the December election, over the course of 2004 Paredes implemented a number of highly visible public works—parks, plazas, gardens, and bridges—across El Alto (Revilla 2009). He spent significant money making sure residents were aware of these projects, with city hall's advertising budget quadrupling between 2000 and 2005. In highly visible billboards across the city, Paredes portrayed himself as the city's benefactor, presenting public works as personal gifts to residents. Billboards featured quotes from residents expressing gratitude to the mayor for these gifts (Revilla 2009). To appeal to the memory of 2003, Paredes associated himself with a discourse of "resistance." His administration erected large billboards in El Alto's central La Ceja district that said, "El Alto is not a problem for Bolivia, it's a solution" and "We've already warned you, the Aymara man is better than the System." Paredes also constructed a Che Guevara monument in La Ceja and used

FIGURE 6.3 "El Alto is not a problem for Bolivia, it's a solution."

Source: Photo by author.

FIGURE 6.4 Che Guevara statue.

Source: Photo by author.

images of the *chakana* (the Andean cross) and the Indigenous Wiphala flag to further associate his administration with support for the 2003 uprising.

Paredes departed the mayor's office in 2005, the first year of his second term, when he was elected prefect of La Paz. El Alto's city council selected Fanor Nava Santiesteban, a city councillor from Paredes's Plan Progreso party, as mayor. Fanor Nava (as he is known) retained this position until his term ended in 2010. Available evidence suggests El Alto's transition to inverted clientelism occurred under him. Civic leaders, municipal officials, and scholars I spoke to about him said Fanor Nava suffered from a lack of legitimacy since he came to office through city council, not an election. To consolidate his authority he sought to establish control over neighborhood councils. Accounts suggest he did so in a thoroughly clientelistic and relatively successful way. But the result was not a simple imposition of the local state over civil society. Civic associations appear to have exerted significant control over Fanor Nava. One form this took was associations "kidnapping the mayor"—detaining him in a given space until he agreed to their demands. Members of the Edgar Patana administration, which succeeded Fanor Nava's, allege that this occurred with great frequency and generated an immense deficit of 500 million bolivianos, since (to end his kidnappings) he would repeatedly agree to projects he lacked funds to complete.

PERPETUATING INVERTED CLIENTELISM UNDER MAS RULE (2010–2015)

In April 2010, MAS's candidate, Edgar Patana, was elected El Alto's mayor. This was doubly historic: it marked the first time a leftist party would control the mayor's office and a social movement leader would be mayor. Patana entered office with big plans to change how El Alto was governed. But these plans were not what one might have expected of a social movement mayor from a movement-left party taking office in "one of the most rebellious urban locales in contemporary Latin America." As detailed in the next section, Patana and his top advisers came to office intensely focused on reshaping city hall's relationship with social organizations, the goal being to *restrict* rather than expand social control and popular participation in decision-making.

The Patana administration's demobilizing governance strategy can be seen as a refraction of MAS's passive revolutionary national strategy. This is less than surprising since Morales handpicked him to be MAS's mayoral candidate for El Alto's 2010 election, reportedly due to Patana's loyalty. His strategy can also be understood in terms of local factors, as a reaction to Patana's and his top advisers' perception that El Alto's dire fiscal situation was due, in large part, to the excessive control social organizations exerted over Fanor Nava. Both national and local factors can thus be seen as contributing to Patana's demobilizing governance strategy.

The combination of this strategy and El Alto's popular power balance of class forces helps account for the perpetuation of inverted clientelism. El Alto's popular power balance of class forces is rooted in the city's class structure. As noted, more than 90 percent of economically active Alteños are from the popular classes. The city's social organizations are clearly rooted in the popular classes. This popular power class force balance helps account for the socially controlled nature of El Alto's clientelistic rule. The key indicators of this social control are having social movement leaders in top positions within the city's government (e.g., the mayor and the head of city council) and institutional mechanisms giving civil society significant (albeit clientelistic) control over the local state.

ASSESSING EL ALTO'S INVERTED CLIENTELISTIC URBAN REGIME

El Alto's inverted clientelistic regime facilitated more extensive and higher-quality popular control over decision-making than Santa Cruz's technocratic clientelistic regime but performed worse on both measures compared to Torres's participatory and Sucre's administered democratic regimes. El Alto performed extremely poorly in terms of institutional and political effectiveness, scoring worse than all the other study cities.

EXTENT OF POPULAR CONTROL

El Alto featured extensive popular input into local political decision-making but limited popular control over decision-making. Popular input into decisions occurred in several ways, including a form of participatory budgeting (PB). (For ease I refer to El Alto's PB in the following discussion, although this term was not used.) Conversations with NC members and leaders suggest El Alto's participatory budget-like system had taken the form described here by around 2006. In 2010, when Patana took office, 20 percent of the city's budget was subject to participatory decision-making. This budget totaled 616 million bolivianos, about 87.9 million USD. Eighty-four percent of the budget (518.4 million bolivianos) was programmed for investment, with the rest allocated to administrative costs.

El Alto's PB had four phases. The first was a pre-*cumbre* (presummit), labeled so since it preceded District Summits, the PB's second phase. I was able to attend the 2010 pre-cumbre, although this took some doing (including paying my own way) as my presence as a foreigner and researcher elicited some suspicion. It took place over two days in October at a resort-style hotel in the Yungas, a beautiful tropical and subtropical forested region a four-hour drive from El Alto. On the drive over in one of the buses hired by the city government, I asked an official I was chatting with why the event was being held so far away. 'So the mayor doesn't get kidnapped,' he replied.

After everyone had checked into their rooms, the pre-cumbre began. One hundred and twenty-five people were present, including the mayor, the heads from city departments and some of their staff, the full staff of the Department of Planning, each district's submayor and Oversight Committee (OC) representative, city councillors, and the leaders of the city's key social organizations, including FEJUVE, COR, and various smaller organizations. The formal portion of the event was a two-day meeting held in a large lecture hall at the resort.

Oscar Cazorla, the director of planning, kicked things off. He explained that the goal was to 'achieve consensus around the 2011 Annual Operating Plan' (POA). Most of the meeting involved the mayor and various officials explaining the relevant laws and regulations covering the 2011 budget process and discussing their goals for the upcoming District Summits. During his opening speech, Patana spoke of wanting to govern differently than in the past. 'We have to do this in a different manner, in a way that is different from what happened before.' This idea of doing things differently, with less conflict and more cooperation from civil society, was a key theme over the two days. After the mayor spoke there was a long round of questions and comments from the assembly. This consisted of specific queries on procedures and the airing of grievances about bureaucracy and limited funds.

At various points Patana spoke about his wish to have a bigger budget. Throughout he pleaded with those assembled to understand the administration's difficult situation due to its large fiscal deficit, limited budget, and lack of options for getting significant new funds any time soon. Various other municipal officials and Zacarías Maquera, the head of city council, answered questions as well.

The pre-cumbre also served a second, quite important, function: providing a space for Patana, who had been in office just four months, to socialize with the leaders of El Alto's key civic associations. Patana and his advisers knew the mayor's success would depend on establishing and maintaining good relations with these leaders. This social portion of the event took place over several relatively lavish lunches and a dinner, as well as a party held the first night of the pre-cumbre. The party involved heavy drinking, as I learned firsthand, when civic leaders and then the mayor himself repeatedly toasted each other and me, proclaiming *al Alteño* and *vacío*, i.e., "bottoms up," as they did so. By all accounts the social portion of the pre-cumbre was a success for the mayor.

It was also very useful to me as a researcher, since the drinking and joking I did with municipal officials, civic leaders, and the mayor seemed to considerably ease their suspicions of me. The morning after the party, however, I learned that some suspicions remained. At one point someone half-jokingly asked, 'How did Obama like your report last night?' I elicited some laughs by responding that he wasn't pleased since it had more errors than usual. On my way to breakfast, an official I had hung out with at the party intercepted me and invited me to a drinking session. This was moments after I evaded a similar invitation from Ruben Paz, a neighborhood council president (and soon-to-be FEJUVE president), whom I saw nodding off hours later. But I could not evade this invitation and followed the official. While my stomach was not pleased, the session appeared to ease officials' suspicions. Carlos Lima, an architect and close confidante of Patana's, grilled me about who I was, why I was here, and if I was with U.S. intelligence. I spoke of my own leftist politics and organizing experience in the United States (including recent efforts to fight budget cuts at UC Berkeley, where I was doing my PhD), and shared my critique of U.S. imperialism and desire to learn from

Latin America's left turn. Carlos appeared impressed, saying, 'It's been my dream to think there are people like this in the U.S. I hope this is all true, and that you're not just going to take the information here and give it to U.S. intelligence.' Whatever lingering doubts he had, Carlos enthusiastically shook my hand several times. I optimistically took this to mean he believed me and was satisfied with my account of myself. Carlos and Gustavo, another official, then told me, 'We believe in the mayor and we'll stay by his side as long as he's leading a true process of change, but as revolutionaries we'll oppose him if he turns his back on this.' The two of them then debated whether the Bolivian Communist Party, which they both belonged to, had betrayed Che Guevara before his death. Carlos insisted the party had, while Gustavo swore it had not.

The relationships I built during the pre-cumbre helped me access the second phase of the PB: District Summits held across the city in October and November. I was able to attend four of the fourteen summits before my presence elicited new suspicions, which led officials to tell me I could not attend any more of them. The summits brought together the mayor, the full Planning Department, district officials (the submayor and OC representative), and presidents of district neighborhood councils (with El Alto having over six hundred councils). The format of the District Summits was similar to the pre-cumbre. Planning Department officials first explained the rules and regulations of the budget process, detailing how much money the district had that year. Patana then spoke of his vision, priorities, hopes, and the challenges his administration faced. This was followed by a period of often-contentious comments, questions, and answers.

The PB's third phase was the neighborhood assemblies, where decisions about spending a zone's funds were made. My own observations and accounts of others indicate that these discussions were typically well attended, deliberative, and consequential, with officials accepting what the assemblies decide. The PB's fourth and final phase was implementation, done by the city or private companies contracted to carry out work, under the supervision of a neighborhood council's president, and the district submayor and OC representative. Accounts suggest this phase was rife with problems of corruption and malfeasance.

El Alto resembled Torres in having consistently high turnout for its PB. Each District Summit I attended in October 2010 was well attended. My quick counts of participants, and the packed auditoriums and meeting rooms where the summits occurred, suggest almost all neighborhood council presidents attended. Neighborhood assemblies also appeared to be well attended. In an assembly I attended in 2010, thirty residents came in a zone of fifty families, suggesting over 50 percent of families were represented. Officials, residents, and civic leaders consistently said turnout was high throughout the PB process.

There was also significant popular input into nonbudgetary decisions in El Alto. This led to some real popular control over decision-making. But my fieldwork suggests that it more often resulted in the clientelistic social control of the state that characterizes inverted clientelism. This input occurred in four ways.

The first was protest, which as noted has been a crucial means by which ordinary Alteños have asserted their demands and met their needs throughout the city's history. Protest itself takes many forms, including marches, road blockades, and "kidnapping" the mayor.

Patana officials I spoke to were highly critical of protest, which they felt undermined their ability to work. In a June 2010 interview, Rosio, an analyst who had worked in the Planning Department since 2007, complained that when a neighborhood wanted a project and could not obtain it through "proper" channels it would take to the streets to demand the project. Like others she said this occurred constantly under Fanor Nava, who she said agreed to projects he had no legal authority to grant. Rosio gave an example from district 5, in which she had a meeting with a neighborhood, and knew the project they wanted could not technically come from the funding source that was available to them. She was about to explain this to the community when the group called the mayor directly and put him on speakerphone so she could hear as he agreed to the project. To her consternation, the community then said, 'It doesn't matter what the law says, nothing can go above the head of the mayor.' According to Rosio, the promises the doctor (as she called Fanor Nava) made led to El Alto's deficit of 500 million bolivianos.

A second form of popular control over nonbudgetary issues was the selection of districts' submayors by neighborhood council presidents. The presidents voted for three candidates. I was told the mayor typically accepted the candidate with the most votes. But this was not always the case; for instance, when the mayor did not trust a choice made by a district's presidents, he would seek to choose the second- or third-place candidate, which unsurprisingly resulted in conflict. In June 2010 road blockades erupted in several districts when Patana choose submayors who were not the first choice of a district's NC presidents.

The third form of nonbudgetary popular input was tripartite bargaining involving the mayor's office, trade unions, and civic associations. An instance of this occurred between February and May 2011 when a conflict erupted between transport unions and FEJUVE over raising bus fares. The unions sought a fare increase, which FEJUVE opposed. Both groups held mobilizations, which threatened to significantly disrupt everyday life in El Alto. This prompted Patana to intervene. He invited both sides to his office to iron out a compromise, though an agreement had not been reached by May 2011, when I left El Alto to travel to Santa Cruz. Officials and civic leaders I spoke to about this dispute said that such negotiations were common in the city.

The fourth form of nonbudgetary popular input into decision-making was the ability of civic associations to impose their personnel choices on the mayor's office in areas corresponding to the association's interest. An example of this would be the Federation of Parents selecting the city's Education Department director. In a June 2010 interview Rosio noted an example of this occurring in the Office of the Promotion of Entrepreneurial and Micro-Enterprise Investments. She said Patana had selected a director for the office earlier that month, but the federation rejected the mayor's choice and forced him to rescind it. He had yet to choose someone, several weeks later, but Rosio was sure the federation would choose someone they could control.

Other officials also complained of this "problem" of social organizations forcing the mayor to appoint one of their leaders to a top municipal post and the official being loyal to the organization rather than the mayor. Officials said this practice had been widespread under Fanor Nava, and they wanted it to end. Evidence suggests they were not successful. In July 2016 I interviewed David Minaya, the director of the Department of Planning in the administration of Patana's successor, Soledad Chapetón. Minaya spoke of the mayor's goal of 'putting our house in order' by hiring more professionals. He complained that 'the social organizations just tried to get people into positions.' He continued, 'Without minimizing social leaders . . . they don't have the academic formation' needed to succeed as municipal officials. According to him, the practice of social organizations putting "their people" into office was systemic under Patana. 'This led to very bad quality works. . . . We're trying to end this *mamadera*,'; this term, which literally means milk bottle, refers to the practice of city officials being forced to grant (what they feel are) unwarranted, politically derived privileges to civic leaders.

Minaya's analysis, which of course cannot be considered unbiased, is supported by Carlos Revilla, a researcher with UNITAS (National Network of Institutions for Social Action Work); Carlos is also the brother of former La Paz mayor Luis Revilla, of the center-left Movimiento Sin Miedo (MSM or Fearless Movement) party, and a resident of El Alto.[4] I spoke with Carlos several times during my fieldwork, including in July 2016. In this interview, he told me that social organizations, and particularly COR, the street vendors' union, and transport unions, were the main organizational base of the Patana administration. Carlos said these organizations 'managed to insert themselves or their children into all the spaces within City Hall. . . . There was a total occupation of City Hall by social leaders.'

The analysis provided by Minaya and Carlos is also supported by what top Patana administration officials told me. These officials felt social organizations wielded far too much power over the mayor and that undermined bureaucratic coherence within the administration. Several of Patana's top advisers told me of the folk theory they developed to make sense of this situation, which they called "the thesis of the dictatorship of the social organizations." I asked one of the officials who regularly used this phrase, Heriberto Mamani, director of the Office of the Environment, what it meant. He replied, 'We need to have participatory planning . . . but when participation is greater than what is expected, this leads to projects being done without any planning . . . [and] the dictatorship of the social structures [as he also referred to the "thesis"] prevents us from having ordered planning.' Heriberto pointed to "social pressure," meaning "threats, blockades, marches," as part of this "dictatorship," and said that this pressure 'distorts ordered planning.'

I pressed Heriberto on what could be done to resolve the situation. He said, 'We want to generate a level of responsibility, and not just have a small group running things. . . . We want to recover the role as the municipal authority . . . to have the mayor be the authority who defines what roles' different groups will have.' He complained that 'in the name of social control, people always ask for more' than they should. One example of this was neighborhood council presidents controlling the process of selecting sub mayors. 'According to the law, the mayor is supposed to name these, as people whom he trusts . . . but the [council] presidents have gained control.' Heriberto hoped the mayor could reassert his authority but acknowledged it could take several years and be difficult. 'This is the dictatorship of society over the municipality,' he said with exasperation. I continued to press him on how to stop this. He said, 'We want to have limited participation.' A minute later he added, 'Projects have to be managed in a technical manner.'

Heriberto was far from alone in wanting to have "limited participation." Patana administration officials repeatedly made similar statements when I asked about participation. In October 2010 I gave a brief presentation to the Planning Department about Torres's PB. I naively expected the officials to be excited about ways they might emulate Torres's highly participatory model of planning. Officials were excited about my presentation, but it was not because of how participatory Torres was but rather how *orderly* it was. After I finished my presentation, one of the officials commented, 'The participation of the people is important, but in this moment the most important thing is to make sure that rules are put in place. And we have to start internally.'

These examples perfectly capture the Patana administration's attitude toward popular participation, which was seen as important but clearly secondary to the much more pressing goal of establishing order. In the months I spent meeting with Patana's officials, I repeatedly heard them speak of the need to "put our house in order" and get residents and civic associations and leaders to "follow the rules." All this points to how El Alto compares to the three other study cities. The lip service Patana officials universally paid to participation contrasts with the full-throated rejection of participation by Santa Cruz officials. Yet El Alto resembles Santa Cruz in prioritizing order over participation and adopting a demobilizing governance strategy as a means of achieving this. In both respects El Alto differs from Torres and Sucre, where participation was central and was pursued through a strategy of organizing and mobilizing popular classes (with this going significantly further in Torres than Sucre). These similarities between El Alto and Santa Cruz, on one hand, and Torres and Sucre, on the other, were a surprise to me during my fieldwork (as noted) and pushed me to develop the general theoretical argument of the book, that a country's national political regime can shape how local governance plays out, and the specific argument that the presence or absence of leftist hegemony at the national level is key to understanding participatory success and failure in the four cases.

QUALITY OF POPULAR CONTROL

Evidence indicates that decision-making in El Alto's PB was deliberative. As noted, decision-making occurred in the PB's third phase, neighborhood assemblies. I attended such an assembly on November 6, 2010, in the 6 de Junio zone of district 3. The zone contains approximately fifty families, and the assembly had thirty participants, suggesting more than half the zone's families had someone present. Don Felix Choque, the neighborhood council president, facilitated the discussion. Residents debated two projects: paving a section of road or constructing a sidewalk. The discussion lasted an hour. Due to traffic, I arrived toward the end. Doña Beatrice, a resident of the zone, walked me through what was discussed before I arrived. Residents favoring the street-paving project argued that it would help reduce dust and problems related to rain. Those favoring the sidewalk countered that paving the road was too expensive; because of the lack of funding they would be unable to use asphalt, which was the best but also the costliest material for the job. Beatrice said she herself favored the sidewalk and had told the assembly, 'We need the sidewalk because when it rains the water gets into the houses.' She and other residents said the assembly had unanimously voted to approve the sidewalk, with residents favoring the street paving also supporting this once it was clear the sidewalk project would win. My conversations about neighborhood assemblies with other city residents, officials, and civic leaders suggest that this assembly was typical of what occurred across El Alto, with interviewees all saying decision-making in these assemblies was deliberative and binding, with district and municipal officials moving forward with residents' decisions.

My research indicates El Alto's PB was highly inclusive in terms of class and race and ethnicity. This is likely at least partially a reflection of the city's demography. As noted, over 80 percent of Alteños self-identify as Indigenous and over 90 percent are from the popular classes. Participation in El Alto's PB reflected this, with most participants being Indigenous and from the popular classes. According to residents, officials, and civic leaders, participation in assemblies (including but not only for PB) was highest in the city's peripheral zones, where recently arrived migrants (who were among the poorest in the city and also those most closely connected to highland community practices) lived.

I found that El Alto's PB and civic spaces generally were less inclusive in terms of gender. Information I gathered through interviews and direct observation suggested that women held 10 percent or fewer neighborhood council presidencies. This post is a key conduit to higher positions within FEJUVE, which itself is seen as a "trampoline" for local political careers. This makes the 2010 election of Fanny Nina as FEJUVE's president a historic moment, with Fanny the first woman to ever lead the organization. But she did not last long as president. She faced fierce resistance throughout her four months and was then ousted, for two reasons: her conflictual relationship to MAS and the often-open misogyny she faced from FEJUVE's largely male organizational- and neighborhood-level leadership. Among other things, Fanny's saga points to the marginalization of women within FEJUVE. Available information suggests women made up between a third and half of participants in neighborhood council meetings. In NC meetings I attended I saw women speak at a rate about a third that of men, with interviews about this issue indicating that this was generally the case.

El Alto's PB and civic spaces generally appeared reasonably inclusive vis-à-vis political views. I asked dozens of NC presidents I met during my research about their political views, and I was always told "we are civic." FEJUVE members and leaders from the top to the bottom of the organization repeated this mantra. But this civic ideology masked a more complex reality: NC members and presidents said councils typically sought to align themselves with the party holding power locally. Santiago Chino, a leader from a NC in district 3, put it this way: 'The presidents are like wheat stalks. . . . When the wind blows this way, they go this way, [and] when it blows that way, they go that way. . . . They're always putting out their hands.' Additionally, as detailed in the next section, clientelism persisted under Patana, albeit in an inverted form.

I found no evidence of anyone being excluded from neighborhood assemblies or District Summits based on their political views. There did appear to be some exclusion based on age, with young people saying they were largely barred from holding leadership positions in neighborhood councils or FEJUVE itself. The youth who told me this tended to have more radical, and explicitly leftist, views, which might indicate some implicit exclusion of such views in the leadership of NCs and FEJUVE. I did collect very solid evidence that MAS sought to increase its representation in FEJUVE and NCs' leadership. Evidence about this in FEJUVE is presented in the section below on political effectiveness. Another piece of evidence came from a series of conversations I had with Don Elias Segara, who was the district 4 Oversight Committee representative when I first met him in November 2010, but he was removed from this position in January 2011. When I spoke to Don Elias about this, he said MAS was behind it. 'They want to dominate everything.' Don Elias said he was removed from the OC because he was seen as being too close to the district's former submayor, whom Patana had recently deposed. According to him, 'The sub mayors say that they have to be with the mayor or they won't get projects from him.' I was unable to systematically verify this allegation but evidence presented in the next two sections shows MAS made a concerted and relatively successful effort in 2010 and 2011 to assert control over El Alto's local state and civil society.

INSTITUTIONAL EFFECTIVENESS

The most glaring deficiency of El Alto's inverted clientelistic regime is its institutional ineffectiveness. Objective and subjective indicators both show the municipal government's persistent and severe difficulties implementing projects. Figure 6.5 presents data, compiled by the Office of the Vice President, on budgetary execution in El Alto compared to the average of Bolivia's six largest cities from 2005 to 2011. (Unfortunately the office did not make data available after 2011.) As the figure shows, with the exception of 2009, El Alto's budgetary execution rate was below the

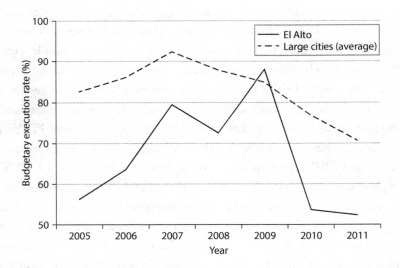

FIGURE 6.5 Budgetary execution in El Alto versus Bolivia's large-city average, 2005–2011. (The average is of Bolivia's six largest cities: Cochabamba, El Alto, La Paz, Oruro, Potosi, Sucre and Santa Cruz.)

Source: Ejecución Presupuestaria, http://vmpc.economiayfinanzas.gob.bo /EjecucionPresupuestariaVarios.asp?t=GM, April 1, 2012.

large-city average for this entire period. In 2010, El Alto's rate plunged to 54 percent, a decrease of over thirty points, which is twenty points below the large-city average. The rate fell slightly in 2011, rose modestly to 59 percent in 2012 (La Razón 2013), and then fell to a new low of 40 percent in 2013, which earned El Alto a rare public rebuke from Vice President Álvaro García Linera.[5]

Subjective indicators also point to a high degree of institutional ineffectiveness in El Alto. In the more than a hundred interviews and conversations I had during my fieldwork in El Alto with residents, base- and higher-level civic leaders, MAS members and leaders, municipal officials, and others, the subject of corruption regularly came up. I was told without fail that it was a very significant problem. I asked nearly everyone I spoke with to estimate how extensive corruption was in neighborhood councils, and I specifically asked for the percentage of NC presidents the person estimated to be corrupt. The lowest estimate I was given was 50 percent, and the highest was 90 percent. While my collection methods were imprecise, the answers give a sense of Alteños' near-universal view that corruption was pervasive.

In an October 2010 interview, Willy Paco, a youth leader of an Indianist *autodeterminación* (self-determination) group that was dubbed "Los Talibanes" after the group put out a pamphlet sometime in 2002 or 2003 analyzing conflict in the Mideast and the United States' role in it, provided his analysis of corruption in El Alto. Willy said it worked through NC presidents, who typically acted in cahoots with the district submayor and OC representative. 'They get the [budget] money and invite companies run by their friends, or a family member, or someone they know. . . . They ask for a percentage of the project, often known as *diesmo* [based on 10 percent being asked for] . . . and often this diesmo also goes to the submayor, to the neighborhood councils and the Oversight Committee, though in some cases not.' He added, 'It's similar in the municipality as a whole, with diesmo, and sometimes six, seven, [or] eight times this.'

Willy's account matches what others told me. During the 2010 precumbre, I sat down with Victor Hugo Rodríguez, who had worked in El Alto's government for six years and was then the coordinator of the Office of Works and the Environment. Like Willy, Victor Hugo said corruption operates through NC presidents working with the submayor and OC representative. Victor Hugo said they channel projects to friends, family, or their own small businesses, in exchange for a percentage of the cost. 'And if the president, the Oversight Committee [representative] and the submayor are all getting a certain percentage, you know the quality of the project will be poor.' An NC leader from district 8 offered similar thoughts on how corruption worked: 'For a street project it might cost 50,000 bolivianos for the paving, the work, everything . . . but they submit an elevated amount, and then this amount gets certified by the submayor.'

Many people said corruption was often small scale; for instance, an NC president might act alone or with others to siphon off a portion of physical materials delivered for a zonal project. In a meeting in district 5 that included the submayor and other district officials, an engineer from the city government discussed a recent case of corruption in which five hundred bags of cement and other materials had gone missing. She said this had prompted a change in the city's policy. 'We will do public handovers of materials. You should tell the [neighborhood council] presidents this, and the bases, those who will receive the materials, should be there for the handover.'

Patana administration officials knew and worried about the seemingly pervasive corruption within the city, but their promises to end this appeared to bear little fruit. In my October 2010 interview with him, I asked Willy if corruption was still occurring under Patana and how he could know if it was. He said, 'It's still happening. . . . We know because we've asked for projects, and the full amount has already been paid, but the project hasn't been completed.' In July 2016, when Patana had been out of office for a year and a half, Carlos Revilla said, 'There were many very major acts of corruption, and Patana is in jail now because of this. . . . Contractors said that they had to pay 10 percent to obtain contracts. And this was generalized' throughout city hall. As Carlos noted, Patana was then in jail, having been sent there in late 2015, less than a year after he left office, on charges of misappropriating thirty-three municipal vehicles. In 2017 Patana was convicted of this and related charges and sentenced to serve four years (La Razón 2017).

POLITICAL EFFECTIVENESS

El Alto is the most institutionally and politically ineffective of the four cases. This is unlikely to be a coincidence since an incumbent party that consistently fails to deliver reliable policy outputs is likely to suffer politically. Patana's fate is consistent with this view. In March 2015 he was trounced in his reelection bid, with Soledad Chapetón of the center-right Unidad Nacional party winning 54 percent to his 32 percent.[6] Unidad Nacional also won a city council majority, taking six of the council's eleven seats. It is likely that the widespread belief that Patana was an inept and corrupt mayor was a significant factor in the election. After he took office in mid-2010, Patana's brief honeymoon period lasted six months at most, with civic leaders criticizing him strongly from early in his term. These critiques centered on his inability or unwillingness to complete unfinished projects. Whatever outside chance Patana might have had in 2015 was dashed a few weeks before the election when a video from 2008—when he was the head of COR—was released showing him accepting an envelope (believed to contain wads of cash) from then-mayor Fanor Nava.[7] To Patana's many critics, the video offered incontrovertible proof of his corruption, which (if the video is to be believed) started years before he became mayor.

The high degree of conflict within and between civil society, political society, and the local state is another indicator of the political ineffectiveness of El Alto's inverted clientelistic regime. Gramsci's (1971, 181) concept of the "economic-corporate level" of class formation provides a useful way to understand this. This is "the first and most elementary" of three levels. It is characterized by a very limited form of solidarity that extends only to others in a particular branch of trade: "a tradesman feels *obliged* to stand by another tradesman, a manufacturer by another manufacturer, etc., but the tradesman does not yet feel solidarity with the manufacturer; in other words, the members of the professional group are conscious of its unity and homogeneity, and of the need to organise it, but in the case of the wider social group this is not yet so" (emphasis in original). The second level of class formation is the "economic class," in which there is solidarity across branches among all members of a given class, such that workers feel solidarity with other workers, and manufacturers with manufacturers, across trades. The third, and highest, level of class formation is the hegemonic; as discussed earlier in the book, this is the "purely political" level in which a ruling bloc succeeds in representing its interests as the interests of all. Among other things, it involves a state-mediated process of class compromise through the coordination of inter- and intra-class interests.

During the primary period of my fieldwork in 2010 and 2011, I found that the actions of the local state, incumbent party, and civic associations resembled the limited solidarity Gramsci ascribes to economic-corporate class politics. Different organizations openly pursued their particularistic organizational interests and made little effort to coordinate their interests with the interests of other organizations. Using language that could have come straight from Gramsci, in March 2011 Carlos Lima, who as noted was one of Patana's top advisers, criticized the city's social organizations. 'They don't have a breadth. The street vendors just have a street vendor vision [*los gremialistas solamente tiene una vision gremialista*]. They see things according to their sectoral interests, but don't see beyond that. There's a lack of a bigger vision.' Evidence presented suggests the local state itself also operated in an economic-corporate way, with department heads pursuing the interests of the organization that put them in office rather than following the mayor's, or his trusted advisers', directives.

MAS's actions in El Alto at this time also followed an economic-corporate logic, as can be seen in the party's highly conflictual relations with both the mayor's office and FEJUVE. Patana's relationship with MAS, the party he ran and governed with, was strained from the time his 2010 candidacy was announced because he was not an "organic" MASista, i.e., a party militant who gradually rose through the ranks and was chosen by grassroots party members. As noted, Morales, not the party's base in El Alto, chose Patana. MASistas in the city told me there was significant grassroots opposition to what was seen as an imposition from above. Rosalía del Villar, an organic MASista and *constituyente*, i.e., delegate in the 2006–2008 constituent assembly, told me in 2010 that grassroots party members did not trust Patana due to rumors of his and his family's corruption and close relations with traditional parties and politicians, like ex-mayor Fanor Nava.

The contentious relationship between MAS and the Patana administration was on display during the December 2010 "gasolinazo." On December 26, Álvaro García Linera, acting as interim president while Morales was abroad, issued a decree abruptly raising the price of gas. This prompted a nationwide social explosion. In El Alto protesters attacked and seriously damaged city hall along with the offices of MAS, FEJUVE, and COR. I was away when this occurred but arrived back to El Alto in January 2011, just a few weeks after. I spoke with several of Patana's top advisers about what had transpired. They were furious with MAS-El Alto since the party had not mobilized to defend city hall. The officials felt this was a betrayal of the mayor.

These officials called MAS 'a bunch of *buscapegas*,' a disparaging term for someone who tries to use their political connections to obtain a government job (*pega*). Patana's top advisers were not the only ones who used this term

FIGURE 6.6 Broken windows of COR-El Alto office after the "gasolinazo" protest.

Source: Photo by author.

to describe MAS-El Alto; on multiple occasions I heard others, including grassroots MASistas, use the term. I spent February 2011 investigating this charge, by shadowing the MAS-El Alto director, Pascual Arellano, on his daily rounds. My investigation led me to the unambiguous conclusion that whatever its linguistic merits, the term buscapegas was analytically appropriate since pegas were MAS-El Alto's overriding focus. In the weeks I shadowed him, Pascual began his day by gathering a group of fifteen to twenty-five party members in La Ceja. For the next several hours or more, Pascual and the group would visit local, regional, and national government offices to ask about pegas. He and the other group members used the term pega openly and matter-of-factly. Lucío, a tailor and MASista from district 6 whom I spoke to regularly during my time shadowing Pascual, at one point commented, 'The point of political parties is pegas . . . [and] the [point of] neighborhood councils is to get projects.' The following day another MASista from Pascual's group said, 'We can have ideology, and we can be with the process of change . . . but the people need jobs.' In addition to showing the group's focus on pegas, these comments also point to the demographic reality of El Alto's high rates of unemployment and poverty. As these MASistas said, the people needed jobs. Pascual needed pegas because they gave him followers, which he badly needed since his position of leadership was at the time contested by two other leaders within MAS-El Alto. Each of the leaders commanded around fifteen to thirty followers, with Pascual at the time commanding the most. But this command was precarious and dependent on pegas.

This provides a context for understanding his open and even gleeful efforts at the time to "break" one of the municipal unions. I learned of these efforts during lunch with him and his group on February 8, 2011, when Pascual announced, 'We have to break the union.' He then outlined a plan to do so, noting that it would open up 'hundreds of pegas.' In coming weeks he and other MAS-El Alto leaders strategized about this. In a February 15 party meeting in district 13, Delia Peñaloza, a MAS city councillor, said a significant number of pegas could open up soon. 'This would involve breaking the union . . . and there could be up to four hundred positions.' Two days after this, Pascual held a press conference outside the Alcaldía

Quemada, where many of the city's offices were housed. (The name referenced the fact that the building had been partially destroyed by a fire set during a protest years before.) During his press conference Pascual put in place a key part of the strategy to break the union: denouncing 'irregularities among city workers.'

A few months before this event MAS had engaged in what could be termed an effort to "break" FEJUVE and gain control over the organization. The focus of this effort, which was at its height from September through November 2010, was removing FEJUVE's recently elected president, Fanny Nina, the first woman to hold this post. Fanny had incurred the national MAS's wrath for the conflictual way in which she related to Morales, such as publishing a *pliego petitorio* (petition sheet) and pushing him hard to fulfill the demands it listed. There were also rumors that Fanny was close to MSM, a center-left party that held La Paz's mayoralty and was seen as one of MAS's main competitors. The effort to oust Fanny was openly misogynist. Her critics spread the fact that she was hospitalized for menstrual bleeding after a critic in an NC meeting physically attacked her.

In November 2010, the campaign against Fanny succeeded. FEJUVE's vice president, Claudio Luna, who was understood to be close to MAS, replaced Fanny. All this was costly for FEJUVE. During the conflict and for months after, the organization was split at all levels, from neighborhood councils to the executive council, between pro- and anti-Fanny factions. After Claudio replaced her, Fanny was physically locked out of her old office. She responded by setting up a desk in the hallway outside the office and holding office hours. Fanny continued her efforts to regain the presidency for months. Claudio might have held on as president were it not for the gasolinazo and his allegedly "wishy-washy" response to it. At the height of the protests, Claudio stayed home. He said he feared for his life, which is very plausible given the destructive protest directed at FEJUVE's office (and that of other organizations) at the time. But in the eyes of FEJUVE's leadership and base, Claudio's actions looked weak and indecisive, and he was ousted weeks later. Rubén Paz (whom I got to know during the precumbre) was installed as FEJUVE's new president. Months of uncertainty followed, with Claudio briefly reinstated as president in May 2011 before

Rubén was finally able to consolidate his presidency. All the while Fanny continued to denounce her removal.

These conflicts played out amid the most sustained popular-sector criticism Morales had faced since being elected, with major protests around rising food prices happening. The gasolinazo had contributed to rising prices, which the measure's abrogation had not managed to halt. In March 2011 FEJUVE and COR held separate marches the same week against MAS and Morales to protest the rising prices. This is another indicator of the economic-corporate character of politics in El Alto. The dueling marches contrast with coordinated actions that occurred in 2008 at the height of Morales's conflict with the Right. A major difference was that in 2008 MAS's actions helped coordinate different social organizations, but by 2011 the party had ceased to play this role. Instead, as the protests made evident, the party was increasingly the target of popular sector wrath.

FIGURE 6.7 COR march (from El Alto to La Paz) against rising food prices, March 2011.

Source: Photo by author.

While this section has highlighted the criticisms MAS faced in El Alto and nationally, it is important to underscore the complexity of Alteños' relationship to the party in these years. Many criticized MAS at the local and national level but still strongly identified with the "process of change" that Morales and MAS were now seen as embodying. A key reason many Alteños (and others) identified with this was the sense that Morales's election had struck a major blow against racism. Consider what Fausto, a base-level MASista from district 13, told me when I asked him about the process of change:

> The process of change is about reforming the laws, it's about reorganiza-
> tion, as with the new constitution, about laws like the new law against
> racism and the law against corruption. . . . And the process of change
> has brought us a sense of recognition and respect. . . . Before we were
> forgotten. We weren't seen as being a part [of this country]. We weren't
> seen as Bolivians [mentions how the ancestors of the Indigenous were
> slaves]. . . . Now we can say that we're Bolivians. We have a vote and a
> voice now. The process of change has made them respect us as people.
> We were discriminated against . . . but now we can enter the govern-
> ment, now we can enter a five-star restaurant, even a *Chola* wearing the
> *pollera*. We have respect now. . . . But the difficulty now is to put these
> laws into practice, which won't be easy. . . . An example is the law against
> racism. The Right is behind the press, and is also behind the Church. . . .
> This is the idea of change . . . There are now 40 languages of ours that
> are recognized. Before you could only speak Spanish, and now we can
> speak our languages, and the public functionaries need to speak two
> languages . . . Before we had to express ourselves in Spanish, but we'd
> feel embarrassed because we couldn't and so we'd remain silent, but now
> we can speak any language, in parliament, in the media . . . The ideo-
> logical struggle of the original peoples . . . it's to manage the republic of
> Bolivia ourselves, to rule ourselves, instead of being ruled. . . . In 50 years
> or more we'll get there. . . . It's a long process, not overnight. . . . We have
> to have Aymara projects, professionals. . . . This will be our liberation,
> those governing will never give this to us. . . . The day that we have our

own Aymara businesses then we can say we've won the war. Until then we've won the battle but not the war. . . . We're also interested in helping Bolivians abroad [he spent several years working in Argentina, and was working on voting rights for Bolivians abroad]. . . . We're millions, exploited, working without any schedule, discriminated against, expelled, killed. . . . There are millions of Bolivians abroad.

There is a great deal to unpack in this quote. The point I emphasize here is the many positive ways ordinary Alteños related to Morales, MAS, and the process of change, which MAS and Morales were increasingly identified with, though it originated in the 2000—2005 protest cycle.

The political ineffectiveness of Patana, and the inverted clientelistic regime he presided over, can also be seen in his stormy relationship with social organizations. This was apparent during the October 2010 District Summits, just a few months into his term. In contrast to Torres and (to a lesser extent) Sucre, where PB appeared to largely elicit consent, I observed frequent expressions of dissent in El Alto's District Summits. This occurred in two of the four summits I attended, in districts 3 and 4. (Both are urban, and I notably observed less dissent in the two rural District Summits I attended. This may be due to MAS's greater strength in rural areas.) To illustrate this dissent I provide a number of the comments NC presidents made in the district 4 summit. While some NC presidents offered praise, most were highly critical, particularly of bureaucratic red tape and the lack of funding for and execution of projects:

- We presidents work voluntarily, without pay . . . but the card [required to submit a project] requires things that cost money. . . . We're entering into more bureaucracy. . . . I'd like an easier, more direct way to enter projects . . . directly to the Oversight Committee.
- I have an avenue, and the paperwork, and don't have anywhere to go to get help. . . . For three years this has gone on . . . [so] when will it be approved? Never. When will we see improvements in the zones? Never. . . . These resources are nothing. . . . Give us more.

- The Planning Department is mistaken. . . . Before, they would tell us how much it would cost for filling out the card. . . . Now they're doubling the bureaucracy . . . making things more complicated [scattered applause greets this].

- I'm a bit indignant with this proposal, where we have to have zonification [i.e., official status as a zone before submitting projects]. . . . This means that we won't be doing projects. . . . If we're not doing projects, where are we going? This is not going to lead to projects being completed. . . . And a question: what's the fear of deconcentrating projects that are under five hundred thousand [bolivianos]? We know the requirements in our zones. . . . I ask you to annul the requirement for the zonification. You, Director Cazorla, are hurting the municipal government. . . . This is not [going to lead to] completing projects. I ask that this be annulled. (This speech was followed by strong applause.)

- Unfortunately, we're worried. . . . There are more papers, more bureaucracy. . . . W're asking that you help us, Mr. Mayor in the small zones,. . . . The big zones have [resources] and can complete projects. . . . Will you help the small zones? With four to five thousand [bolivianos] what can we do?

- [First comment from a woman] Please do more to help, submayor and in the central office, because those of us presidents who are new don't know what to do. . . . We're told to go here and there, and that takes up days. . . . Give us an orientation. . . . Functionaries [elsewhere] are more open, in Santa Cruz and Cochabamba, but they're very closed in La Paz, and El Alto. . . . In my zone we don't have any streets paved. . . . This isn't enough. I'm registering this complaint in the name of my bases and asking for your help . . . to get more money in the budget. . . . We need a sewer system. . . . This whole sector is abandoned. . . . Thank you.

- Thanks, mayor, for your presence, to explain how the POA is handled. . . . On the technical card, we have to comply with all of these requirements. . . . So thanks for making this more flexible [others shout "hurry"]. . . . I want to register a complaint that the low zones are forgotten, they get flooded with water [more shouts].

- Mr. Mayor, we want you to come and look at the lower zones, . . . What can we do with fifteen thousand [bolivianos]. . . . We ask for participation and rotation. . . . We want smaller projects to be administered by the submayor. . . . We have no paved streets.
- [Many more comments occur, with the mayor and other officials occasionally responding.]
- [Third comment from a woman, with all other comments from men] Where's the change? There are no projects. We need projects. What are you doing, Mr. Mayor? How much was spent on your vacation to Coroico [for the pre-cumbre]? You're spending money on advertising, but what are you advertising? Mr. Mayor, let's work for the district and for the city of El Alto. [applause]
- We've seen nothing. . . . Until this point we have no projects. . . . There's lots of propaganda and no projects. . . . In [my zone] we don't have good [transportation] or public lighting. . . . How long will we wait, Mr. Mayor?
- [Rare comment offering some support, and some criticism, to the mayor] I'll speak up in support of the mayor, who has come and is committed to the full execution of the first project package. It's a million and a bit, which is nothing for the first package. . . . How much money from the president? . . . I believed that we would be discussing what we want here, but there's no money. . . . The first package of projects has to be finished completely, and then the second package of projects should be started. . . . But how much money is there?

Over the coming months things deteriorated even more for Patana. By January 2011 FEJUVE leaders were openly musing about seeking a recall referendum against him. In July 2011 a FEJUVE executive council member from district 14 told me, 'The mayor is still very weak because of the lack of project execution. In district 14 we've asked to hold a revocation referendum on the mayor.' While Patana did not face a recall, his term cannot be considered a success politically given his opponent's landslide victory in the 2015 election and Patana's subsequent jailing.

THE END OF INVERTED CLIENTELISM?

In 2015, Soledad Chapetón became the first woman elected mayor of El Alto. Like her predecessors, Chapetón promised to end clientelism and corruption. In a July 2016 interview, approximately a year into her term, David Minaya, her director of planning, spoke of the need to "order the house." He also commented that social organizations had grown accustomed to doing as they pleased. What is striking about his comments is how similar they are to what I heard from Patana's top advisers. This similarity points to the continuity of many long-standing patterns found in El Alto, where a new administration feels vexed by the "excessive" power of social organizations and expresses its determination to bring these organizations to heel.

But the Chapetón administration stands out for its expressed desire to bypass social organizations entirely. In a July 2016 interview, Gumercindo Flores, the director of culture, said, 'The mayor is trying to apply the concept of government, to apply the laws.' He said she 'isn't going to work with the social organizations, not directly.' I am not able to assess whether Chapetón succeeded in this goal. Evidence presented from earlier administrations suggests doing so would be far from easy. Chapetón learned this fact in March 2016 when a protest outside city hall resulted in a fire that killed six people. Her administration blamed the fire on school councils, which they said had been promised contracts to run "dignified schools" by Patana before he left office. The councils were apparently pressing her to make good on his promise. Her refusal led to the protest that resulted in the fire at city hall.

When I started my research I thought that El Alto was likely to be the most successful of the four cities I would study. On paper, it seemed exceedingly well positioned for robust participatory reform. The city was globally famous because of its truly impressive social movements, which had toppled consecutive presidents just a few years before. And in 2010, the year I commenced my fieldwork, El Alto elected its first-ever leftist mayor, a social movement leader backed by MAS, Bolivia's movement-left ruling party. What more could one ask for in terms of conditions favoring participatory success?

As this chapter has shown, El Alto was anything but a success in participatory terms. As detailed in the preceding pages, the city's social organizations have continued to flex their muscles and exerted significant control over the local state. But instead of leading to participatory democracy, it instead created an inverted clientelistic regime; resources were distributed in a particularistic fashion, but civic leaders rather than local state officials played leading roles. The city's social organizations effectively held the city government hostage (sometimes quite literally) by regularly forcing the mayor to appoint civic leaders who were loyal to their organizations rather than the mayor. The mayor reacted to this by governing in a manner unexpectedly similar to his counterpart in Santa Cruz: seeking to limit participation and control civil society.

To explain this unexpected outcome I have pointed to local and national factors, in particular the local dynamics just described and MAS's post-2010 passive revolutionary turn. El Alto's MASista mayor governed in a manner that bore a notable resemblance to the party's national strategy, with an emphasis on demobilizing movements and establishing control and order. As with the other three cases, my case study of El Alto points to the need to pay attention to how national political dynamics can shape urban governance, in sometimes surprising ways, namely by inducing mayors like Percy Fernandez and Edgar Patana, who are on opposite sides of the political spectrum and administered notably different cities, to govern in a strikingly similar, antiparticipatory way.

CONCLUSION

From Making Democracy Safe to Making It Real

Donald Trump's effort to overturn the 2020 U.S. presidential election and Jair Bolsonaro's copycat attempt to overturn Brazil's 2022 election provide stark reminders that the political Right's opposition to democracy is not a thing of the past. This opposition has led many to conclude that democracy is possible only when it is safe for elites. (And even then there are no guarantees.) The logic of the argument goes like this. Democracy constitutes an inherent threat to elite power and privilege, the defense of which is the Right's raison d'être. Ipso facto, the Right is inherently suspicious of democracy. The intensity of this suspicion depends on the degree to which democracy threatens elites, or appears to do so. The lower the threat, the more tolerant the Right will be, and vice versa. Since political forces of the Left have historically fought for a deeper and more extensive, i.e., more real and more threatening, vision of democracy (which critics and some adherents see as incompatible with liberal democracy), the Right's tolerance for democracy is likely to be at its lowest when the Left holds political power or appears on the cusp of doing so.

The historical record provides ample support for this argument. Across time and space, the Right has regularly opposed democracy when it becomes threatening to elites and shown greater willingness to tolerate democracy when it appears relatively safe. Consider the Right's relationship to democracy in Latin America over the course of the twentieth century. From the turn of the century through the 1970s the Right viewed democracy with great suspicion and showed no scruples in ending it when it appeared too dangerous for dominant classes. The frequency of right-wing coups (backed by the United States in more and less covert ways) against democratically elected leftist presidents during this time attests to this fact; such coups occurred in Venezuela, Guatemala, Brazil, Bolivia, the Dominican Republic, Chile, and elsewhere. During the 1980s and 1990s the Latin American Right (and the U.S. government) largely came to accept democracy. There are multiple reasons for this, but the most important were the defanging of the Left, due to decades of brutal repression, and neoliberalism's regional and global ascendance. Together these related processes ensured that democracy would be safe for elites.

This points to the paradox of modern democracy: it appears to be possible only when subordinate classes are sufficiently strong to overcome dominant classes' initially fierce resistance to any form of popular rule yet not so strong as to appear existentially threatening to elites and trigger a conservative reaction that ends democracy. This paradox has led scholars to conclude that the optimal sociopolitical configuration for making democracy (and making it more real) is a strong but moderate left political force that can organize and mobilize subordinate classes *and* keep their demands within acceptable bounds (Rueschemeyer et al. 1992; Sandbrook et al. 2007). Scholars have also argued that democracy is most likely to endure in the presence of one or more cohesive, well-organized conservative political parties, which can effectively channel and defend elite interests within the political arena, inducing elites to see democracy as less threatening (Rueschemeyer et al. 1992; Gibson 1996; Middlebrook 2000; Ziblatt 2017).

It would thus appear that there are relatively firm limits to how real democracy can be. If these limits are transgressed the powerful will ensure that democracy ceases to exist. Leading classic and contemporary works on democracy, such as Rueschemeyer, Stephens, and Stephens's

Capitalist Development and Democracy, Sandbrook et al.'s *Social Democracy in the Global Periphery*, and Ziblatt's *Conservative Parties and the Birth of Democracy* all support this idea.[1] Ziblatt (2017, 367–68) concludes his book by stating, "The price that advocates of democracy must pay is that the propertied and powerful not only have a diffuse but disproportionate influence on society all the time, but also that it be protected by organizationally strong and well-endowed political parties that have the chance of winning elections at least some of the time."

But is "a compromised version of democracy" the best that can be hoped for (as Ziblatt reluctantly contends)? Must the Left embrace moderation as the price of democracy's existence? Is democracy possible only if it is safe? I reject these conclusions and have sought to show that the possibilities for real democracy are greater than most existing scholarship allows for. The key to understanding why lies in the concept of leftist hegemony, in which a left bloc not only achieves political power but also succeeds in establishing "moral and intellectual unity, posing all the questions around which the struggle rages not on a corporate but on a 'universal' plane" (Gramsci 1971, 182).

LEFTIST HEGEMONY AND THE RIGHT, OR HUGO CHÁVEZ AS THE LEFT'S MARGARET THATCHER

My central argument is that the establishment of leftist hegemony forces the Right to "play the game" of politics on the Left's terrain. This is analogous to the better-known effect of the right-wing, neoliberal hegemony established by figures such as Margaret Thatcher, who as noted in the introduction boasted that her "greatest accomplishment" was "Tony Blair and New Labour." Thatcher's subsequent quip, "We forced our opponents to change their minds"—referencing New Labour's abandonment of socialism and enthusiastic embrace of free-market capitalism—provides as good a summation of the general effect of hegemony, whether left or right, as any critical theorist. One of the main contributions of *Democracy on the Ground* is to show that leftist hegemony produces a similar effect as right-wing hegemony: it compels the Right to "change its mind" and embrace ideas and practices associated with the Left.

This insight was developed to make sense of the doubly unexpected findings of my comparison of participatory reform in cities governed by left and right parties in Venezuela and Bolivia at the height of the Latin American left turn. As detailed in the introduction, I expected to find more participatory success in the two left-run cities than the two right-governed cities. I also expected to find relatively greater success in the Bolivian rather than Venezuelan cities.

My findings did not match either expectation. I found relatively successful participatory reform in the left- and right-governed Venezuelan cities and unsuccessful reform in the left- and right-governed Bolivian cities. I have sought to demonstrate that a central reason for this is the presence of leftist hegemony in Venezuela and not Bolivia at the left turn's height. Specifically I endeavored to show that Venezuela developed a left-populist hegemonic regime that transformed politics such that all parties, including right-wing opposition parties, were forced to operate on Chavismo's left-populist terrain. Among other things, this pushed right-wing parties to promote participatory democracy to an extent rarely if ever seen in Latin America, or anywhere.

The chapter on Sucre documented the surprising case of a right-of-center, anti-Chavista mayor annually devoting tens of millions of U.S. dollars and thousands of staff hours to participatory budgeting; referencing the experience using Chavismo's left-populist language of "popular power;" and recruiting hundreds of Chavistas to participate. Lest this experience be dismissed as exceptional it should be noted that the party that led it, Primero Justicia, was the opposition's leading force from 2009 to 2013. As discussed in chapter 1, in the 2012 and 2013 presidential elections, Primero Justicia's candidate, Henrique Capriles, campaigned on a platform of extending democracy, explicitly promising to expand and better manage Chávez's signature social missions. It is not coincidental that Sucre's Participatory Budget and Capriles's presidential campaigns occurred at the height of Venezuela's period of left-populist hegemony. Had he lived, Chávez could have referred to Capriles as his "greatest accomplishment."

Another notable feature of Sucre is its unexpected similarity to Torres. As chapter 2 showed, Torres is the most successful of the four cases. Under successive movement-left mayors, Torres's citizens exercised a degree of control over budgetary and nonbudgetary decisions that approximates if not exceeds that of paradigmatic cases of participatory success like Porto Alegre. Torres also went some way to justify being labeled Venezuela's "first socialist city" by establishing an impressive degree of popular control over economic decision-making. Torres's greater success versus Sucre is unsurprising given the political and ideological differences of the cities' mayors. What is surprising is that the cities resemble each other at all, with both having robust mechanisms allowing popular input into decisions and translating this input into government output. The cities' strikingly similar path to participatory governance is also surprising. Left-populist hegemony, along with its contradictions, was central to this path in both cases.

Bolivia forms a marked contrast to Venezuela, with Morales failing to establish leftist hegemony.[2] As detailed in chapter 4, under Morales Bolivia developed a passive revolutionary regime that transformed politics in important ways but in a different manner and to a seemingly lesser extent than what occurred in Venezuela under Chávez. The arguably lesser degree of transformation is most visible in urban politics, where my research shows that preexisting patterns of clientelistic rule continued largely as before Morales took office. From the standpoint of this book, a key consequence of the Morales administration's failure to achieve leftist hegemony was that local politicians of the Right and, more surprisingly, also the Left faced little to no pressure to govern in accord with the ruling MAS's rhetoric of "ruling by obeying."

The chapters on Santa Cruz and El Alto document this partially unexpected reality. The difference between governance in Santa Cruz and Sucre is night and day, starkly illustrating my argument that the presence or absence of leftist hegemony shapes the Right's actions toward democracy. As chapter 5 detailed, Santa Cruz's center-right opposition mayor, Percy Fernández, firmly opposed popular input into political decision-making. Percy's antidemocratic governance strategy appears notable when contrasted to Carlos Ocariz's embrace of participation, but it is Percy and not Ocariz who better fits what one would expect of a right-of-center mayor. What is more surprising is that El Alto's leftist mayor, Edgar Patana, of the ruling MAS, embraced a strategy similar to Percy's, with the Patana administration seeking to reduce participation and end the "dictatorship of the social organizations." As with the surprising similarity of the left- and right-run cities in Venezuela, I have sought to demonstrate that Bolivia's national context, and specifically the establishment of a passive revolutionary regime, is central to explaining the unexpectedly similar outcomes found in right-governed Santa Cruz and left-governed El Alto.

A NOVEL FRAMEWORK FOR UNDERSTANDING PARTICIPATORY URBAN GOVERNANCE OUTCOMES

Democracy on the Ground also contributes to thinking about urban participation. Building off Baiocchi's (2005) notion of state-society regimes, I introduce the idea of the urban political regime as a way to understand participatory urban governance outcomes. I categorize the four study cities as four urban regime types, based on the combination of each city's "form of rule" and "state-society balance." Torres is a participatory democracy, with socially controlled democratic rule. There is significant popular participation and universalistic access to decisions and resources, and social actors largely determine the form of rule. Torres's motto is "It's better to err with the people than be right without the people." Sucre is an administered democracy, with state-controlled democratic rule. There is significant participation and universalistic access to decisions and resources, and local state actors primarily determine the form of rule. Sucre's motto appears to be "Give the people some but not too much power." Santa Cruz is a case of technocratic clientelism, with state-controlled clientelistic rule. Political and civic elites prevail in decisions, there is clientelistic access to decisions and resources, and state actors determine the form of rule. Officials disdain democracy and proudly affirm, "There's a difference between what residents say they want and what they actually need." El Alto is a case of inverted clientelism, with socially controlled clientelistic rule. Political and particularly civic elites predominate over citizens in decisions, there is clientelistic access to decisions and resources, and social actors are key to determining the form of rule. The motto here is "limited participation" and "putting our house in order."

To get beyond the success versus failure binary used in many studies of urban participation (including this one), I compare cities, and urban regimes, on four axes: the extent and quality of popular control over political decision-making and institutional and political effectiveness. This offers a multidimensional way to see similarities and differences of cities and urban regime types. My findings support the following propositions about urban regime types:

- Participatory democracy (Torres) is characterized by extensive and high-quality popular control over political decision-making, a high degree of institutional effectiveness and a very high degree of political effectiveness.
- Administered democracy (Sucre) is characterized by moderately extensive and moderate-quality popular control over decision-making and a high degree of institutional and political effectiveness.
- Inverted clientelism (El Alto) is characterized by limited and low-quality popular control over decision-making and institutional and political ineffectiveness.
- Technocratic clientelism (Santa Cruz) is characterized by extremely limited and extremely low-quality popular control over decision-making and a moderate degree of institutional and political effectiveness.

My findings permit tentative conclusions about the relationships between these axes. The regimes with the most extensive and highest-quality popular control over decisions, participatory and administered democracy, also show the highest institutional and political effectiveness. This suggests that popular control contributes to institutional and political effectiveness. The apparent link between popular control and institutional effectiveness could be due to more participatory regimes being more transparent (see Goldfrank 2011a). In principle expanding participation limits possibilities for corruption, which my research suggests contributed to institutional ineffectiveness in Santa Cruz's technocratic clientelistic regime and El Alto's inverted clientelistic regime. The apparent link between participation and political effectiveness may be due to the consent participation seems to produce, with this likely benefitting incumbent parties. It is notable that Torres had the most participatory and most politically effective regime; Torres is the only case where the local incumbent party was reelected with a new mayoral candidate.

My findings also suggest a link between institutional and political effectiveness. In the three cases with some degree of institutional effectiveness—Torres, Sucre, and Santa Cruz—there was also some degree of political effectiveness, with the incumbent party reelected in each. In the case without institutional effectiveness, El Alto, the incumbent party badly lost its reelection bid. Institutional effectiveness thus seems necessary for political effectiveness, and this relationship seems to hold irrespective of popular control, which was present in Torres and Sucre but not Santa Cruz.[3]

One of my main concerns has been explaining the outcomes found in the four cases. I have sought to demonstrate the limits of explanatory localism for this task. In each case study I endeavored to show that the outcome could not be adequately explained by pointing to the two local variables existing research posits as particularly important for explaining participatory urban governance outcomes: the character of the local incumbent party and of local civil society. As discussed earlier, there is a near-consensus among scholars that participation is most likely to succeed when there is a movement-left mayor and a strong and autonomous civil society. Based on this, one would expect the cases to range from most to least successful as follows: El Alto should be highly successful due to its movement-left mayor and strong and autonomous society; Torres should be successful due to its movement-left mayor and strong but less autonomous society; and Sucre and Santa Cruz should be unsuccessful due to having right-of-center mayors and weaker and more dependent societies. This ranking does not, of course, correspond to what I found in my research. It does not follow that the character of a city's local incumbent party and civil society are unimportant or irrelevant to explaining participatory governance outcomes.

The argument I advance is, rather, that understanding the causal import of these variables may (and in the cases covered in this study does) require paying close attention to national context. I also make a more specific argument about the contrasting national political regimes found in Venezuela and Bolivia and how these regimes shaped the actions of local incumbent and opposition parties and civic association leaders and members. I hold, further, that this was consequential for the outcome of participatory reform in each city.

I argue that Torres and Sucre achieved participatory success in a strikingly similar way: left-populist hegemony led to participatory clientelism, raising and dashing popular hopes for participatory rule, and generating a popular backlash leading to the election of an opposition party that refracted the ruling party's toolkit into democratic rule. Competitive elections appear to be a necessary condition for this path, which depends on the municipal executive flipping from the ruling party to the opposition. This path led to different urban regimes in the two cases because of Torres and Sucre's distinct balance of class forces, which I contend is key to shaping a city's state-society balance. Torres had a popular power class-force balance, generating socially controlled democratic rule. Sucre had an elite-professional class-force balance, leading to state-controlled democratic rule.

The path to participatory failure in El Alto and Santa Cruz was also unexpectedly similar. Both are cases of refracted passive revolution perpetuating clientelistic rule. This refraction took place under a distinct balance of class forces, which led to distinct regimes. El Alto's popular power balance led to socially controlled clientelistic rule, while Santa Cruz's elite-professional balance led to state-controlled clientelistic rule.

My overall causal argument is that a country's national regime and a city's balance of class forces determines the city's urban regime type. A strength of this argument is that it helps explain the unexpectedly similarly outcomes in cities as different as Torres and Sucre, on the one hand, and El Alto and Santa Cruz, on the other. The fact that this argument appears to be explanatorily useful in a notably, and unexpectedly, broad range of contexts suggests that it may be generalizable well beyond these four cases.

SEEING LEFTIST REGIMES IN A DYNAMIC AND RELATIONAL WAY

Another contribution of *Democracy on the Ground* is to demonstrate the usefulness of seeing leftist regimes in a dynamic and relational way. I show, specifically, that leftist regimes can transform, in sometimes surprising ways, based on how the regimes respond to the conservative backlash their rise elicits. Chapters 1 and 4 detail Venezuela's and Bolivia's distinct "reaction to the reaction" that put the countries on divergent paths to left-populist hegemony and passive revolution.

I draw on Gramsci's writings on crises of hegemony to make sense of this divergence. Venezuela entered the left turn through a top-down involutionary crisis of hegemony. This led to a vaguely left-populist ruling party loosely linked to a relatively weak and disorganized civil society. Bolivia entered the left turn through a bottom-up revolutionary crisis of hegemony, which led in the early left turn to a movement-left ruling party organically linked to a strong and autonomous civil society. These initial state-society configurations shaped how Chávez and Morales responded to conservative backlash, albeit in ways that one might not have expected. Chávez responded with full-out populist mobilization, which I view as an attempt to construct a sturdier popular bulwark to withstand the conservative backlash. In conjunction with the 2003 oil boom this move led to a left-populist hegemonic regime. Morales had a popular bulwark already, and due to his not-unreasonable fear of civil war, he responded to the conservative backlash with a mixed strategy of contained mobilization and demobilization of popular movements. From 2010 on, demobilization escalated, leading to a passive revolutionary regime.

RETHINKING VENEZUELA AND BOLIVIA AS CASES WITHIN THE LEFT TURN

As noted, Venezuela and Bolivia have been seen as falling on the "radical" side of the Latin American left turn. The evidence presented in these pages affirms but also complicates this view. In a number of ways, Chávez and Morales stand out as more radical than their counterparts in moderate left turn countries like Brazil, Chile, and Uruguay. Chávez and Morales are notable for their fiery anti-imperialist discourse, fierce denunciations of capitalism, and greater willingness to challenge domestic and foreign capital by, e.g., nationalizing industry. Such moves have no parallels in the moderate left turn cases. They also stand out in their promotion of nonliberal forms of democracy and measures designed to progressively redistribute resources to subordinate classes. But I have shown that the two cases are very different when it comes to participatory democracy. Participation was rhetorically promoted in both countries, but it was significantly more institutionally central to the ruling party's governance strategy in Venezuela than Bolivia. This suggests that, while the radical left label appears justified for both Venezuela and Bolivia, care should be taken such that the label does not obscure salient differences between the two.

It is also worth remembering that what seems radical in early twenty-first-century Latin America differs from what was considered such in the 1960s and 1970s. In that era, the radical left proposed the wholesale destruction of capitalism and its replacement by a full-scale socialist alternative, and it countenanced guerilla warfare as strategically necessary in many contexts. In the left turn the term radical denotes regimes that break with neoliberal orthodoxy by implementing statist or heterodox economic policy, employ anticapitalist and socialist rhetoric, and seek to extend and deepen democracy. It is telling that the International Monetary Fund (IMF) praised the macroeconomic policies of Morales, who is often considered a radical left leader. This is one indication of how different Latin America is today compared to fifty years ago.

Scholars who distinguish Venezuela and Bolivia as left turn cases often treat Venezuela as a left populist and Bolivia as a movement-left regime (Levitsky and Roberts 2011a; Anria 2018). Evidence I have presented partially supports but also seeks to go beyond these categorizations. I see the categorizations as relatively accurate in characterizing the types of left regime that emerged in Venezuela and Bolivia at the start of the left turn. But as already discussed, I highlight the developmental trajectories of the countries' regimes during the left turn. I contend that the left-populist label is most useful in Venezuela after 2003 when the state's effort to organize popular classes really took off. Additionally, I have sought to demonstrate that Venezuela had a left-populist hegemonic regime from roughly 2005 to 2013. I argue that Bolivia's regime type shifted under Morales from movement-left to passive revolutionary.

As with the question of how to categorize Venezuela and Bolivia as left turn cases, there is a lively debate about how to judge the countries' regimes on various metrics, including democratic quality. Venezuela is a particularly polarizing case. To many, Chávez was an autocrat who transformed Venezuela into a competitive or fully authoritarian regime (Corrales and Penfold 2011; Mainwaring 2012; Weyland 2013; Levitsky and Loxton 2013; Handlin 2017). Others view Venezuela as a shining example of participatory or socialist democracy.[4] A third view is provided through what might be termed critical Chavista scholarship, which is broadly sympathetic to the Chávez administration's emancipatory aims but is critical of the manifold contradictions, ambiguities, and shortcomings of the Bolivarian process (Ellner 2008; Fernandes 2010; Buxton 2011; Smilde and Hellinger 2011; Ciccariello-Maher 2013; Valencia 2015; Azzellini 2016; Schiller 2018; Kingsbury 2018; Cooper 2019).

My analysis is closest to this third strand of scholarship, which, among other things, is notable for providing a "messy" analysis of Chavismo. It is not coincidental that this is often done through works, like this one, which are largely based on ethnographic evidence. Ethnography is particularly well suited to messy analysis of the social and political since it forces researchers to grapple with the uneven nature of sociopolitical reality. Consider the issues of pluralism and civic autonomy. Critics who portray Chavismo as authoritarian (of an unqualified or "competitive" nature) do so in large part because of the Chavista project's alleged assault on both these vaunted features of liberal democracy.

I have worked to show that the reality of Chávez-era Venezuela was considerably more complicated that this view allows for. The chapters on Torres and Sucre show that the ruling party, in its incarnations as the Fifth Republic Movement (MVR) and United Socialist Party of Venezuela (PSUV), infringed on pluralism and civic autonomy in cities it governed;

institutions of the national state, such as Fundacomunal, did so as well. But I have shown that pluralism continued to exist in Chávez-era Venezuela. In Torres, pluralism was vigorously promoted by Julio Chávez and Edgar Carrasco's administrations. It should be noted that while Julio was initially a radical left oppositionist mayor, he joined the PSUV when it was formed in 2007, with Carrasco's entire period in office coming with the PSUV. This shows that the claim that the ruling party always damaged pluralism is less straightforward than critics claim. Sucre is arguably even more interesting and significant on this point. As chapter 3 showed, there were politically mixed (i.e., pluralistic) communal councils in Sucre during the Chávez era. These councils reported facing challenges from Fundacomunal officials who took a nonpluralistic line of not allowing oppositionists in the leadership. At least some councils took creative measures of submitting leadership slates that appeared fully Chavista while retaining fully oppositional or mixed leadership in practice. The need to take such measures substantiates the existence of pressures against pluralism in Chávez-era Venezuela, but the willingness of both Chavistas and oppositionists to figure out a way around this pressure indicates the continued vitality of pluralistic processes in Venezuela at this time and the limits of the state's repressive-regulatory capacity.

Torres and Sucre show that the question of civic autonomy was also complicated in this period. Critics of Chavismo point to the state's efforts to help organize and finance civic associations as proof that these associations lacked autonomy. The chapters on Torres and Sucre show that ruling-party mayors did attempt to exercise control over civic associations; for instance, Torres's Javier Oropeza told Myriam Giménez to "put our people in there" in the participatory budget Myriam organized, and Sucre's José Vicente Rangel Ávalos pushed to have programs involving only MVR supporters. The evidence presented in chapters 2 and 3 shows, however, that civic associations in both cities retained considerable functional autonomy from the ruling party. This is shown clearly in Sucre where a number of Chavista-led communal councils openly and even proudly participated in "Ocariz's" Participatory Budget. Leaders of these councils were unaware or unconcerned that some Fundacomunal officials said Chavistas should not participate. In Torres, communal councils and communes appeared even more autonomous in practice, regularly criticizing and clashing with national state institutions, and criticizing the municipal government as well. In both cases, the ethnographic evidence I present does not support the view that pluralism and civic autonomy were eviscerated in Chávez-era Venezuela. Nor, it should be added, does this evidence support claims that the ruling party and national state fully respected pluralism and autonomy. The reality was messy.

Evidence presented in these pages also speaks to the question of electoral freedom in Chávez-era Venezuela, which many critics contend did not exist. On this point the evidence I present is clear: through at least 2013 there was real electoral competition within Venezuela, with the government conceding defeats. If this were not the case, it would not have been possible for Julio Chávez or Carlos Ocariz to win and hold office. The fact that both mayors faced pressures from the ruling party does not negate this.

Venezuelan democracy in this period was, of course, hardly flawless. But in terms of what is arguably the most significant measure of democracy—ordinary people's ability to influence decisions that affect their lives—evidence presented shows that Venezuelan democracy performed at a high level. In this respect Venezuela compares favorably to countries like the United States, which, as recent scholarship shows, has an essentially oligarchic political system that gives ordinary citizens no ability to influence national policy-making (Gilens and Page 2014).

My findings also speak to how the Venezuelan Right, and the opposition generally, have been represented in scholarly and journalistic accounts of Chávez-era Venezuela. Two contrasting images appear. In mainstream journalism and much of the scholarship critical of Chávez, the opposition is often portrayed, in heroic terms, as a democratic force struggling against a malicious dictatorship. Some critics of Chavismo acknowledge the opposition's less savory moments, like supporting the 2002 coup against Chávez, but usually portray these actions as understandable, if regrettable, reactions to Chávez's overbearing or authoritarian ways.[5]

Scholarship more sympathetic to Chavismo has portrayed the opposition in very different terms—as a violent right-wing and racist antidemocratic force. In part this reflects these scholars' ethnographic embeddedness with grassroots Chavistas, who view the opposition in this way (cf. Fernandes 2010; Ciccariello-Maher 2013; Azzellini 2017; Schiller 2018). This strand of scholarship also emphasizes the upper-class and white nature of the opposition to Chávez. Cooper's (2019, 149) characterization of the opposition illustrates this in exemplary fashion: "Historically, right-wing opposition to Chávez and Maduro reflected the interests of the privileged while displaying indifference or even hostility toward poor and racially marginalized Venezuelans."

The evidence presented in *Democracy on the Ground* does not fit neatly into either interpretation. A first step toward a more accurate portrayal is periodization. The periodization I offer is as follows. From 2001 to 2005 the opposition was led by its right-wing, and at times far-right, faction, which was more than willing to engage in antidemocratic, racist, and violent action, as shown by the 2002 coup against Chávez. (As noted, moderate opponents largely went along with the coup while it was in progress.) The opposition returned to something like this after Chávez's death in 2013, although the government's authoritarian turn in 2016 complicates the analysis. But as I have shown, from 2009 to 2013 the opposition was led by a center-right party that rhetorically supported deepening and extending democracy and took real steps to implement participatory policies at the local level. The party behind this, Primero Justicia, was active in reaching out to the poor and managed to attract Venezuelans of color to its ranks.

My analysis has two implications for thinking about the opposition. The first is the need to view it as a nonmonolithic force, in socioeconomic and ideological terms. Throughout the Chávez and Maduro years the opposition has contained, and was often led by, far-right elements linked to predominantly white dominant classes, who had little toleration for democracy, unless it was safe. The opposition has also contained center-right parties, and factions associated with the Left (with left opposition seemingly greater under Maduro compared to Chávez). And, as the chapter on Sucre shows, at times the opposition had success expanding its base among predominantly Brown and Black popular classes.

Second, I have worked to show that the opposition is not static but dynamic. Specifically, I tried to show that the opposition's actions have shifted according to the presence or absence of leftist hegemony. This factor can be used to account for the shift in the opposition's leadership and predominant strategy toward the government over the course of the Chávez and Maduro years. In the early years, when Chavismo was not yet hegemonic, the opposition was led by its more far-right antidemocratic elements. During the period of left-populist hegemony, the opposition was forced to move left, its far-right elements were relatively marginalized, while center-right forces took the stage and proclaimed support for the poor and for deepening and extending democracy. When the period of left-populist hegemony ended around 2013, the opposition again was dominated by more far-right elements. Consider the difference between Henrique Capriles and Carlos Ocariz circa 2009 to 2013, when they embraced Chávez's social missions and implemented participatory reform, and Juan Guaidó's open calls for military coups and U.S. military intervention from 2019 to 2021.

BOLIVIA UNDER MORALES: A NOTE OF CAUTION CONCERNING THE BOOK'S FINDINGS

I have sought to show that Venezuela under Chávez provided a surprisingly conducive setting for urban participatory reform, while Bolivia under Morales provided a surprisingly unconducive setting for this. It would be easy to extrapolate from this that I view Venezuela under Chávez as a "success" and Bolivia under Morales as a "failure." However, that statement is not accurate for either country. I deal with the questions of "success" and "failure" in Venezuela in the following section. This section makes the simple but critical point that Morales's tenure in Bolivia was far from a failure.

The following is a partial list of highly significant, even unprecedented, ways that Morales's election and the policies his administration implemented transformed Bolivia:

- Indigenous Bolivians felt a newfound sense of dignity and pride due to the election of the country's first Indigenous president and Indigenous representation in the highest reaches of the state.

- Under Morales Bolivia officially committed itself to the goal of decolonization, with this affirmed in the 2009 Constitution, recognizing Bolivia as a plurinational state, with thirty-six official languages. Other laws directly challenged racism and promoted Indigenous culture, rights, and autonomy.

- In his first years in office Morales fulfilled the two outstanding demands of the "October Agenda" by nationalizing Bolivian gas (albeit in a partial manner that was criticized by many on the Left) and convoking and successfully holding a Constituent Assembly. Morales's government also pursued land reform, initially in a far-reaching fashion. These measures earned his administration significant enmity from Bolivian elites and foreign powers, as detailed in chapter 4.

- Bolivia's economic performance during Morales's nearly fourteen years in office was quite impressive by conventional standards. During this time, the economy grew at an annual rate of 3.2 percent, double the Latin American average of 1.6 percent. As Arauz et al. (2019) show, Bolivia's economic achievements came through heterodox economic policy, in which the state took a direct and highly active role. This directly contradicted the dictates of the IMF, which had exercised significant control over Bolivia's economy in the two decades prior to Morales's election. It is notable that the IMF nonetheless praised Morales's policies, which allowed Bolivia to perform better than any other South American country in the years following the 2008–2009 global recession.

- The Morales administration increased social spending by 80 percent in real terms from 2005 to 2017 (though critics argued more could be done). As of 2018, 51.8 percent of the population received direct cash transfers from the government (13).

- These policies contributed to major reductions in poverty, which declined from 59.9 percent to 34.6 percent from 2006 to 2018. Extreme poverty declined even more during this time, from 37.7 to 15.2 percent (15). Inequality also declined under Morales.

- While partial and ambiguous in nature, the government's 2006 "nationalization" of hydrocarbons significantly boosted state revenue. Arauz et al. note that, "In the first eight years of the Morales administration, national government revenue from hydrocarbons increased nearly sevenfold from $731 million to $4.95 billion." (8).

This list should put to rest any notion that Morales's administration was a failure.[6] Whatever its (very real) shortcomings, it is clear that his administration achieved quite a lot. These accomplishments must be seen as one of the factors that led voters to resoundingly return Morales's MAS to the presidency in October 2020.

VENEZUELA'S COLLAPSE (AND ITS SIGNIFICANCE FOR MY CENTRAL ARGUMENT)

If it is important to address, and reject, the notion that Bolivia under Morales is a case of failure, it is even more important to address the idea that Venezuela under Chávez can be considered a success. To many this idea will appear absurd or even offensive. At the time of writing (April 2021), Venezuela is in the eighth year of a multidimensional crisis of world-historic proportions: the economy has collapsed, there is a humanitarian catastrophe, and the country is mired in seemingly intractable political conflict. Among other things, this crisis raises questions about the relevance of this book's findings. To put things starkly: Does the evisceration of Venezuela's left-populist hegemony invalidate the argument that Chávez established such hegemony and that this compelled the Right to embrace leftist ideas and practices regarding democracy?

The wager of this book is that this argument remains valid and relevant despite Venezuela's crisis. The evidence I have presented shows that Venezuela achieved left-populist hegemony in the Chávez years. The end of this hegemony does not negate its prior existence. Nor does it negate the consequences leftist hegemony had, namely the transformation of Venezuela's Right. I have worked to document this transformation, which arguably reached its highest (but not only) expression in Sucre municipality during Carlos Ocariz's administration.

While Venezuela's crisis does not invalidate the findings and analysis I have presented, it does point to the need to think about the contradictions and limits of left-populist hegemony and, most importantly, its conditions of possibility. Close analysis of the Venezuelan case suggests its left-populist hegemony rested on two conditions: historically high commodity (and specifically oil) prices, which formed the material foundation for this hegemony, and Hugo Chávez's charismatic political leadership.

These two conditions were both present during the period of left-populist hegemony. Oil prices were high from 2003 to 2014, with a brief dip in 2008 and 2009. And Hugo Chávez was a notably charismatic politician. This charisma is important in accounting for his ability to shift policy at key moments, such as following the 2002 coup, when he initially adopted a more moderate line in the face of ongoing elite intransigence, and his radicalization of policy from 2004 onward (Ellner 2008). Chávez's charisma allowed him to retain support from different factions, including moderates, military generals, and sectors of business, on the one hand, and radicals, revolutionaries, and grassroots movements, on the other. It is arguable that only someone with Chávez's political acumen and skill could navigate the politics of all this.

Chávez's death brought a much less charismatic leader to office, heightening the difficulties of maintaining the disparate Chavista coalition and making necessary policy changes. Through 2022 (when I write these lines) Maduro has proven adept at surviving in office, but unlike Chávez he has done so through reliance on very significant repression and openly authoritarian politics. Critically, Maduro avoided making necessary policy moves, with respect to critical issues such as currency, which could have averted or lessened Venezuela's crisis, and which it is at least plausible to think Chávez would have been in a better position to make.[7] The crash in oil prices in 2014 revealed the Venezuelan economy and state's continuing hyperdependence on petroleum. The end of the commodity boom also helped bring right-wing leaders back to office throughout Latin America. This resulted in Maduro having far fewer allies compared to Chávez. And it meant the return of more pro-U.S. regimes throughout the hemisphere, with U.S. influence over the region regaining something of its former strength. Left-populist hegemony could not survive the destruction of these foundations.

LEFTIST HEGEMONY BEYOND LATIN AMERICA
AND THE LEFT TURN

This brief exploration of the limits, contradictions, and conditions of possibility of left-populist hegemony points to several related questions. What other forms can leftist hegemony take and what other forms have historically existed? How do these forms compare to left-populist hegemony? In particular, do other forms of leftist hegemony produce the same consequence this study found for left-populist hegemony, namely pushing the Right to "change its mind" and embrace leftist ideas and practices?

There is evidence that leftist hegemony has taken another form beyond its left-populist variant, with similar effects on the Right. This evidence comes from the 1960s and 1970s "golden age" of Scandinavian social democracy. Huber and Stephens (2001, 11) characterize Norway as a case of social democratic "ideological hegemony." This produced an effect analogous to that found in this book for left-populist hegemony, namely forcing the Right to actively embrace policies associated with the Left.

> An alternative path-dependent specification is the argument that the strong social democratic labor movements developed ideological hegemony in society and so thoroughly dominated public opinion formation on social policy that the only way for a bourgeois coalition to win elections was to adopt social democratic policies. This is our ideological hegemony mechanism and we do find instances of bourgeois governments passing policy that had been put on the agenda by labor, such as the Norwegian supplementary pension plan in the mid-1960s. However, we do not find cases of sustained innovation with the social democratic labor movement being able to define the agenda and force policy choices on a series of consecutive bourgeois governments.

The final sentence of the quote points to this question: Can leftist hegemony function, i.e., force the Right to "change its mind," if the Left is out of office? Huber and Stephens find that in the case of social democratic hegemony the answer is no. One can surmise that the reason for this relates to the structural difference between left and right forms of hegemony: leftist hegemony seeks to dismantle the capitalist world system, while right-wing hegemony (in current manifestations) seeks to bolster this system. This structural difference explains why right-wing hegemony can produce durable effects when the Right is out of office, while leftist hegemony is unlikely to do so. Consider Margaret Thatcher's effect on the UK Labour Party or the similar effect of Ronald Reagan on the U.S. Democratic Party. In both instances, the effects of right-wing neoliberal hegemony were lasting, with Tony Blair and Bill Clinton implementing neoliberal policies for consecutive terms in office. Since leftist hegemony is antisystemic, its effects are more fragile and unlikely to be sustained for long if the Left is out of national office.

This discussion points to the classic problem of "socialism in one country." Even if a left party is modestly successful in attempting to construct socialism in a given country, the capitalist world system remains a major constraint. There are two plausible ways to resolve this problem. One would be a worldwide transition to socialism, a process likely to encounter significant challenges, to say the least. Latin America's left turn provided a different, partial solution to this issue, with regional change creating a more hospitable context for national left change to occur. This was very important in particular instances, such as the 2008 right-wing insurgency against Evo Morales, which the Union of South American Nations quickly condemned. This outcome helped Morales stay in office, a marked contrast to the intraright networks in the 1970s that supported right-wing authoritarian governments and made leftist change all the harder to construct.

If social democratic and left-populist hegemony are united in facing a hostile capitalist world, the two forms of leftist hegemony are different in two important ways and arguably similar in one key way. The first difference relates to material base. As noted, Venezuela's left-populist hegemony rested on a fragile, unsustainable oil base. Social democratic hegemony rested on a more diversified industrial base, making it more resilient and sustainable. Second, social democratic hegemony did not suffer from the problem of charismatic leadership found in Venezuela but was more programmatic.

The two forms of leftist hegemony, however, share a similarity that appears significant. Like authoritarian state socialism, both social democracy and left populism have been unable to overcome the problem of statism, in which the state predominates over civil society. As Poulantzas (1980) notes, this manifests in a distrust of popular, bottom-up initiatives. In Venezuela this distrust was kept at bay during the period of right-wing backlash and for a time after, but under Maduro such distrust became more manifest. This is one reason neither social democracy nor left populism has been able to successfully transition to democratic socialism, in which a left ruling party actively mobilizes a strong subaltern civil society but is careful to allow civic autonomy to remain intact.

Overcoming what might be termed "the statist trap" is a significant challenge, which no left party has ever fully resolved at the national level. Torres provides clues about how this problem can be partially resolved at the local level. Julio Chávez arguably came close to doing so through his sustained alliance with mobilized popular classes. Abstracting from the case, the key to achieving some form of democratic socialism, at any level, appears to be a governing left party that is linked to but does not subordinate civil society. The outstanding question is whether and how partially successful attempts to do this might be scaled up and sustained at the national and global levels. The many pressing national and global challenges—rising inequality, pandemics, and climate change—mean that finding an answer to this question is of more than academic interest.

The recent rise of a new crop of leftist leaders in Latin America, the so-called "left turn 2.0" also points to the possibility that new forms of leftist hegemony might be constructed in coming years. If this occurs it will raise interesting and important questions, including the degree to which novel forms of leftist hegemony in the "second left turn" will manage to overcome the limits of the first, in particular its ecological limit, namely the heavy reliance of left governments on revenues derived from fossil fuels. The second left turn will also have to grapple with the challenge of trying to implement major change in what (in August 2022) appears to be a coming period of global recession and economic stagnation. Given the ever-more-real possibility of climate catastrophe it may not be hyperbole to say that the fate of the world rests in the balance.

METHODOLOGICAL APPENDIX

Thinking About the Political in Political Ethnography

Why are you here?

I was starting to sweat as Luis asked me this for the third time (or was it the fourth?). Everything depended on my answer. Well, not everything. In fact, perhaps not very much, in the grand scheme of things. But the moment felt big. Important. Consequential. If I gave the "right" response I would be "in" for El Alto. If I failed I would have to wait to gain access to the city.

Sinclair had tried to prepare me when he gave me his number. "Luis is hardcore."

I thought I was ready.

And so, on June 27, 2008, my first day in Bolivia, I met Luis at the appointed time at Alexander Coffee in Sopocachi, an upscale neighborhood in La Paz. I introduced myself and listened with great interest as Luis provided a brief history of Bolivia. He then launched into a comparative analysis of the state of community politics in the United States, Venezuela (where I had just flown in from), and Bolivia. 'The U.S. is in the Stone Age. Venezuela is in the Middle Ages. And Bolivia is in the Renaissance . . . [with] the most advanced forms of popular movements and community politics anywhere in the world.'

Luis then posed the question: Why are you here? I gave my usual academic answer, mentioning my interests in political sociology, democracy, participation, and the left turn. He was unmoved and asked again. I noted my political interests in leftist politics, socialism—of a new, more participatory, type—and revolution.

Luis was still not satisfied. 'I want to know the *personal reason* why you're here.'

With a mix of desperation, resignation, and a far-from-rhetorical sense of "what do I have to lose?" I dropped my usual defenses and decided to share what I supposed was the "deeper" reason I was in Bolivia. 'I'm interested in the ability of communities to realize their interests and desires . . . and [I gulped] I want to be part of this process. . . . I think critical intellectual work is needed to promote understanding of how participatory democracy, real participatory democracy, might be able to function.'

I waited with bated breath.

'Ah,' said Luis. 'You want to change the world, and so you came down to experience this. That's good.' I breathed a sigh of relief. Luis continued, 'This answer is necessary for me to be able to share my contacts with you. Values are the most important thing. Trust is essential. After I share my contacts, you'll have to figure out your own path. You shouldn't bring preconceived ideas of what to find. You should *feel* what is happening. The more you think you're understanding something the more you should realize you're not understanding it.'

I nodded, but because of my nervousness and the effects of the altitude I was sure I didn't understand everything he was telling me. I supposed that was the point.

My conversation with Luis was the most dramatic instance of "getting in" I experienced, but I had similar encounters throughout my time in the field. As Luis had told me, trust was essential. My research involved me intruding in the lives of people I barely knew and had often just met and asking them probing political questions over and over again. My ability to do this depended heavily on gaining the trust of key people like Luis, who gave the signal to others that "this guy is OK to talk to."

I found that politics, and specifically communicating my own political commitments to (some of) the people I was studying, was central to this. At first it came as a surprise. Many of the methodology books I had read early in grad school had emphasized the importance of being "objective" and "controlling for bias." Few of these texts had talked explicitly about politics or specifically of the need to share my own politics. But over and over again I found out that this was the key to gaining the trust I needed to "enter the field" in my research sites.

On June 11, 2008, my fourth day in Torres, I excitedly followed Julio Chávez's chief of staff, Johnny Murphy, to a conference room in the mayor's office. I had met Johnny the previous summer, on my first trip to Venezuela, when I spent a day in Torres. I was smitten with Torres's Participatory Budget, which was unlike any form of democracy I had personally experienced. I knew immediately that Torres would be a centerpiece of my dissertation. And now I was back to start my research.

As Luis would do a few weeks later, Johnny persistently inquired why I was there. And he made it clear that an academic answer would not suffice. He began our interview with this question: 'Are you a communist, a socialist, or an anarchist?' I was taken aback. Without much time to think, I replied that I had been drawn to anarchism when I was younger and as a result I was always a bit suspicious of rigid large state structures. I said I identified more with socialism now, saying I had seen how capitalism could make people act in ways that seemed inhuman. Johnny appeared satisfied, saying, 'We're more or less in agreement.' He then indicated that I could fire away, and we had the first of many conversations. Johnny explained that Torres had experienced four moments in an ongoing constitutive process: the first was the Municipal Constituent Assembly, the second the Participatory Budget, the third communal councils, and the fourth communes, which were in the process of being formed as we spoke. Johnny told me he had planned to serve as Julio's chief of staff for just two weeks but had served two years. He had stepped down recently. With a grin, he told me, 'My official title now is "advisor to the mayor."'

As with Luis, my conversation with Johnny opened many doors. Both of them made clear that they needed to know who I was, in a political (or "personal"-political) sense, in order to feel comfortable sharing their views and introducing me to others. But I found that I did not need to share my politics with everyone I met. Often I would have an intense conversation that, among other things, involved me answering pointed political questions with one or a few key people, who would then vouch for me to others. When I mentioned I had gotten so-and-so's number from Johnny, Luis, or another key contact, the person I was reaching out to would usually say they were happy to speak with me.

If sharing (something of) my political commitments was crucial to entering the field in the left-governed cities I studied, things were more complicated in the right-run cities. My initial entrée to Sucre was easy enough. I emailed several of Carlos Ocariz's staff a few weeks before I was set to arrive in Caracas. They told me to come to the Fundasucre office and were quite open to speaking to me and having me observe their work. I did not ask why these officials were so open, though I suspect it had something to do with my affiliation with a prestigious university in the United States (the University of California, Berkeley), my light skin color, and my U.S. nationality. The Venezuelan opposition had (and has) good relations with the U.S. government, and its leadership was (and is) predominantly white.

But political questions, that is, questions about my politics, could not be avoided in any of the cities I studied, including the two right-governed cities of Sucre and Santa Cruz. I found things easier in Sucre, where I learned I could bond with Ocariz administration officials over a mutual and (for myself and many of the officials) deeply felt interest in participatory democracy. I also found that some within the administration identified as leftists who had grown frustrated with Chávez and joined the opposition. This led to another means of bonding, in which I felt more open saying that I found the ideals of Chavismo attractive even as I was critical of many government practices. But I felt a contradictory mix of feelings in these conversations: a sense of guilt that I was not being entirely forthcoming; a distinct guilt that I was perhaps being too forthcoming and that, by voicing (my genuine) criticisms of the government, I was betraying Chavistas I had befriended; and a persistent worry that I might be "found out," without a clear sense of what that would mean.

For the first month or so in Sucre I felt capable of managing these complications. But things became hairier when I began spending significant time with oppositionists and Chavistas in the middle of the 2010 parliamentary election. One day in September, weeks before a primary vote (with the election itself in December), I found myself in the open-air bed of a Chavista campaign truck speaking with volunteers for the PSUV's National Assembly candidate. An image of Ocariz administration officials seeing me on the truck popped into my head and struck me with terror. A few blocks later I popped my head in the truck's back window and mentioned that I had forgotten to wear sunscreen that day and wondered if I might finish the ride inside. The PSUV officials in charge quickly said yes, although the young campaigner forced to leave his seat for me did not look particularly happy. With a mixture of emotions—but mostly relief—I sat down.

The tensest moment of my fieldwork came seven months later, when I was back in Sucre for a second round of fieldwork. By then I had spent nearly three months total in the municipality and felt reasonably confident that I had a decent sense of what was going on. Being committed to the idea of public sociology, I arranged to give a public presentation of my preliminary findings on Sucre at the Rómulo Gallegos Center for Latin American Studies (CELARG) a respected state-run cultural and research center in Caracas. I invited Marta Harnecker, a well-known researcher I was in semiregular contact with, to join me for a conversation about what "critical Chavistas" might learn from the case of Sucre. The main point I hoped to get across was that Chavistas would lose elections if they governed in corrupt or bureaucratic ways while innovative opposition leaders like Ocariz were "doing popular power" in relatively clean and efficient ways.

I had not considered the fact that Ocariz administration officials might learn of, and be interested in, my presentation. But just before the presentation was about to begin I received a phone call from Maribel Piñango, one of the officials I was closest to. Maribel said she and four other Fundasucre officials were headed over. And they were pissed off I had not told them I was speaking publicly about my research on Sucre.

I was seized with panic. Not only would I have to redesign my presentation—on the fly—to make it as academic and politically neutral as possible. More importantly, I worried what my lack of foresight would mean for my ability to finish my research in Sucre. Would the door be slammed shut immediately and forever?

As I was pondering this question, the Fundasucre officials arrived. I apologized for not having told them I would be speaking, saying I had not realized they would be interested. The event started. Marta showed the documentary she had made of Torres's Participatory Budget. I offered what felt like a watered-down version of my planned remarks. The discussion that followed was more interesting than I expected. Marta raised the issue of the difference between doing participatory budgeting solely as a means of distributing money and doing it as a means of redistributing wealth and power. She said that in Porto Alegre participatory budgeting had been used to invert the priorities of the municipality and provide more money to poor neighborhoods than wealthy ones.

Marta asked what officials in Sucre thought about participatory budgeting. I (and I assumed Marta) expected that the answer would be that Sucre's Participatory Budget was distributive as opposed to redistributive. But Alexander González, one of the Fundasucre officials present, responded by detailing the formula they used for Sucre's Participatory Budget, which was based on population, poverty, and providing more money to lower- than to higher- income neighborhoods . In other words, it was a redistributive formula. Marta commented on how impressed she was with the work the Ocariz administration was doing. She had heard that he was doing participatory budgeting but had not previously learned any details. A few people present commented on how positive it was that people working on the same issue (participatory budgeting), but from very different ideological points of view, could come together like this.

By the time we concluded the anxiety that had gripped me had dissipated. The event seemed to have been a positive, even generative, experience for those present. In the weeks that followed I learned that a Fundasucre official I was close to was deeply hurt I had failed to tell her and her colleagues that my presentation was happening. It became clear I had lost her trust. But to my relief I was not locked out of Sucre, though my ability to continue my research, in 2011 and on further visits in 2015 and 2016, depended on fence-mending conversations with Maribel, Alexander, and others.

Like in Sucre, I found that my skin color, nationality, and status as a researcher from a well-known foreign university appeared to facilitate my access to officials in Santa Cruz. But unlike Sucre, where I was able to bond with some officials over our mutual fondness for participatory democracy, I found it nearly impossible to bond with officials in Santa Cruz. One reason was their contempt for participation of any form. Another was their open expressions of racism. One instance of this occurred during my interview with a high-level official in the Parks and Garden department. With undisguised contempt, the official said, 'It's the people who come here from the interior of the country [i.e., Bolivia's highlands and valleys] who protest. Cambas generally don't hold up placards and blockade. . . . The majority of the people who come here to complain are from the interior, are *mujeres de pollera*,' meaning highland Indigenous women.

My skin color and nationality likely contributed to this official's willingness to speak in this way. These attributes came across very differently in El Alto, where my presence often elicited suspicion. I could well understand why, given the racism that has long structured Bolivian life, and the history of U.S. intervention in Bolivia and throughout the region. As noted in chapter 6, Alteños on multiple occasions asked me, in a half-joking manner if I worked for U.S. intelligence. I deployed three tactics to navigate the challenges such suspicions posed: discussing my political commitments, social drinking, and joking. When someone asked me, 'How did Obama like your report last night?' following heavy drinking during the first night of El Alto's 2010 pre-cumbre event, I quipped that Obama was 'less than pleased' since my report was riddled with errors. I also regularly told Alteños I met that I was the "president of district 15," which elicited laughs since at the time the city only had fourteen districts.

As my research progressed I found that the relationship between politics and fieldwork was a two-way street, and by this I mean the way in which the unexpected results of my research forced me to rethink my own political assumptions. To be concrete: when I started my research I assumed that the Venezuelan Right would respond to the national government's (contradictory, complicated, and messy) efforts to deepen democracy by seeking to end democracy or make it safer. I did not contemplate the possibility that the Right would seek to copy these efforts (in a contradictory, complicated, and messy way). The surprising findings of my research thus forced me to reassess my view of right-wing political forces in Venezuela and in general. The book in your hands (or on your screen) is the main result of this reassessment.

NOTES

PREFACE

1. For the claim that the United States is essentially oligarchic—in the sense that the rich few have overwhelming influence over political decisions—see Gilens and Page (2014). Former President Jimmy Carter has also made this claim, as has Bernie Sanders.
2. The Left's relationship to electoral democracy is, of course, complex. Leftist forces in Eastern Europe, Latin America, and elsewhere have at times rejected elections as a farce or ruled in authoritarian ways.

INTRODUCTION

1. Throughout this book I use single quote marks to denote quotes taken from fieldnotes, which are close to but not always verbatim. Double quote marks are used for citations from published sources and verbatim quotes that come from tape-recorded interviews.
2. This amount is calculated using the official exchange rate. In 2009 it was 2.14 bolivares to 1 USD. At this rate, 850,400 bolivares = 397,355 USD. This amount would, of course, be lower if calculated using the black market rate, which in 2009 was two to three times above the official rate.
3. See, for example, Walker, McQuarrie, and Lee 2015, 13.
4. See, for example, Heller 2001; Baiocchi 2003, 2005, 2018; Goldfrank 2011a; Wampler 2007.

5. Brazil's Workers' Party, Uruguay's Broad Front, Venezuela's La Causa R (The Radical Cause), and Bolivia's MAS are examples of movement-left parties. Brazil's Democratic Labor Party (PDT) and Venezuela's United Socialist Party (PSUV) are examples of left-populist parties.

6. This shift refers to Chávez's leftward radicalization during his time in office. As detailed later, Chávez's successor, Nicolás Maduro, has governed as a pseudo-leftist authoritarian.

7. To be sure, the surge in participatory experimentation that the expression *participatory revolution* seeks to capture has multiple origins, but it is hard to dispute that one of these was Latin American cities governed by novel leftist parties in the 1980s and 1990s.

8. Participatory Budgeting Project, https://www.participatorybudgeting.org/what-is-pb/. Accessed April 3, 2022.

9. The argument is that participatory budgeting is antidemocratic and/or totalitarian because it undermines elected local representatives.

10. This is not meant to deny the variation and evolution of the European Left(s) during the twentieth century but merely to point out that socialism was the main political horizon for much of the Left from the late nineteenth through the mid to late twentieth century.

11. Per Rueschemeyer et al. (1992, 143), "the optimal configuration of working-class organization for the development of democracy would be one in which the class was well organized, both in unions and a party, but that these organizations were not radical." See Sandbrook et al.'s (2007) similar argument on social democracy in the global periphery.

12. Stuart Hall (1988) masterfully details how Margaret Thatcher made neoliberalism hegemonic in the United Kingdom by disorganizing British political "common sense," "combining different elements of conservatism [free markets, the family, law and order] in a radically distinctive and original way," becoming "the *leading* political and ideological force," and winning "popular consent among significant sections of the dominated classes, successfully presenting itself as a force on the side of the people" (39–40).

13. In the first reform, which created residents' committees (*Comites de Colonos*), ordinary citizens' participation was limited to electing eight committee representatives, who made decisions about issues to bring up with the local government. A committee president Montambeault interviewed said, "It's us [representatives] who decides," making clear that citizens had no role in the process apart from initially selecting the representatives. Montambeault's data also indicate the residents' committees' lack of influence on municipal government. Citizen Wednesdays (*Miercoles Ciudadanos*), the second reform, let citizens meet with municipal staff. But the meetings were individual with no promise or expectation that the government would take action to resolve issues citizens raised.

14. From 1993 to 2000, PB was implemented in Recife under a succession of two center-right parties, PMDB and PFL. Montambeault's analysis indicates that ordinary citizens had no direct role in PB in Recife during these years. Citizens' role in the process was limited to selecting half the budget delegates who directly participated in the process, with the municipal government selecting the other half. The process was further limited due to rampant clientelism. Wampler's analysis is generally consistent, but he notes a difference between how PB was run under the centrist PMDB government (led by a mayor with

semi-leftist roots) from 1993 to 1997 and a technocratic conservative mayor under the PFL from 1997 to 1999. In the centrist 1993–97 period 84 percent of projects approved in the PB were implemented, but only 18 percent of projects approved through PB during the conservative mayoral period of 1997–99 were. Wampler agrees with Montambeault that ordinary citizens played no direct role in the PB process during both periods (1993–2000). Another study that examines participation, of a different type than that found in this book, in right-run governments is Tarlau's (2019) study of the MST's education reforms in Brazil.

15. Goldfrank (2011a, 265–66) writes, "It remains to be seen whether or not political forces that do not have an ideological commitment to deepening democracy through expanding citizen participation can make PB work, and do so in contexts for which it was not initially designed. My expectation is that PB will *not* successfully serve as a politically neutral 'tool' for democracy and development, as many international donors are advertising. My fear is that as it spreads, participatory budgeting will continue to be designed in such a way as to *restrict its potential*" (emphasis added).

16. This definition draws on Jansen (2011), Roberts (1995), and Weyland (2001).

17. Honduras's Manuel Zelaya turned to the left while in office. On Ecuador see Riofrancos (2020).

18. Luna and Rovira Kaltwasser's (2014) edited volume is one of the few recent works that has attempted to address the place of the Right within the left turn.

19. Scholars with widely varying views on the left turn have characterized Venezuela and Bolivia in approximately this way. See Castañeda (2006), Ciccariello-Maher (2013), and several edited collections on the left turn, including Ellner (2014), Levitsky and Roberts (2011b), Weyland, Madrid, and Hunter (2010), and Cameron and Hershberg (2010). Some of these works seek to complicate the radical/moderate, populist/non-populist, good/bad dichotomies, but in each grouping Venezuela and Bolivia are treated as more similar to each other than to so-called moderate cases like Chile, Brazil, and Uruguay.

20. Brazil went further than Chile, and there were relatively impressive and successful efforts to extend (and to some extent deepen) democracy in Uruguay, a third left turn case often identified as "moderate." For more on these cases see Anria (2018, 168–91).

21. Ecuador in the Correa years is also frequently seen as part of the "radical left." Riofrancos (2020) provides an excellent examination of this period, with a focus on the intra-left clash between Correa, a supporter of radical resource nationalism, and an emergent anti-extractivist left.

22. In Venezuela I visited Sucre, El Hatillo, Baruta, Libertador (Caracas), Barquisimeto, Torres, Libertador (Carabobo), and Maracaibo. In Bolivia I visited El Alto, Achacachi, La Paz, Santa Cruz, and Cochabamba, where I also interviewed Villa Tunari's mayor.

23. I did not seek to find cities that are "representative" of Venezuela and Bolivia, partly because I doubt such cities exist. My concern instead was finding left- and right-governed cities in each country that at the outset of my research appeared to have similar prospects for success or failure. While not representative of Venezuela or Bolivia, the four cities do show the importance of national processes. A central claim of the book is that the unexpected

similarities between the cross-ideological, within-country city pairs (Torres and Sucre, and El Alto and Santa Cruz) are in large part due to national processes, which play out in surprisingly similar but far from identical ways in the within-nation city pairs.

24. By asking "Who rules?" I follow in the footsteps of classics like Dahl's *Who Governs?*

25. Ethnography, of course, has a complicated history. As many scholars, particularly within anthropology, have noted, ethnographers were often complicit with colonialism. For a brief discussion of this, see Burawoy (2009, 118–19).

26. This multidimensional framework helps address two interrelated problems common to the urban participation literature. First, many studies compellingly assess specific features of participatory urban governance processes such as turnout, participant socioeconomic profiles, percent of participants speaking in meetings, budgetary percent subject to popular control (Avritzer 2009:90–99), and whether participatory processes persist through mayoral turnover or are formally open to all (Van Cott 2008, 30). However, with a handful of exceptions (Wampler 2007; Goldfrank 2011a; Baiocchi et al. 2011; Montambeault 2015), few studies employ systematic frameworks facilitating compelling comparative assessment of cases. Second, as Baiocchi et al. (2011, 71) note, studies of participation often fail to examine if participatory inputs are effectively linked to policy outputs, which are a key measure of the efficacy of participatory urban governance reforms.

27. Projects are considered implemented if credible data indicate the project is completed (in the sense of being physically built or established in accord with a project proposal). This leaves the question of a project's broader "success" (its ability to fulfill social or other goals beyond just being finished) unaddressed. Data constraints dictated the choice to focus on project implementation rather than "success," as I obtained data on project success for the two more transparently governed cities, Torres and Sucre, but not for the two less transparent cities, El Alto and Santa Cruz. In Santa Cruz significant evidence indicates projects listed as implemented are such only on paper. This is one reason I use subjective data, which allows me to crosscheck the validity of "objective" or harder data.

28. Van Cott (2008) and Goldfrank (2011a) are two exceptions.

29. Modonesi points to the degree of political repression in distinguishing progressive and regressive passive revolutions, with repression low in progressive passive revolutions and high in regressive passive revolutions. He also points, more ambiguously, to demobilization and cooptation of movements: it is unclear if this should be considered a feature of passive revolution in general (as he largely appears to argue) or only of regressive passive revolutions.

1. VENEZUELA: FROM CRISIS TO LEFT-POPULIST HEGEMONY

1. Classic works on Punto Fijo are Karl (1997), Coronil (1997), and more recently Tinker Salas (2009).

2. Velasco (2015, 196) notes "estimate[s of] between 750 and 1,000 fatalities," and Silva (2009, 204) estimates 276–1,500 killed in the Caracazo. Some estimates are even higher.

3. Gamboa (2017) characterizes the opposition's strategy in this period as radical and extra-institutional, meaning it prioritized using aggressive tactics, such as the 2002 coup and 2002–2003 oil strike/lockout, and on immediately removing Chávez.

4. Per Gamboa (2017, 465) the forty-nine decrees "enraged middle- and upper-class sectors."

5. I use the term civil society to denote the voluntary associational sphere between state and economy. In Chávez-era Venezuela the opposition claimed a near-monopoly over the term's use.

6. This excludes 2004 when growth was a whopping 18.3 percent, largely due to the recovery from the 2002–2003 crisis years. Including 2004 gives a 5.9 percent annual rate for the 2004–2013 period. Growth was spectacularly high, averaging 10.5 percent, from 2004 to 2008.

7. "Venezuela Foreign Exchange Reserves," Trading Economics, http://www.tradingeconomics .com/venezuela/foreign-exchange-reserves, accessed October 24, 2022.

8. This and the following statistical data are taken from Johnston and Kozameh (2013).

9. Jiménez (2021) offers a very different take on the opposition's shift in these years, which she attributes to a change from low to medium repression within Venezuela.

10. "Venezuela Situation," UNHCR, https://www.unhcr.org/en-us/venezuela-emergency.html, accessed October 24, 2022.

11. I am indebted to David Smilde for his clarification of the timing of U.S. sanctions in these years.

12. In some cases the Supreme Court could argue that the National Assembly had over-stepped its bounds in Spring 2016; for instance the assembly attempted to free imprisoned opposition leader Leopoldo López despite lacking the authority to do so. But the Court's blanket refusal to let the National Assembly function constituted a clear consolidation of authoritarian rule.

2. TORRES: PARTICIPATORY DEMOCRACY IN "VENEZUELA'S FIRST SOCIALIST CITY"

1. This claim cannot be proven but is plausible given the impressive degree of popular control over decision-making found in Torres in these years and the decline of Porto Alegre's famed Participatory Budget after the 2005 election of a conservative mayor.

2. http://www.encarora.com/agricultura.htm, last accessed April 12, 2016.

3. This quote, and subsequent information, come from the following document: http://gentur .infocentro.net.ve/comun/sitios/rafael_rodriguez_194/asentamiento_montana_verde /index.php?id_seccion=7, last accessed April 12, 2016.

4. Information about this here: http://www.pueblodelapastora.8m.com/custom.html, last accessed April 12, 2016.

5. In 2013 a computer virus destroyed critical files in the CLPP office in Torres relating to, among other things, PB turnout. The estimate of 15,000 people comes from multiplying the number of communal councils in Torres by the number of participants attending PB

community assemblies. Using conservative estimates of 500 communal councils (versus the true figure of 560) and 30 participants per assembly yields the number 15,000. The figure of 30 attendants per assembly is likely a very low estimate. Non-PB community assemblies I attended had 200 to 300 people present. Attendance in PB assemblies was likely as high or higher, given PB's importance to peoples' lives. A less conservative estimate is that anywhere from 30,000 to 45,000 people in Torres attend PB events annually.

6. The only partial exception to this statement is the urban sectional discussion in the Trinidad Samuel parish assembly, where the facilitator appeared to make decisions rather than participants. This, however, did not appear to follow a command-and-control logic but appeared due to a combination of chaos and backstage preassembly negotiations.

7. Another major example of voceros approving projects officials opposed was the 13 percent of PB funding in the first year allocated to evangelical churches.

8. In many parish assemblies I did not have sufficient time to ask participants their ethnoracial self-identification in a systematic manner; at times I was told how participants identified, but I also utilized what officials and others told me of participants' race or ethnicity.

9. In some parts of Venezuela, such as Miranda state where Sucre municipality is, those identified or identifying as Black (Negro) in Torres self-identified as Afro-Venezuelan, but this category was not widely used in Torres, perhaps due to its small Black population.

10. This report is available here: http://notasdetorresycarora.blogspot.com/2013/03/alcalde-de-torres-edgar-carrasco.html, accessed April 30, 2018.

11. The official name of the factory is Planta Socialista de Ensamblaje de Contadores de Energía Eléctrica. See Metrocontadores, "PDVSA Industrial firma memorando para construir fábrica de medidores eléctricos," http://metrocontadores.blogspot.com/, accessed August 18, 2018.

3. SUCRE: ADMINISTERED DEMOCRACY IN A RIGHT-GOVERNED "CHAVISTA CITY"

1. República Bolivariana de Venezuela, XIV Censo Nacional de Población y Vivienda, http://www.ine.gov.ve/documentos/Demografia/CensodePoblacionyVivienda/pdf/miranda.pdf, last accessed January 19, 2023.

2. Father Renaud still lives in Petare; he has remained active in popular movements and is highly critical of Venezuela's Catholic leadership for its conservative politics.

3. http://pjcarlosocariz.blogspot.com/2007/05/cada-tres-das-matan-cuatro-personas-en.html, accessed May 1, 2015.

4. Housing data comes from Venezuela's 2011 census, http://www.ine.gob.ve/, accessed May 1, 2015.

5. These officials told me that they did receive proposals from communities during the José Vicente years, but that there was no specific set of proposals labeled (or otherwise thought of) as "participatory budgeting." This suggests that proposals gathered in community

assemblies—through what José Vicente termed participatory budgeting—were handled just the same as any other community proposals, with officials having full say to accept or reject the proposals; at best this experience gave citizens quite limited influence over decision-making.

6. In addition to apparently helping deliver Sucre to Ocariz, the choice of Chacón as the PSUV's Sucre mayoral candidate in 2008 is notable because it foreclosed the possibility that Sucre could go down a Torres-like path toward left-led participatory democracy. This is because Chacón defeated Carlos Molina (Pitufo) in the June 2008 PSUV primary. A key reason, according to Chavistas, was that Hugo Chávez 'raised Jesse's hand' (publicly supported Chacón in the primary). This surely reduced Molina's chances.

7. The single exception is Caucagüita in the 2010 parliamentary election when the PSUV won 55 percent of the vote, which still gave it a 10 percent margin of victory over the opposition.

8. Alexander also mentioned Venezuela's constitution, which as noted mandated that all municipalities practice PB. This, however, is insufficient for explaining why Ocariz implemented PB in a much more robust way than most mayors.

9. Initially there were thirty-eight zones, with three additional zones added later.

10. http://www.alcaldiamunicipiosucre.gob.ve/contenido/2011/04/30/7816_arranco-en -sucre-el-presupuesto-participativo-2012/, accessed March 2017. In an April 2011 PB assembly Ocariz put PB turnout at 2,500.

11. Officials hoped it would be less subject to critique, but the same argument—that the program amounted to a hidden semiprivatization of education—could still be leveled, as Uno+Uno made public education more dependent on private (parents') contributions. The program could also be critiqued for exacerbating inequalities among schools, since wealthier schools would receive more funding compared to poorer schools.

12. I attended three of these assemblies and a PB facilitator from the municipal government collected data on three additional assemblies she attended around the same time. Apart from all being held in the beginning of the 2011 PB cycle, these assemblies were essentially selected at random and appear to be reasonably representative. The changes recorded here accord with what appears to have happened across Sucre in this period.

13. In explaining why they did not participate in Sucre's PB, some Chavistas told me they felt no need to, given the resources they could access through the national government. For instance, Amelia Sanchez, a Chavista leader from Guaicoco, commented, 'If we get three to four projects from the central government, why would we also go to City Hall?'

14. The Lista de Tascón, or Tascón's List, is an infamous document that Luis Tascón, an MVR national assembly member, published on his personal website in 2004, listing everyone who signed in favor of holding a recall referendum against Hugo Chávez. Signatories complained of being discriminated against, as Violeta brags about doing.

15. Partido Socialista Unido de Venezuela, "Jorge Amorin: El 27 de septiembre activaremos un referéndum revocatorio a Carlos Ocariz," http://www.psuv.org.ve/portada/jorge -amorin-27-septiembre-referendum-revocatorio-carlos-ocariz/#.Y-aC5-nYqRs, last accessed February 10, 2023.

16. This does not negate that Ocariz may have been more inclined than other opposition politicians to embrace participation due to his own history, which includes experimenting with participation in a modest way during his work in the Miranda state government in the 1990s.

4. BOLIVIA: FROM ACTIVE TO PASSIVE REVOLUTION

1. This discussion draws on Hylton and Thomson 2007 (138–42), Postero 2017 (chapter 2), Farthing and Kohl 2014 (40–43), among other sources, cited in the text.
2. Almaraz is also the son of Sergio Almaraz, a cofounder of the Bolivian Communist Party and socialist who helped facilitate the 1969 nationalization of gas (Gustafson 2020, 1).

5. SANTA CRUZ: TECHNOCRATIC CLIENTELISM, OR FEAR OF THE MASSES

1. Bolivian vote data is from http://www.oep.org.bo/. Municipal turnout data is missing for 2010. Department-level municipal election turnout data for 2010 show La Paz at 89.2 percent and Santa Cruz at 86.3 percent. See also http://www.lostiempos.com/resultados-elecciones-municipales-departamentales-bolivia-2010.php; http://www.bolivia.com/Especiales/2004/Elecciones_Municipales/resultados/Santacruz.asp, last accessed April 4, 2016.
2. Santa Cruz's newspaper *El Día* reported similar struggles in districts 9 and 10 at this time, indicating that the patterns I observed in districts 8 and 12 were not unique.

6. EL ALTO: INVERTED CLIENTELISM IN THE REBEL CITY

1. This is discussed in the chapter on MAS in García Linera et al. (2004). See also Grisaffi (2019), who offers a less positive view of MAS in the Chapare.
2. As Roberts (1995) and Weyland (1999) show in the cases of Peru, Brazil, and Argentina, support for neoliberalism was a key feature of other neopopulist parties.
3. Goni is the widely used nickname of President Gonzalo Sánchez de Lozada.
4. Revilla himself cannot be considered unbiased, given who his brother is and with MSM becoming a prominent foe of MAS in the 2010s. However, Revilla was never a municipal official in El Alto (where he was born and lived) and thus is not as clearly interested as current members of the municipal government.
5. "Vicepresidente critica baja ejecución presupuestaria de municipos del país," Agencia de Noticias de Bolivia, http://anbolivia.blogspot.com/2014/01/vicepresidente-critica-baja-ejecucion.html, accessed January 8, 2014.
6. Official electoral statistics from Órgano Electoral Plurinacional are available here: https://www.oep.org.bo/wp-content/uploads/2017/02/elecciones_subnacionales_2015.pdf.

7. "Exalcalde de El Alto, Fanor Nava, entrega un "paquete" a Édgar Patana," YouTube, https://www.youtube.com/watch?v=ETmHnv2WYfU, accessed July 4, 2015.

CONCLUSION: FROM MAKING DEMOCRACY SAFE TO MAKING IT REAL

1. To be sure, Rueschemeyer et al. and Sandbrook et al. both show that the limits of democracy are historically variable; they depend on the balance of class and social forces in given global, regional, and national conjunctures. Yet their analysis is clear that a radical Left party that pushes too far runs a very high risk of setting off a conservative reaction that ends democracy.

2. As noted in the introduction, scholars of Gramsci continue to debate whether or not passive revolution is compatible with certain forms of hegemony. There is also debate about whether or not Morales achieved hegemony. This book contributes to this debate but will not resolve it. I hope, however, to have established that there are notable and theoretically and empirically consequential differences between the national regimes established in Venezuela under Chávez and Bolivia under Morales.

3. These conclusions are tentative, as they are based on limited evidence. The conclusions can most usefully be taken as informed hypotheses, which could shape further research.

4. This is the Venezuelan government's self-assessment. A version of this argument can also be found, to a lesser degree, among some pro-Venezuela solidarity activists, who through the time of writing (March 2021) continue to defend the democratic credentials of the Maduro administration and vociferously reject arguments that Maduro has transformed Venezuela into an authoritarian regime.

5. Corrales and Penfold (2011, 22), for instance, argue that the opposition's support for the 2002 coup can only be understood in the context of a "series of coups," the first being "Chávez's coup against institutions of checks and balances." They also criticize Chávez for eschewing "reconciliation" and instead "provoking the opposition to irrational acts" (22–23). The clear takeaway is that while this period of confrontation "left few leaders in Venezuela guilt-free" (22), Chávez bears ultimate responsibility, including for the anti- and undemocratic actions of the opposition. Handlin (2017, 155) presents a similar argument that Chávez bears chief or at least very significant responsibility for the opposition's undemocratic tactics, which are due to "the 'winner-take-all' nature of polarized politics [that] *incentivized the opposition* to resort to non-electoral and highly undemocratic strategies to oust Chávez" (emphasis added). Handlin thus also argues that Chávez bears ultimate responsible for the opposition's temporary deviation from its democratic ways.

6. Gustafson (2020) provides an excellent account of the Morales years.

7. But it should be noted that Chávez himself failed to make critical changes to Venezuela's currency regime, for instance.

REFERENCES

Abers, Rebecca. 2000. *Inventing Local Democracy: Grassroots Politics in Brazil.* Boulder, CO: Lynne Rienner.

Achtenberg, Emily. 2017. "Why Is Evo Morales Reviving Bolivia's Controversial TIPNIS Road?" *NACLA*, August 21.

———. 2016. "After the Referendum, What's Next for Bolivia's Progressive Left?" *NACLA*, April 15.

Alcaldía de Torres. 2011. "Plan de Desarollo." Unpublished.

Aliendre, Freddy. 2002. *Diagnóstico Político y de Gestión Del Gobierno Municipal de El Alto.* El Alto, Bolivia: Centro de Promoción de la Mujer Gregoria Apaza.

Almaraz, Alejandro. 2015. "Luchas Políticas y Legales por la Tierra en Bolivia." In *Memoria Seminario: Recientes Transformaciones Agrarias en Bolivia.* La Paz, Bolivia: Fundación Tierra.

Anderson, Perry. 2000. "Renewals." *New Left Review* 1 (February): 5–24.

Anria, Santiago. 2018. *When Movements Become Parties: The Bolivian MAS in Comparative Perspective.* Cambridge: Cambridge University Press.

Arauz, Andrés, Mark Weisbrot, Andrew Bunker, and Jake Johnston. 2019. "Bolivia's Economic Transformation: Macroeconomic Policies, Institutional Changes, and Results." Washington, DC: Center for Economic and Policy Research.

Arbona, Juan, and Benjamin Kohl. 2004. "La Paz-El Alto." *Cities* 21(8): 255–65.

Auyero, Javier. 2000. *Poor People's Politics: Peronist Survival Networks and the Legacy of Evita.* Durham, NC: Duke University Press.

Avritzer, Leonardo. 2009. *Participatory Institutions in Democratic Brazil.* Baltimore, MD: Johns Hopkins University Press.

REFERENCES

Azzellini, Dario N. 2017. *Communes and Workers' Control in Venezuela: Building 21st Century Socialism from Below*. Leiden: Brill.

Baiocchi, Gianpaolo. 2018. *We, the Sovereign*. Cambridge: Polity.

——. 2005. *Militants and Citizens: The Politics of Participatory Democracy in Porto Alegre*. Stanford, CA: Stanford University Press.

——, ed. 2003. *Radicals in Power: The Workers' Party and Experiments in Urban Democracy in Brazil*. London: Zed.

Baiocchi, Gianpaolo, and Ernesto Ganuza. 2014. "Participatory Budgeting as If Emancipation Mattered." *Politics & Society* 42(1): 29–50.

——. 2017. *Popular Democracy: The Paradox of Participation*. Stanford, CA: Stanford University Press.

Baiocchi, Gianpaolo, Patrick Heller, and Marcelo Silva. 2011. *Bootstrapping Democracy: Transforming Local Governance and Civil Society in Brazil*. Stanford, CA: Stanford University Press.

Baptista, Félix, Diliana Domínguez, and Angel Reyes. 1993. "El Barrio Cuenta Su Historia. Alto Lebrún: El Uso de La Tierra En La Conformación de Un Barrio." In *Boletín Del Centro de Historia Regional de Petare 2*. Caracas, Venezuela: Alcaldía del Municipio Sucre.

Bethell, Leslie, and Ian Roxborough. 1992. "Conclusion: The Postwar Conjuncture in Latin America and Its Consequences." In *Latin America between the Second World War and the Cold War: Crisis and Containment, 1944–1948*, ed. Leslie Bethell and Ian Roxborough, 327–34. Cambridge: Cambridge University Press.

Bjork-James, Carwil. 2020. *The Sovereign Street: Making Revolution in Urban Bolivia*. Tucson: University of Arizona Press.

Block, Fred. 1977. "The Ruling Class Does Not Rule: Notes on the Marxist Theory of the State." *Socialist Revolution* 33 (June): 6–28.

Brewer-Carías, Allan R. 2010. *Dismantling Democracy in Venezuela: The Chávez Authoritarian Experiment*. Cambridge: Cambridge University Press.

Burawoy, Michael. 2009. *The Extended Case Method: Four Countries, Four Decades, Four Great Transformations, and One Theoretical Tradition*. Berkeley: University of California Press.

Buxton, Julia. 2016. "Venezuela After Chávez." *New Left Review* II(99): 5–25.

——. 2011. "Foreword." In *Venezuela's Bolivarian Democracy: Participation, Politics, and Culture under Chávez*, ed. David Smilde and Daniel Hellinger, ix–xxii. Durham, NC: Duke University Press.

Cameron, Maxwell A., and Eric Hershberg, eds. 2010. *Latin America's Left Turns: Politics, Policies, and Trajectories of Change*. Boulder, CO: Lynne Rienner.

Canel, Eduardo. 2010. *Barrio Democracy in Latin America: Participatory Decentralization and Community Activism in Montevideo*. University Park: Pennsylvania State University Press.

Cardoso, Fernando Henrique. 1979. "On the Characterization of Authoritarian Regimes in Latin America." In *The New Authoritarianism in Latin America*, ed. David Collier, 33–58. Princeton, NJ: Princeton University Press.

Castañeda, Jorge. 2006. "Latin America's Left Turn." *Foreign Affairs* 85(3): 28–43.

Chávez Crespo, Hermes. 2010. *Hermes Chávez y La Revolución Bolivariana*. Carora, Venezuela: Fondo Editorial Ali Lameda.

REFERENCES

Chavez, Daniel, and Benjamin Goldfrank, eds. 2004. *The Left in the City: Participatory Local Governments in Latin America.* London: Latin America Bureau.

Ciccariello-Maher, George. 2013. *We Created Chávez: A People's History of the Venezuelan Revolution.* Durham, NC: Duke University Press.

Collier, Ruth Berins, and David Collier. 1991. *Shaping the Political Arena: Critical Junctures, the Labor Movement, and Regime Dynamics in Latin America.* Notre Dame, IN: University of Notre Dame Press.

Cooper, Amy. 2019. *State of Health: Pleasure and Politics in Venezuelan Health Care under Chávez.* Berkeley: University of California Press.

Coronil, Fernando. 1997. *The Magical State: Nature, Money, and Modernity in Venezuela.* Chicago: University of Chicago Press.

Corrales, Javier, and Michael Penfold. 2011. *Dragon in the Tropics: Hugo Chavez and the Political Economy of Revolution in Venezuela.* Washington, DC: The Brookings Institution.

Cortés Riera, Luis E. 2007. "La godarria caroreña-Una singularidad social republicana." http://luiscortesriera.blogspot.com/2007/09/la-godarria-carorea-una-singularidad.html, September 19.

Couto, Claudio Gonclaves. 2003. "The Second Time Around: Marta Suplicy's PT Administration in São Paulo." In *Radicals in Power: The Workers' Party and Experiments in Urban Democracy in Brazil,* ed. Gianpaolo Baiocchi, 79–90. London: Zed.

Curiel, John, and Jack Williams. 2020. "Analysis | Bolivia Dismissed Its October Elections as Fraudulent. Our Research Found No Reason to Suspect Fraud." *Washington Post,* February 27.

Dangl, Benjamin. 2009. "Bolivia Looking Forward: New Constitution Passed, Celebrations Hit the Streets." *NACLA,* January 27.

Davis, Diane, and Arturo Alvarado. 2004. "Mexico City: The Challenge of Political Transition." In *The Left in the City: Participatory Local Governments in Latin America,* ed. Daniel Chavez and Benjamin Goldfrank, 135–68. London: Latin America Bureau.

della Porta, Donatella, Joseba Fernández, Hara Kouki, and Lorenzo Mosca. 2017. *Movement Parties Against Austerity.* Hoboken, NJ: Wiley.

Denis, Roland. 2015. "Chávez Didn't Dare Do What He Had to Between 2002 and 2003." Venezuelanalysis.com, June 12.

Desafío. 2013. *Análisis Del Presupuesto Municipal 2013: Santa Cruz de la Sierra.* Santa Cruz de la Sierra: Observatorio de Presupuestos Publicos.

Dunning, Thad. 2008. *Crude Democracy: Natural Resource Wealth and Political Regimes.* Cambridge: Cambridge University Press.

Eaton, Kent. 2014. "New Strategies of the Latin American Right: Beyond Parties and Elections." In *The Resilience of the Latin American Right,* ed. Juan Pablo Luna and Cristóbal Rovira Kaltwasser, 75–93. Baltimore, MD: Johns Hopkins University Press.

——. 2007. "Backlash in Bolivia: Regional Autonomy as a Reaction against Indigenous Mobilization." *Politics & Society* 35(1): 71–102.

ECLAC (Economic Commission for Latin America and the Caribbean). 2017. "Social Panorama of Latin America 2016." Briefing paper.

El Deber (Santa Cruz de la Sierra). 2014. "Para García Linera, Solo Santa Cruz Ejecutó Bien Su Presupuesto." January 8.

Eley, Geoff. 2002. *Forging Democracy: The History of the Left in Europe, 1850–2000*. Oxford: Oxford University Press.

Ellner, Steve. 2008. *Rethinking Venezuelan Politics: Class, Conflict, and the Chavez Phenomenon*. Boulder, CO: Lynne Rienner.

———. 2014. *Latin America's Radical Left: Challenges and Complexities of Political Power in the Twenty-first Century*. Lanham, MD: Rowman and Littlefield.

Ellner, Steve, and David J. Myers. 2002. "Caracas: Incomplete Empowerment Amid Geopolitical Feudalism." In *Capital City Politics in Latin America: Democratization and Empowerment*, 95–131. Boulder, CO: Lynne Rienner.

Ellner, Steve, and Miguel Tinker Salas. 2007. "The Venezuelan Exceptionalism Thesis: Separating Myth from Reality." In *Venezuela: Hugo Chavez and the Decline of an "Exceptional Democracy,"* ed. Steve Ellner and Miguel Tinker Tinker Salas, 3–15. Rowman & Littlefield.

Farthing, Linda C., and Benjamin H. Kohl. 2014. *Evo's Bolivia: Continuity and Change*. Austin: University of Texas Press.

Fernandes, Sujatha. 2010. *Who Can Stop the Drums? Urban Social Movements in Chávez's Venezuela*. Durham, NC: Duke University Press.

Ferreira, Reymi. 2010a. *Las logias en Santa Cruz (Vol 1)*. Santa Cruz de la Sierra, Bolivia: Fondo de Ediciones Municipales.

———. 2010b. *Las logias en Santa Cruz: (Vol 2) 1994–2010*. Santa Cruz de la Sierra, Bolivia: Fondo de Ediciones Municipales.

Friedman, Milton. 1962. *Capitalism and Freedom*. Chicago: University of Chicago Press.

FUDECO. 2010. *Estado Lara Dossier 2009*. Barquisimeto: Vicepresidencia de la República Bolivariana de Venezuela.

Fung, Archon, and Erik Olin Wright. 2003. *Deepening Democracy: Institutional Innovations in Empowered Participatory Governance*. London: Verso.

Garcés, Fernando. 2011. "The Domestication of Indigenous Autonomies in Bolivia: From the Pact of Unity to the New Constitution." In *Remapping Bolivia: Resources, Territory, and Indigeneity in a Plurinational State*, ed. Nicole Fabricant and Bret Gustafson, 46–67. Santa Fe, NM: School for Advanced Research Press.

García Linera, Álvaro, Marxa Chávez Léon, and Patricia Costas Monje. 2008. *Sociologia De Los Movimientos Sociales En Bolivia*. La Paz: Plural Editores.

García Ponce, Antonio. 1986. *Crisis Oligarquía y Latifundio: Carora (1929–1935)*. Barquisimeto, Venezuela: Fondo Editorial Buría.

García-Guadilla, María Pilar. 2011. "Urban Land Committees: Co-optation, Autonomy, and Protagonism." In *Venezuela's Bolivarian Democracy: Participation, Politics, and Culture under Chávez*, ed. David Smilde and Daniel Hellinger, 80–103. Durham, NC: Duke University Press.

Gibson, Edward L. 1996. *Class and Conservative Parties: Argentina in Comparative Perspective*. Baltimore, MD: Johns Hopkins University Press.

Gibson, Christopher L. 2019. *Movement-Driven Development: The Politics of Health and Democracy in Brazil*. Stanford, CA: Stanford University Press.

Gilens, Martin, and Benjamin I. Page. 2014. "Testing Theories of American Politics: Elites, Interest Groups, and Average Citizens." *Perspectives on Politics* 12(3): 564–81.

Gill, Lesley. 2000. *Teetering on the Rim.* New York: Columbia University Press.

Gill, Timothy. 2019. "Shifting Imperial Strategies in Contemporary Latin America: The U.S. Empire and Venezuela under Hugo Chávez." *Journal of Historical Sociology* 32(3): 294–310.

_____. 2022. *Encountering US Empire in Socialist Venezuela: The Legacy of Race, Neo-Colonialism, and Democracy Promotion.* Pittsburgh, PA: University of Pittsburgh Press.

Gilly, Adolfo. 2007. "Prologue: The Spirit of Revolt." In *Revolutionary Horizons: Past and Present in Bolivian Politics,* ed. Forrest Hylton and Sinclair Thomson, xiii–xix. London: Verso.

Giménez de García, Myriam. 2008. "Historia de Las Cooperativas En Torres." In *Antecedentes Comunitarios en El Municipio Torres,* 77–86. Carora, Venezuela: Fondo Editorial Ali Lameda.

Giusti, Roberto, and Tony De Viveiros. 2012. *Carlos Ocariz: El Mandato de la Calle Una Gestión Municipal Existosa.* Caracas: Alcaldía del Municipio Sucre.

Gleijeses, Piero. 1992. *Shattered Hope: The Guatemalan Revolution and the United States, 1944–1954.* Princeton, NJ: Princeton University Press.

Goldfrank, Benjamin. 2011a. *Deepening Local Democracy in Latin America: Participation, Decentralization, and the Left.* University Park: Pennsylvania State University Press.

——. 2011b. "The Left and Participatory Democracy." In *The Resurgence of the Latin American Left,* ed. Steven Levitsky and Kenneth M. Roberts, 162–83. Baltimore, MD: Johns Hopkins University Press.

——. 2007. "Lessons from Latin America's Experience with Participatory Budgeting." In *Participatory Budgeting,* ed. Anwar Shah. Washington, DC: World Bank Institute.

Golinger, Eva. 2006. *The Chavez Code: Cracking U.S. Intervention in Venezuela.* Northampton, MA: Interlink.

Gamboa, Laura. 2017. "Opposition at the Margins: Strategies against the Erosion of Democracy in Colombia and Venezuela." *Comparative Politics* 49(4): 457–77.

Gotkowitz, Laura. 2007. *A Revolution for Our Rights: Indigenous Struggles for Land and Justice in Bolivia, 1880–1952.* Durham, NC: Duke University Press.

Gramsci, Antonio. 1971. *Prison Notebooks.* New York: International.

Grandin, Greg. 2011. *The Last Colonial Massacre: Latin America in the Cold War. Updated Edition.* Chicago: University of Chicago Press.

_____. 2013. "On the Legacy of Hugo Chávez." The Nation, March 6.

Grisaffi, Thomas. 2019. *Coca Yes, Cocaine No: How Bolivia's Coca Growers Reshaped Democracy.* Durham, NC: Duke University Press.

Gustafson, Bret. 2020. *Bolivia in the Age of Gas.* Durham, NC: Duke University Press.

Gutiérrez Aguilar, Raquel. 2014. *Rhythms of the Pachakuti: Indigenous Uprising and State Power in Bolivia.* Durham, NC: Duke University Press.

Hale, Charles R. 2005. "Neoliberal Multiculturalism: The Remaking of Cultural Rights and Racial Dominance in Central America." *Political and Legal Anthropology Review* 28(1): 10–28.

Hall, Stuart. 1988. "The Toad in the Garden: Thatcherism among the Theorists." In *Marxism and the Interpretation of Culture,* ed. Cary Nelson et al., 35–58. Chicago: University of Illinois Press.

REFERENCES

Handlin, Samuel. 2017. *State Crisis in Fragile Democracies: Polarization and Political Regimes in South America*. Cambridge: Cambridge University Press.

——. 2013. "Social Protection and the Politicization of Class Cleavages During Latin America's Left Turn." *Comparative Political Studies* 46(12): 1582–1609.

Harnecker, Marta. 2008. *Transfiriendo poder a la gente: municipio Torres, estado Lara, Venezuela*. Caracas: Centro Internacional Miranda.

Harvey, David. 2005. *A Brief History of Neoliberalism*. Oxford University Press.

Hawkins, Kirk. 2010. *Venezuela's Chavismo and Populism in Comparative Perspective*. Cambridge: Cambridge University Press.

Heller, Patrick. 2001. "Moving the State: The Politics of Democratic Decentralization in Kerala, South Africa, and Porto Alegre." *Politics & Society* 29(1): 131–63.

Hetland, Gabriel. 2020. "If Democracy Is Restored in Bolivia, Thank Protesters and Not the U.S. or the OAS." *Washington Post*, August 26.

——. 2019. "What the UN Report Gets Right—and Wrong—About the Crisis in Venezuela." *The Nation*. July 24.

Huber, Evelyne, and John D. Stephens. 2012. *Democracy and the Left*. Chicago: University of Chicago Press.

——. 2001. *Development and Crisis of the Welfare State*. Chicago: University of Chicago Press.

Hylton, Forrest, and Sinclair Thomson. 2007. *Revolutionary Horizons: Past and Present in Bolivian Politics*. London: Verso.

Idrobo, Nicolás, Dorothy Kronick, and Francisco Rodríguez. 2022. "Do Shifts in Late-Counted Votes Signal Fraud? Evidence from Bolivia." *The Journal of Politics* (March).

International Human Rights Clinic. 2020. "'They Shot Us Like Animals': Black November and Bolivia's Interim Government." Report. Human Rights Program and Harvard Law School, http://hrp.law.harvard.edu/wp-content/uploads/2020/07/Black-November-English-Final _Accessible.pdf.

Jansen, Robert. 2011. "Populist Mobilization: A New Theoretical Approach to Populism." *Sociological Theory* 29(2): 75–96.

Jiménez, Maryhen. 2021. "Contesting Autocracy: Repression and Opposition Coordination in Venezuela." *Political Studies* (May).

Johnston, Jake, and Sara Kozameh. 2013. "Venezuelan Economic and Social Performance Under Hugo Chávez, in Graphs." Washington, DC: Center for Economic and Policy Research.

Karl, Terry. 1997. *The Paradox of Plenty: Oil Booms and Petro-States*. Berkeley: University of California Press.

Kingsbury, Donald V. 2018. *Only the People Can Save the People: Constituent Power, Revolution, and Counterrevolution in Venezuela*. Albany: State University of New York Press.

Kirshner, Joshua. 2013. "City Profile: Santa Cruz de La Sierra." *Cities* 31 (April): 544–52.

Kohl, Benjamin, and Linda Farthing. 2006. *Impasse in Bolivia: Neoliberal Hegemony and Popular Resistance*. London: Zed.

Kreidler Flores, Bismarck. 2010. *Municipio Cruceño*. Santa Cruz de la Sierra.

REFERENCES

Kurmanaev, Anatoly. 2017. "How Hundreds of Mysterious Votes Flipped a Venezuelan Election." *Wall Street Journal*, November 2.

La Razón. 2013. "El Gobierno Edil Cruceño Lidera La Ejecución Presupuestaria Con 64 percent." January 5, 2013.

Lander, Edgardo. 2016. "The Implosion of Venezuela's Rentier State." *New Politics Papers* 1 (September).

——. 2008. "Venezuela. Populism and the Left: Alternatives to Neo-Liberalism." In *The New Latin American Left: Utopia Reborn*, ed. Patrick Barrett, Daniel Chavez, and César Rodríguez-Garavito, 69–98. London: Pluto.

Latinobarómetro. 1995. *Informe 1995–2018*. Santiago de Chile: Latinobarómetro.

Lazar, Sian. 2008. *El Alto, Rebel City: Self and Citizenship in Andean Bolivia*. Durham, NC: Duke University Press.

Levitsky, Steven, and James Loxton. 2013. "Populism and Competitive Authoritarianism in the Andes." *Democratization* 20(1): 107–36.

Levitsky, Steven, and Kenneth M. Roberts. 2011a. "Introduction: Latin America's 'Left Turn': A Framework for Analysis." In *The Resurgence of the Latin American Left*, ed. Steven Levitsky and Kenneth M. Roberts, 1–28. Baltimore, MD: Johns Hopkins University Press.

——. 2011b. Eds. *The Resurgence of the Latin American Left*. Baltimore, MD: Johns Hopkins University Press.

Linárez, Pedro Pablo. 2004. *La lucha armada en las montañas de Lara*. Unión Editorial Gayón.

——. 2006. *La lucha armada en Venezuela: apuntes sobre guerra de guerrillas venezolanas en el contexto de la Guerra Fría (1959–1979) y el rescate de los desaparecidos*. Ediciones Universidad Bolivariana de Venezuela.

López Maya, Margarita. 2014. "Iglesia Católica y democracia participativa y protágonica en Venezuela." *Latin American Research Review, Volume 49 Special Issue: 45–60*.

López Maya, Margarita, and Luis Lander. 2011. "Participatory Democracy in Venezuela: Origins, Ideas, and Implementation." In *Venezuela's Bolivarian Democracy: Participation, Politics, and Culture under Chávez*, ed. David Smilde and Daniel Hellinger, 58–79. Durham, NC: Duke University Press.

Loxton, James. 2014. "The Authoritarian Roots of New Right Party Success in Latin America." In *The Resilience of the Latin American Right*, ed. Juan Pablo Luna and Cristóbal Rovira Kaltwasser, 117–40. Baltimore, MD: Johns Hopkins University Press.

——. 2021. *Conservative Party-Building in Latin America: Authoritarian Inheritance and Counterrevolutionary Struggle*. Oxford: Oxford University Press.

Luna, Juan Pablo, and Cristóbal Rovira Kaltwasser. eds. 2014. *The Resilience of the Latin American Right*. Baltimore, MD: Johns Hopkins University Press.

Mainwaring, Scott. 2012. "From Representative Democracy to Participatory Competitive Authoritarianism: Hugo Chávez and Venezuelan Politics." *Perspectives on Politics* 10(4): 955–67.

Mallen, Ana L., and María Pilar García-Guadilla. 2017. *Venezuela's Polarized Politics: The Paradox of Direct Democracy Under Chávez*. Boulder, CO: Lynne Rienner.

Mamani Ramírez, Pablo. 2011. "Cartographies of Indigenous Power: Identity and Territoriality in Bolivia." In *Remapping Bolivia: Resources, Territory, and Indigeneity in a Plurinational State*, ed. Nicole Fabricant and Bret Gustafson, 30–45. Santa Fe, NM: School for Advanced Research Press.

———. 2005. *Microgobiernos Barriales: Levantamiento de La Ciudad de El Alto (Octubre 2003)*. La Paz: CADES.

———. 2004. *El rugir de las multitudes: la fuerza de los levantamientos indígenas en Bolivia/Qullasuyu*. La Paz: Aruwiyiri.

Mayorga, Fernando. 1997. *Ejemonias? Democracia representativa y liderazgos locales: Percy Fernández, Manfred Reyes Villa, Mónica Medina*. La Paz: PIEB/SINERGIA.

———. 2002. *Neopopulismo y democracia: compadres y padrinos en la política boliviana (1988–1999)*. Centro de Estudios Superiores Universitarios.

McNulty, Stephanie L. 2011. *Voice and Vote: Decentralization and Participation in Post-Fujimori Peru*. Stanford, CA: Stanford University Press.

Middlebrook, Kevin. 2000. *Conservative Parties, the Right, and Democracy in Latin America*. Baltimore, MD: Johns Hopkins University Press.

Modonesi, Massimo. 2017. *Revoluciones pasivas en América*. Mexico City, Mexico: Editorial Itaca.

Monaldi, Francisco. 2018. "The Collapse of the Venezuelan Oil Industry and Its Global Consequences." *The Atlantic Council* 16.

Montambeault, Françoise. 2015. *The Politics of Local Participatory Democracy in Latin America: Institutions, Actors, and Interactions*. Stanford, CA: Stanford University Press.

Morgan, Jana. 2011. *Bankrupt Representation and Party System Collapse*. University Park: Pennsylvania State University Press.

Mudge, Stephanie L. 2018. *Leftism Reinvented: Western Parties from Socialism to Neoliberalism*. Cambridge, MA: Harvard University Press.

Nohlen, Dieter. 2005. *Elections in the Americas: A Data Handbook: Volume II: South America*. Oxford: Oxford University Press.

Olsen, Niklas. 2019. *The Sovereign Consumer: A New Intellectual History of Neoliberalism*. London: Palgrave Macmillan.

Peruzzotti, Enrique. 2013. "Populism in Democratic Times: Populism, Representative Democracy, and the Debate on Democratic Deepening." In *Latin American Populism in the Twenty-First Century*, ed. Carlos de la Torre and Cynthia J. Arnson, 61–84. Washington, DC: Woodrow Wilson Center Press.

Polanyi, Karl. 1994 [2003]. *The Great Transformation: The Political and Economic Origins of Our Time*. Boston: Beacon.

Poliszuk, Joseph. 2016. "Rangel Ávalos & Co." Berlin: Transparency International.

Portes, Alejandro, and Kelly Hoffman. 2003. "Latin American Class Structures: Their Composition and Change during the Neoliberal Era." *Latin American Research Review* 38(1): 41–82.

Postero, Nancy. 2017. *The Indigenous State*. Berkeley: University of California Press.

———. 2010. "The Struggle to Create a Radical Democracy in Bolivia." *Latin American Research Review* 45: 59–78.

——. 2007. *Now We Are Citizens: Indigenous Politics in Postmulticultural Bolivia*. Stanford, CA: Stanford University Press.

Poulantzas, Nicos. 1980. *State, Power, Socialism*. London: Verso.

Powell, John Duncan. 1971. *Political Mobilization of the Venezuelan Peasant*. Cambridge, MA: Harvard University Press.

Prado, Fernando Salmon. 2005. *Santa Cruz y Su Gente*. Santa Cruz de la Sierra, Bolivia: CEDURE.

Przeworski, Adam. 1985. *Capitalism and Social Democracy*. Cambridge: Cambridge University Press.

Quisbert Quispe, Máximo. 2003. *Fejuve el Alto, 1990–1998 : dilemas del clientelismo colectivo en un mercado político en expansión*. La Paz, Bolivia: Ediciones Aruwiyiri.

Revilla Herrero, Carlos J. 2009. "La Visibilidad y El Obrismo Desde La Estrategia Política Del Movimiento Plan Progreso En La Ciudad de El Alto." *Villa Libre* 4: 86–114.

Richmond, Matthew Aaron. 2018. "Bolsonaro's Conservative Revolution." Jacobin.com. October 17. https://jacobin.com/2018/10/brazil-election-bolsonaro-evangelicals-security.

Riley, Dylan. 2010. *The Civic Foundations of Fascism in Europe: Italy, Spain, and Romania, 1870–1945*. Baltimore, MD: Johns Hopkins University Press.

Riofrancos, Thea. 2020. *Resource Radicals: From Petro-Nationalism to Post-Extractivism in Ecuador*. Durham, NC: Duke University Press.

Rivera Cusicanqui, Silvia. 1984. *Oprimidos Pero No Vencidos : Luchas Del Campesinado Aymara y Qhechwa de Bolivia, 1900–1980*. Informe/Instituto de Investigaciones de Las Naciones Unidas Para El Desarrollo Social 85.1. La Paz, Bolivia: Aruwiyiri.

Roberts, Kenneth. 2015. *Changing Course in Latin America: Party Systems in the Neoliberal Era*. Cambridge: Cambridge University Press.

——. 2003. "Social Polarization and the Populist Resurgence in Venezuela." In *Venezuelan Politics in the Chavez Era: Class, Polarization, and Conflict*, ed. Steve Ellner and Daniel Hellinger, 55–72. Boulder, CO: Lynne Rienner.

——. 1998. *Deepening Democracy? The Modern Left and Social Movements in Chile and Peru*. Stanford, CA: Stanford University Press.

——. 1995. "Neoliberalism and the Transformation of Populism in Latin America: The Peruvian Case." *World Politics* 48(1): 82–116.

Romero, Simon. 2008. "A Vote That May Strengthen Bolivian Leader." *New York Times*. August 8.

Rueschemeyer, Dietrich, Evelyne Huber Stephens, and John D. Stephens. 1992. *Capitalist Development and Democracy*. Chicago: University of Chicago Press.

Salazar, Juan José. 2007. *Antropología de La Madre Tierra: El Latifundio Caroreño Un Estudio de Caso*. Quíbor: Museo Antropológico de Quíbor.

Sánchez-Uribarri, Raul. 2008. "Venezuela: The Left Turning Further Left?" In *Leftovers: Tales of the Latin American Left*, ed. Jorge Castañeda and Marco Morales. London: Routledge.

Sandbrook, Richard, Marc Edelman, Patrick Heller, and Judith Teichman. 2007. *Social Democracy in the Global Periphery: Origins, Challenges, Prospects*. Cambridge: Cambridge University Press.

Schiller, Naomi. 2018. *Channeling the State: Community Media and Popular Politics in Venezuela.* Durham, NC: Duke University Press.

Schumpeter, Joseph. 1942. *Capitalism, Socialism, and Democracy.* New York: Harper.

Silva, Eduardo. 2009. *Challenging Neoliberalism in Latin America.* Cambridge: Cambridge University Press.

Sintomer, Yves, Carsten Herzberg, and Giovanni Allegretti. 2010. *Learning from the South: Participatory Budgeting Worldwide.* Bonn, Germany: InWEnt gGmbH—Capacity Building International.

Slobodian, Quinn. 2018. *Globalists: The End of Empire and the Birth of Neoliberalism.* Cambridge, MA: Harvard University Press.

Smilde, David. 2011. "Introduction." In *Venezuela's Bolivarian Democracy: Participation, Politics, and Culture under Chávez,* ed. David Smilde and Daniel Hellinger, 1–27. Durham, NC: Duke University Press.

Smilde, David, and Daniel Hellinger, eds. 2011. *Venezuela's Bolivarian Democracy: Participation, Politics, and Culture under Chávez.* Durham, NC: Duke University Press.

Soliz, Carmen. 2021. *Fields of Revolution: Agrarian Reform and Rural State Formation in Bolivia, 1935-1964.* Pittsburgh, PA: University of Pittsburgh Press.

Sousa Santos, Boaventura de. 1998. "Participatory Budgeting in Porto Alegre: Toward a Redistributive Democracy." *Politics & Society* 26(4): 461–510.

Tarlau, Rebecca. 2019. *Occupying Schools, Occupying Land: How the Landless Workers Movement Transformed Brazilian Education.* Oxford: Oxford University Press.

Thomson, Sinclair. 2002. *We Alone Will Rule: Native Andean Politics in the Age of Insurgency.* Madison: University of Wisconsin Press.

Tinker Salas, Miguel. 2009. *The Enduring Legacy: Oil, Culture, and Society in Venezuela.* Durham, NC: Duke University Press.

Trigo, María Silvia, Anatoly Kurmanaev, and Allison McCann. 2020. "As Politicians Clashed, Bolivia's Pandemic Death Rate Soared." *New York Times,* August 22.

Trotsky, Leon. 1980. *The History of the Russian Revolution.* New York: Pathfinder.

Valencia, Cristobal. 2015. *We Are the State! Barrio Activism in Venezuela's Bolivarian Revolution.* Tucson: University of Arizona Press.

Van Cott, Donna Lee. 2008. *Radical Democracy in the Andes.* Cambridge: Cambridge University Press.

Velasco, Alejandro. 2022. "The Many Faces of Chavismo." *NACLA* 54(1): 20–73.

——. 2015. *Barrio Rising: Urban Popular Politics and the Making of Modern Venezuela.* Berkeley: University of California Press.

Wampler, Brian. 2007. *Participatory Budgeting in Brazil: Contestation, Cooperation, and Accountability.* University Park: Pennsylvania State University Press.

Wampler, Brian, and Leonardo Avritzer. 2005. "The Spread of Participatory Budgeting in Brazil: From Radical Democracy to Participatory Good Government." *Journal of Latin American Urban Studies* 7 (Fall 2005/Spring 2006): 37–52.

Webber, Jeffery. 2017. *The Last Day of Oppression, and the First Day of the Same: The Politics and Economics of the New Latin American Left.* Chicago: Haymarket.

———. 2011a. *From Rebellion to Reform in Bolivia: Class Struggle, Indigenous Liberation, and the Politics of Evo Morales.* Chicago: Haymarket.

———. 2011b. *Red October.* Leiden: Brill.

———. 2010. "Venezuela Under Chávez: The Prospects and Limitations of Twenty-First Century Socialism, 1998–2009." *Socialist Studies* 6(1): 11–44.

Weisbrot, Mark. 2019. "The Organization of American States Has Deceived the Public, Terribly, on the Bolivian Election." Center for Economic and Policy Research, November 19.

———. 2017. "Trump's Sanctions Make Economic Recovery in Venezuela Nearly Impossible." *The Nation*, September 7, 2017.

Weyland, Kurt. 2013. "The Threat from the Populist Left." *Journal of Democracy* 24(3): 18–32.

———. 2004. "Neoliberalism and Democracy in Latin America: A Mixed Record." *Latin American Politics & Society* 46(1): 135–57.

———. 2001. "Clarifying a Contested Concept: Populism in the Study of Latin American Politics *Comparative Politics* 34(1):1–22.

———. 1999. "Populism in the Age of Neoliberalism." In *Populism in Latin America*, ed. Michael Conniff, 172–90. Tuscaloosa: University of Alabama Press.

Weyland, Kurt, Raúl Madrid, and Wendy Hunter. 2010. *Leftist Governments in Latin America: Successes and Shortcomings.* Cambridge: Cambridge University Press.

Wilpert, Gregory. 2007. *Changing Venezuela by Taking Power: The History and Policies of the Chavez Government.* London: Verso.

Winn, Peter. 1986. *Weavers of Revolution: The Yarur Workers and Chile's Road to Socialism.* Oxford: Oxford University Press.

World Bank. 1998. "Project Appraisal Document on a Proposed Loan in the Amount of US$60.7 Million to Venezuela for a Caracas Slum-Upgrading Project." Washington, DC: World Bank.

Wright, Erik Olin. 2010. *Envisioning Real Utopias.* London: Verso.

Yarrington, Doug. 1997. *A Coffee Frontier: Land, Society, and Politics in Duaca, Venezuela, 1830–1936.* Pittsburgh, PA: University of Pittsburgh Press.

Young, Kevin. 2017. *Blood of the Earth: Resource Nationalism, Revolution, and Empire in Bolivia.* Austin: University of Texas Press.

Ziblatt, Daniel. 2017. *Conservative Political Parties and the Birth of Modern Democracy in Europe.* Cambridge: Cambridge University Press.

INDEX

Page numbers in *italics* refer to figures or tables.